Hélène Miard-Delacroix is Professor in the History and Civilisation of Contemporary Germany at the Université Paris Sorbonne (Paris IV).

‘Like his contemporary, John F. Kennedy, Willy Brandt remained for a long time the archetype of political modernity, the opposite of yesterday’s Europe.’

Le Monde

‘Hélène Miard-Delacroix … succeeds in capturing the eventful life, through the tragedies of Germany in the 20th century, of Herbert Frahm, born with no known father, but who eventually become known under his resistance pseudonym, “Willy Brandt”.’

Libération

‘This is a must-have book for anyone who wants an insight into a century of Germany’s history.’

Vingtième siècle

‘Offering a lively biography of the old chancellor, Miard-Delacroix recounts both the history of a country and the life story of a man. Although Brandt’s life has been dominated by his political career, the author delves into his personal life restoring the humanity of this historical figure.’

Yann-Sven Rittelmeyer,
Politique étrangère (website)

Willy Brandt

The Life of a Statesman

Hélène Miard-Delacroix

Translated by Isabelle Chaize

English translation supported by the Federal Chancellor Willy Brandt Foundation (Berlin)

Published in 2016 by
I.B.Tauris & Co. Ltd
London • New York
www.ibtauris.com

ISBN: 978 1 78453 688 6
eISBN: 978 1 78672 024 5
ePDF: 978 1 78673 024 4

A full CIP record for this book is available from the British Library
A full CIP record is available from the Library of Congress

Library of Congress Catalog Card Number: available

Typeset by JCS Publishing Services Ltd, www.jcs-publishing.co.uk
Printed and bound in Great Britain by T.J. International, Padstow, Cornwall

Contents

Illustrations

1 Two-year-old Herbert Frahm with his mother Martha Frahm in Lübeck, 1915 (© Willy-Brandt-Archiv im Archiv der sozialen Demokratie, Bonn)

2 Willy Brandt, presumably Paris, 1937 (© fredstein.com)

3 Willy Brandt as Norwegian press correspondent on the press gallery at the International Military Tribunal (bottom section, third row from the front, fourth from the right), Nuremberg, 1946 (© Jewgeni Chaldej/Sammlung Ernst Volland und Heinz Krimmer)

4 Governing Mayor of West Berlin Willy Brandt in front of Rathaus Schöneberg, Berlin, 1957 (© Archiv der sozialen Demokratie der Friedrich-Ebert-Stiftung, Bonn)

5 President John F. Kennedy and Willy Brandt, Governing Mayor of West Berlin, in front of Rathaus Schöneberg, 26 June 1963 (© Polizeihistorische Sammlung beim Polizeipräsidenten Berlin)

6 Federal Minister of Foreign Affairs Willy Brandt and Queen Elizabeth II at a meeting of the Council of Europe, Banqueting House, London, 5 May 1969 (© Bundesregierung/Ludwig Wegmann)

7 Appointment of the cabinet members of Federal Chancellor Willy Brandt by Federal President Gustav Heinemann at Villa Hammerschmidt, Bonn, 22 October 1969 (*first row, from left*: Gerhard Jahn, Käte Strobel, Gustav Heinemann, Willy Brandt, Walter Scheel, Karl Schiller, Georg Leber; *second row, from left*: Helmut Schmidt, Alex Möller, Erhard

Eppler, Hans-Dietrich Genscher, Walter Arendt; *third row, from left*: Egon Franke, Lauritz Lauritzen, Hans Leussink, Horst Ehmke, Josef Ertl) (© Bundesregierung/Ludwig Wegmann)

8 Federal Chancellor Willy Brandt on his knees in front of the Monument of the Ghetto Heroes, Warsaw, 7 December 1970 (© bpk/Hanns Hubmann)

9 Chairman of the SPD parliamentary group Herbert Wehner, Federal Chancellor Willy Brandt and Federal Minister of Finance and Economic Affairs Helmut Schmidt at the convention of the Social Democratic Party (the so-called 'Troika'), Dortmund, 1972 (© Bundesregierung/ Engelbert Reineke)

10 Federal Chancellor Willy Brandt in dialogue with Vice-Chancellor and Minister of Foreign Affairs Walter Scheel, Fuerteventura, 1973 (© Willy-Brandt-Archiv im Archiv der sozialen Demokratie, Bonn)

11 Federal Chancellor Willy Brandt, President Richard Nixon and Secretary of State Henry Kissinger at the Oval Office, Washington DC, 29 September 1973 (© Bundesregierung/ Ludwig Wegmann)

12 Welcome for Willy Brandt and members of the North–South Commission after its inaugural meeting by Federal President Walter Scheel at Schloss Gymnich near Bonn, 9 December 1977 (© J.H. Darchinger/ Friedrich-Ebert-Stiftung)

13 Willy Brandt and Shridath Ramphal handing over the 'Brandt Report' to President Jimmy Carter, Washington DC, 15 February 1980 (© picture alliance/UPI)

14 Willy Brandt, Edward Heath and Federal Chancellor Helmut Schmidt at a reception at Schloss Charlottenburg during the meeting of the North–South Commission in Berlin, 29 May 1981 (© Bundesregierung/Klaus Lehnartz)

15 Official celebration of Willy Brandt's seventy-fifth birthday at the invitation of Federal President Richard von Weizsäcker at Villa Hammerschmidt, Bonn, 20 January 1989 (*back row, from left*: Björn Engholm, Peter Glotz, Holger Börner, Shepard Stone, Walter Scheel, Oskar Lafontaine, Bruno Kreisky, Ernst Breit, Karel van Miert, Kurt Scharf, Egon Bahr, Friedbert Pflüger, Basil Mathiopoulos, Hans Katzer; *middle row, from left*: Johannes Rau, Helmut Kohl, Layachi Yaker, Jacques Delors, Ingvar Carlsson, Hans-Jochen Vogel, Shridath S. Ramphal, Franz Vranitzky, Alan Boesek, Georg Leber, Valentin Falin, Rainer Barzel; *front row, from left*: Marianne von Weizsäcker, François Mitterrand, Gro Harlem Brundtland, Brigitte Seebacher-Brandt, Mieczslaw Rakowski, Willy Brandt, Richard von Weizsäcker, Mário Soares, Hans-Dietrich Genscher, Shimon Peres) (© Bundesregierung/ Arne Schambeck)

16 Willy Brandt at the Brandenburg Gate the day after the fall of the Berlin Wall, 10 November 1989 (© William Palmer Mikkelsen)

Abbreviations

ACC	Allied Control Council
CDU	Christian Democratic Union
CPSU	Communist Party of the Soviet Union
CSCE	Conference for Security and Cooperation in Europe
CSU	Christian Social Union
DNA	Norwegian Labour Party
DNVP	German National People's Party
EEC	European Economic Community
EKD	Evangelical Church in Germany
FDP	Free Democratic Party (liberal and classical-liberal)
FRG	Federal Republic of Germany
GDR	German Democratic Republic
GVP	All-German People's Party
HVA	(GDR) Main Directorate for Reconnaissance
IDA	International Development Association
KPD	German Communist Party
MBFR	Mutual Balanced Forces Reduction
NATO	North Atlantic Treaty Organisation
NKVD	People's Commissariat for Internal Affairs (Soviet secret service)
NPD	National Democratic Party (neo-Nazi)
NSDAP	National Socialist German Workers' Party (Nazi Party)
ONA	Overseas News Agency
POUM	Workers' Party of Marxist Unification
PS	(French) Socialist Party
PSOE	Spanish Socialist Workers' Party

SA Sturmabteilung – the original paramilitary wing of the Nazi Party
SAJ Socialist Labour Youth
SAP Socialist Workers' Party
SDP (GDR) Social Democratic Party
SDS Socialist German Student League
SED (GDR) Socialist Unity Party of Germany
SPD Social Democratic Party
Stasi Staatssicherheit, abbreviation of Ministerium für Staatssicherheit, GDR secret service
UEF Union of European Federalists
UN United Nations
USSR Union of Soviet Socialist Republics

Abbreviations Used in Notes and Bibliography

AAPD *Akten zur Auswärtigen Politik der Bundesrepublik Deutschland*
AdsD Archiv der sozialen Demokratie (Archive of Social Democracy), Friedrich Ebert Foundation, Bonn
AN Archives Nationales, Pierrefitte (National Archives of France)
BA *Berliner Ausgabe*
BStU Behörde des Bundesbeauftragten für die Unterlagen des Staatssicherheitsdienstes der ehemaligen DDR (Archive of the State Security Services of the GDR)
BWBS Federal Chancellor Willy Brandt Foundation
DDF *Documents diplomatiques Français*
WBA Willy Brandt Archive (in AdsD)

Preface

'Now Hitler has finally lost the war!' These were Willy Brandt's words in response to his election by the members of the Bundestag to the position of chancellor, on 21 October 1969. For a former resistance fighter from the extreme left, a man of uncertain paternity who had been accused of treason, to become the democratically elected head of state of the Federal Republic of Germany was indeed a sign of a new Germany. And yet many of us in Europe are still blinded by Nazism when we look at Germany. Hitler, his henchmen, his regime and his crimes stop us recognising the existence of another twentieth-century German history.

Willy Brandt's life, from 1913 to 1992, is the remarkable journey of a German democrat, although he is best known for having been betrayed by a spy from the East. His almost 80 years were marked by brutal ruptures as well as slow changes in Germany: tragedies and attempts at reparation, chaos, despair and physical and moral reconstruction. He was also touched by and involved in the Cold War, with threats to Berlin, Ostpolitik and the European project. Brandt is probably one of the only politicians ever to have become head of state after a change of identity. What other political leader can say they escaped death by wearing a foreign uniform after being captured by their own country's army? Even more remarkably, while Hitler managed to acquire German nationality, Brandt was stripped of his – a strange twist of fate that should have caught our attention long ago.

Apart from a small circle of academic specialists, there is widespread ignorance about what Germany became after 1945. There is equally widespread astonishment among those who learn about the internal German resistance to Nazism, and about the fierce struggle between the various democrats who took charge of the country's reconstruction, or who find out what the Cold War really meant as an everyday reality in the representations and political practices of a divided Berlin, and in the rest of West Germany. Willy Brandt embodies this whole story.

There are many stereotypical views of the man who received the Nobel Peace Prize in 1971 for his policies of reconciliation with his neighbours in the Eastern Bloc. The image of the Chancellor on his knees in front of the Warsaw Ghetto Memorial is certainly well known internationally, but in Germany his name just as commonly conjures up the triumphant Social Democrat, the dynamic reformer, the great seducer, the melancholic … This man, who moved from the extreme left to the centre, who reformed the oldest party in Germany and made it capable of governing, who defended the values of social democracy wherein the welfare state guarantees the rights and concrete freedoms of the individual – this committed European remains little known to us, his neighbours.

And yet the questions raised by his life are not unique to Germany. His life is also the history of the heart of the continent, *our* history as Europeans, and with it come the questions of our era: questions about loyalty and the duty of resistance, the problems of memory and reconciliation, the sharing and redistribution of wealth, and the importance of the construction of Europe. His life also poses questions about the concept of nationhood before and after the fall of the Berlin Wall. What sort of German, what sort of patriot was Willy Brandt? In October 1969 he singled out Hitler's betrayal of the German nation as the origin of Germany's divisions and problems. He admired General de Gaulle because he thought it right and just for the state to be founded on resistance, but he wanted to guide his convalescent people while still demanding the best from them. Embattled, attacked and opposed, he demanded respect and insisted on political openness. Was he wrong not to hide his weaknesses? According to his adviser Egon Bahr, 'his weakness is what made him human; it's precisely what made him so popular and so appealing to so many people. His vulnerability became his strength.'[1]

Willy Brandt's life is a voyage through the storms of the twentieth century. It has everything we need to inspire us in the present.

Prologue

Berlin, October 1936

'What is this regime where criminals are deemed to be within the law and those who oppose them are breaking it?' This and similar thoughts ran through the mind of a history student with a strong Norwegian accent, who spent his mornings at the library in Berlin studying *Mein Kampf* and other Nazi texts. Every month he had to go personally to the Reichsbank to withdraw the money sent to him from Oslo and to show his passport; the German police could confiscate it at any moment, despite his Aryan looks and suitably Nordic name: Gunnar Gaasland. There was a strange atmosphere in this Germany that had just hosted the Olympic Games, and it was setting the scene for the show of power, energy and cold efficiency that was to come. In 1936, in an attempt to rehabilitate its international image after the remilitarisation of the Rhineland, Berlin had slightly relaxed the repressive regime that had ruled the country for the last three years. Nevertheless, opponents of the ruling party were still being detained in prisons and in the first concentration camps, which had been created for that purpose in March 1933. Such was the fate of the socialist Kurt Schumacher, arrested soon after Hitler's rise to power and never forgiven by the Nazis for his public declaration in the Reichstag, in February 1932, that Nazism was 'an ongoing appeal to every man's inner swine'. In the streets of Berlin, in that autumn of 1936, the population seemed to be getting used to its new rulers, whose economic policies had already reduced unemployment and convinced people to believe their miraculous promises.

The student was lodging in a furnished flat in the house of one Frau Hamel, close to the Kranzler café, on the corner of Kurfürstendamm and Joachimthaler Street. He lived frugally, but allowed himself a small luxury in the evenings: a cheap ticket to hear Wilhelm Furtwängler conducting the symphony orchestra at the Berlin Philharmonie.[1] He had to be on his guard at all times – more so than any other foreigner in the city. One day, at the bank, an employee introduced him to another Norwegian, a friendly man who offered to take him along to a club of Scandinavian Nazis. Gaasland answered evasively, wanting to say as little about his life as possible. In a café on another day he noticed one of his former teachers from his secondary school in Lübeck. The old teacher's eyes warned the young man not to approach him – the heavy weight of silent understanding. 'If all Germans are Nazis, why can Hitler not rule without terror, without the Gestapo and without the camps where he imprisons his opponents?'[2]

In fact, the Norwegian student was German. He had memorised the life story of the real Gunnar Gaasland, whose name he had borrowed for his fake Norwegian passport. He needed to know how to answer convincingly if he was interrogated or tortured. From September to December 1936, the young German socialist spent three months in *Metro*, the code name for Berlin, entrusted with a special mission: he was to provide information and support to the members of the small Socialist Labour Party, SAP, which still survived in secret in Nazi Germany. Every afternoon he would meet a contact, in disguise, in a park or in one of the woods north of Berlin. His task was to identify those members of the resistance who would be able to attend a clandestine meeting set to take place in a few weeks at Mährisch-Ostrau (now Ostrava), while always making sure to mention Kattowitz, in Poland, as the venue in case the Gestapo got wind of the preparations. He also had to report his impressions of the situation in Germany to other members of the network who were exiled in the various capitals of Europe. This was done in a few phrases hidden in mundane letters where he observed that, even under a dictatorship, for most people 'life is not about *isms*, but about eating and drinking, love and football'.[3] Already, in 1930, he had seen the effectiveness of Nazi propaganda on the young people in his hometown, Lübeck.[4] The student's name was Willy Brandt, but that was not his real name either.

Chapter 1

Between Attachment and Emigration

Lübeck

At about midday on 18 December 1913, a little boy named Herbert was born at 16 Meierstrasse, in a working-class area of Lübeck. His mother, Martha Frahm, was 19 years old, and the boy was recorded at the registrar's office as her son, with her surname. For 35 years this name, Herbert Ernst Karl Frahm, would be the legal name of the man who would not officially become Willy Brandt until 1949.

In Lübeck, the roads were cobbled and the port had the rancid smell of boats, familiar to all those who live where a river meets the open sea. Goods were hoisted and lowered and moved around, and sweat formed on salty hands that were dry in summer and numb in winter when the cold froze the north of Germany. The city lived off its iron- and wood-processing industries, as well as the activities of the port, which is connected to the Baltic Sea by the River Trave. In December 1913 the Trave was white with snow, as it is every winter. To its inhabitants, Lübeck is 'the city of the seven towers', with its vertiginous Gothic church clock-towers as well as the massive towers at the gateway to the city. It has been a free, independent city-state since medieval times. It is made of the dark-red brick of the Hanseatic city, and the houses have the Flemish-style pediments seen all around the shores of the North and Baltic seas, from Bergen to Danzig – which at that time was still a German city.

When Herbert Frahm came into this world, Europe was in the midst of the last winter before the Great War. The alliances that would lead to conflict were already in place. In contrast to France and Great Britain, where the parliamentary system was well established, Germany was still an imperial state. It was a large country in the full flow of modernisation, but markedly behind its neighbours in terms of democracy, with its capricious and power-hungry Emperor Wilhelm II, passionate about military uniforms and warships.

The first photographs of little Herbert are deceptive; they are not a good illustration of the condition of the German working class at the beginning of the twentieth century. The little blond boy in the pictures is chubby and fashionably dressed in the sailor suit beloved by the bourgeoisie all over Europe when they had their children's pictures taken. Martha, a working-class girl and an unmarried mother, loved to treat herself to these photographs on Sundays, the only day she was able to spend with her child. During the rest of the week he was in the care of a neighbour, Paula, so that Martha could work as a cashier in a cooperative shop, earning an income she supplemented by working as a domestic cleaner, washerwoman and seamstress. He called her Mama, she was loving and cheerful, a little plump, and he had her round face and high cheekbones. Martha was conscious of class. She learned about it in the socialist circles that provided education for workers and acted as their extended family. She knew German, although everyone spoke *platt*, the northern dialect, and she sought out culture in books and at the Volksbühne theatre, where cheap seats were available.[1]

The future Willy Brandt did not know who his father was. It was not a rare circumstance in the working-class environment of the time, but in his future political battles he would be repeatedly and viciously reminded of this shortcoming. As an older man he looked back in amazement at his inability to come up with a simple answer to these attacks, frozen as he was by shame.[2] A pastor was willing to baptise the infant on

26 February 1914, but in his rectory rather than in the area's Lutheran church.

At home the masculine figure was his grandfather, Ludwig Frahm, whom the little boy called Papa despite having not met him until he was five years old, when this surrogate father returned from the war. A grandfather playing the role of father – in fact, Ludwig was not even the boy's real grandfather. Brandt only found out the truth from his uncle Ernst in 1934. When Ludwig met his first wife, Wilhelmine, he had agreed to take on responsibility for her daughter Martha, Herbert's mother. Martha may have been born after Wilhelmine was claimed by a provincial squire under the *droit de seigneur* still exercised by the minor gentry over their female servants at the end of the nineteenth century. After Wilhelmine's death, Ludwig married Dora Sahlmann in 1919, and Martha, now an adult with a child of her own, stayed with him. Herbert's grandfather's wife, Dora, with whom the little boy did not get on well, was therefore not his real grandmother either. He called her 'my aunt', a common German name for adults close to a child, whether or not they are related. To add to the confusion, he called Emil Kuhlmann, the construction foreman whom his mother married in 1927 and the father of his half-brother Günter, 'my uncle'.[3]

Did this complicated family history perhaps contribute to Brandt's habit of playing hide-and-seek with the truth and with people, and, indeed, of never staying in one place for too long?[4] It was certainly a slightly chaotic home, but it taught him the values and reference points of socialism, that universe that was called simply 'the Movement'. Its official name was the Social Democratic Party, or SPD, and it organised the social life and leisure activities of the workers, from Saturday dances to excursions and fishing or sailing trips, not to mention that great hub of German working-class socialising, skittles matches.

Herbert's grandfather sometimes went on strike, with all the inevitable consequences for his family: no money, no food. A former farmhand from a forgotten part of eastern Germany on the Baltic Sea near Wismar,[5] Ludwig had come to the city to become a coachman and then a driver, part of the great rural exodus of a country that did not become industrialised until the end of the nineteenth century. For a long time there had been numerous obstacles to modernisation in Germany: the land was divided into tiny parcels controlled by mercantile guilds that were self-sufficient as a matter of principle. These parcels were separated by countless borders, each with its own customs duties, and all had different systems of weights, measures and money.

Ludwig became a labourer in Lübeck, and as soon as his young grandson was old enough, he taught him about the dignity of the class struggle. So when little Herbert, at eight years old, proudly brought home the two loaves of bread that one of the directors of the striking factory had given him, his grandfather made him give them back, lecturing him severely that 'they can't bribe us like that. We are not beggars receiving charity. We want what is our right, not hand-outs!'[6]

At the beginning of the 1920s the Weimar Republic was having difficulty gaining stability. The first chaotic postwar months had seen the proclamation of the German Republic on 9 November 1918, the crushing of the Spartacist uprising that winter[7] and the signing of the Treaty of Versailles at the end of June 1919. A humiliated country that had lost 15 per cent of its territory, the government of the first German Republic had a great deal of work to do to convince large swathes of the population they were in good hands. In March 1920, the Kapp Putsch, an uprising of the military Freikorps,[8] showed just how strong anti-republican sentiment was among the demobilised soldiers, and moreover revealed the army's passive resistance to the Republic. Using the excuse that 'the Reichswehr does not fire on the Reichswehr', the army was unwilling to defend the Republic – which the French monarchists called 'La Gueuse' (The Harlot) – against the rioting soldiers. The SPD, along with the liberals, supported the new democratic order, but at the same time, anchored as it was in the traditions of the labour movement, it continued its social struggle on behalf of the proletariat and the workforce.

In 1927, at the end of his seven years at the local elementary school in St Lorenz, Herbert Frahm found out that through his grandfather's efforts and with the help of one of his teachers, he had been awarded a scholarship for gifted students. He was given a place at the Johanneum Gymnasium (*Gymnasien* are secondary schools with an academic focus, designed to prepare students for university) and so gained access to a stronghold of the affluent, cultured families of Lübeck. He was the only working-class child in the school; at that time *Gymnasien* accepted only 1 per cent of German teenagers. Herbert was a natural writer and speaker, and he soon became a charismatic figure in his class, in stark contrast to the traditional image of the solitary working-class child rejected by the sons of the bourgeois.[9] His teachers rated him highly because he was a voracious reader, both out of curiosity and because he wanted to absorb the culture of the ruling class. On the other hand, it was not rare for him to skip class, writing his excuse notes himself, so that he could continue to lead his second life with other young socialists.

The different spheres of his social life soon began to interlock and complement each other: school, family, the party's youth movement. From the age of eight Herbert had taken part in activities organised by the socialist youth organisation, the Kinderfreunde (Friends of the Children), playing sport and learning the mandolin, and he had also joined the related youth movement the Red Falcons, with their uniform of blue shirt and red necktie. When he was 15 he joined the Socialist Labour Youth Organisation (SAJ) and became head of a local group called 'Karl Marx'. The SAJ was the youth version of the adult movement Reichsbanner Schwarz-Rot-Gold (Black-Red-Gold Banner of the Reich), created by the defenders of the Weimar Republic in 1924 to counter the various groups of reactionary agitators who would have liked to overthrow the regime. From the beginning of the twentieth century, the socialists had been at the heart of the extraordinary growth of youth movements in Germany. These movements were ideologically very varied, but they all provided a haven for young people searching for an answer to the brutal changes brought by modernity. Herbert, like many other young people, held enthusiastically to an ideal of moral and physical purity. At the gatherings of the movement, known as the 'Children's Republics', he experienced life as part of a diverse community and was encouraged to be independent. There was a strong ideological element in both the Red Falcons and the SAJ. Their rallying cry was: 'The Republic is just a start, socialism is our goal!'[10]

From a young age Herbert Frahm was steeped in this culture of the glorification of labour; he said later that his early books and fairy tales were texts by Karl Marx and Eduard Bernstein.[11] His first article, describing what it was like to be a Red Falcon, was published in the local daily *Lübecker Volksbote* in December 1928. At just 15, he was full of passion for the young people learning to 'brandish the scarlet torch in the shadows of ignorance and to carry the red flag on towards to the socialist republic!'[12] His regular articles in the local paper made him a bit of money and started him dreaming of becoming a real journalist, but his overriding interest was always the politics of the economically unstable Weimar Germany. Although the Republic had shored up its political bases, in 1923 there had been a bout of hyperinflation in which small savers lost everything, reducing their children's inheritance to ghostly wheelbarrows piled with notes in completely worthless astronomical amounts. In 1929 American investments in Germany were repatriated to the United States on a massive scale, and the crisis struck hard: there were 5 million unemployed in Germany in 1931, and the country could no longer pay the reparations imposed after its defeat in World War I. As a consequence, the welfare system completely collapsed.

In Lübeck, as everywhere in Germany at that time, extremism flourished. On the right, a nationalist bloc quickly grew, comprising the reactionary, anti-republican and militaristic German National People's Party (DNVP); the Stahlhelm (Steel Helmet), a paramilitary organisation that attracted former soldiers; and above all, the National Socialist German Workers' Party (NSDAP, hereafter referred to as the Nazi Party), which emerged out of the rumbling discontent and hardship that abounded in 1920s Germany. At the other extreme, the ranks of communism swelled as tensions with the socialists grew more intense. Comintern, the Communist International, had designated the socialists 'social traitors' because the SPD supported the parliamentary regime and rejected Moscow's revolutionary radicalism. Since the Communist International had shifted towards Stalinism, young Herbert Frahm had been leaning further and further away from the German Communist Party (KPD) and its intransigence. 'They are defiling the name of the proletariat!' he exclaimed on 28 April 1931 in an article in the *Volksbote*.[13] Instead, he joined the SPD, by special exemption as he was only 16. This labour party, created in 1875, was his first political party, although he would later turn away from it for some time. In 1932 he passed his high-school leaving exam, the *Abitur*. His best marks were in history, which was his favourite subject – along with German – because of a 'brilliant' teacher, Herr Pauls.[14] In one of his long history essays he discussed the great figure of the SPD during the Imperial period, August Bebel. Bebel was the 'workers' emperor', a veritable legend before World War I, at a time when the SPD, with its reformist and revolutionary branches, took almost 35 per cent of the vote in the Reichstag elections of 1912.[15] Bebel died in August 1913, a few months before Willy Brandt's birth. For the fatherless boy, Bebel always remained an elusive father-figure.

Brandt had plenty of father-figures throughout his life. Politicians, an orchestra conductor, a Mecklenburg count, even a Bulgarian communist.[16] He waited until February 1947, when he had to make contact with the civil registry office about something, before finally asking his mother to tell him who his real father was. He had never been spoken of at home, and so Herbert had never asked about him. Martha responded by letter, with few details: 'Dear Herbert, your father's name is John Möller, he has always lived in Hamburg, and he was an accountant at the cooperative shop.'[17] A former high-school teacher who had been fired because of his social democratic sympathies, Möller may have sent Martha some money, but his son knew nothing about it, and he learned little more when a cousin who appeared out of nowhere in June 1961 told him about this 'calm, collected' father. Later, at the end of the 1980s, Brandt wrote in his memoirs: 'Even later I thought it would be wrong to try tracing him, since he so clearly did not want to know about me.'[18]

Among the young Herbert's heroes was Abraham Lincoln, a model of upward social mobility who particularly fascinated the European working class, but it was the figure of Julius Leber that dominated Herbert's personal pantheon. A Francophile from the Alsace region, Leber was the editor-in-chief of the newspaper Herbert wrote for, and was chairman of Lübeck's SPD branch. In 1924 he became a member of the Reichstag. In Lübeck he was known as 'the king of the little people'.[19] Herbert admired this socialist, who was also a lovechild raised by his grandfather in a working-class family. Like Herbert, Leber had talent that allowed him to improve his social situation, and both men preferred action to theory, as well as sharing a penchant for women and alcohol. Leber would always be a figure Brandt looked up to and learned from, despite their later disagreement. He was a true hero, who had been decorated in the Great War and taken part in the crushing of the Freikorps putsch in 1920. He was a member of the German resistance to Nazism and when he was arrested in 1933 he felt, in the depths of his cell, that the socialists had 'become drunk on their own impotence' when facing the Nazis.[20] He was finally executed for his role in the failed attempt on Hitler's life on 20 July 1944.

The youth of the party, who were generally more inclined towards the left, had exactly the same reproach. Herbert felt it in Lübeck: he thought the party's direction had stagnated with its support for the 'bourgeois' government of Catholic Centre Party Chancellor Brüning, which had shown its clear inability to deal with the Nazi threat. In October 1931 Leber attended a meeting at the trade union office at which the young socialists, Herbert Frahm prominent among them, started hissing in disapproval. There was uproar. Leber was furious and railed against the young agitators, who were eventually physically removed from the meeting room. Not far away, those who had been ejected met in a workers' gym and, enraged, decided to leave the SPD altogether and set up a local branch of a party that had recently been launched in Germany, the Socialist Workers' Party, SAP. So began a phase that Brandt later described as one of political error and 'sectarian impasse',[21] following the mirage of a 'third way' between the SPD's socialism and Stalinist communism.

The SAP had been founded in Berlin on 4 October 1931 by several SPD members, including Max Seydewitz and Kurt Rosenfeld, who had been expelled from the SPD because of their criticism of the party's 'lesser evil policy'.[22] The SAP was made up of socialists of a more left-wing persuasion and communists who disagreed with the pro-Soviet decisions of the leader of the KPD, Ernst Thälmann. Numerous other small groups with loose links to socialism also joined. At the head of this new party was Jacob Walcher, who had been a founding member of the KPD in January 1919, along with Wilhelm Pieck, who 30 years later became the first president of the GDR (German Democratic Republic).

The SAP never really managed to make an impression: its total number of members throughout Germany is estimated to have been about 15,000. In Lübeck, a city of 100,000 inhabitants, there were 200 members in 1932, in contrast to the SPD's 10,000.[23] On the other hand, the SAP's share of young supporters – who were not yet old enough to vote – was much larger; in Lübeck, half the SPD's youth had moved to the SAP. Herbert Frahm's role included producing agitprop materials and writing pamphlets which he handed out to workers on the docks; his writing expressed stronger and stronger criticism of parliamentarianism, even going so far as to accuse the SPD of having betrayed the workers.[24] He was now also writing for other socialist publications, having become *persona non grata* at the *Volksbote*. Julius Leber could not forgive him for leaving the SPD, and the break between mentor and young man was final. According to his third wife, Brigitte Seebacher, Herbert managed to disappoint all three of his father-figures in one stroke: his grandfather Ludwig, his teacher Herr Pauls and Julius Leber.[25] Thanks to Leber's support, he had been in line to receive a scholarship from the SPD to study at university, but his change of political direction meant he had to give up this dream. Instead he was employed by S.H. Bertling, a shipping agent, where his job was to deal with customs formalities for the small boats arriving from Scandinavia and the Netherlands. This at least gave him the opportunity to learn the languages spoken by the sailors, and quite soon he could manage well in Flemish, Swedish and Norwegian.[26]

There was certainly a good deal of naivety in thinking that the workers' movement could be revitalised simply by founding another party that advocated a third way between socialism and communism. Was it the best response to the rise of authoritarianism and the extreme right? On 20 July 1932 the reactionary Papen, then chancellor of the Reich, launched a coup in Prussia and dismissed the Social Democratic prime minister of the region, Otto Braun. It was an illegal move according to German federalism, which was built on firm respect for the autonomy of the member states. Papen's goal was to force the SPD to capitulate in its stronghold of Prussia, the largest province of Germany, with 60 per cent of the population and three-fifths of the country's surface area. The question was whether to respond by sending policemen loyal to the government, along with the workers of the Reichsbanner movement, to fight Papen's army in the streets; or whether the

Iron Front of socialists and trade unions should surrender to the Harzburg Front: a broad alliance of nationalists and anti-republicans, from the Nazis to the DNVP via the Stahlhelm, as well as former soldiers and Pan-Germanists of all persuasions. Brandt was always convinced that the Iron Front had been wrong to surrender.[27]

Together with his friends and girlfriend, Gertrud Meyer, he threw himself into the SAP's campaign in the run-up to the Reichstag elections on 31 July 1932. While Hitler's party received a record result of 37 per cent of the votes, the SAP managed only 0.2 per cent, and half as many again at the next round of elections in November. In Lübeck, the Nazis even overtook the SPD, with more than 41 per cent of the votes, and the SAP's result was hardly worth mentioning. On 30 January 1933, Adolf Hitler was named chancellor of the Reich. The young Frahm believed that it was the SPD's reformism that had made it easier for the Nazis to take power, although despite this conviction he himself had not become a communist. The day after the Reichstag Fire, 28 February, all civil and political liberties were suspended throughout the country by order of President Hindenburg. The SAP was dissolved by its own leaders, who encouraged its members to rally to the SPD, in Seydewitz's case, and the KPD, in Rosenfeld's. This was a desperate measure in hindsight, given the fate that awaited first the left and eventually all opposition parties, which were banned on 14 July 1933.

On 11 and 12 March, a week after the election fiasco at the Reichstag, where the communists' votes were declared invalid after voting had taken place, the left wing of the SAP, centred around Jacob Walcher and Paul Frölich, met in a Dresden suburb and decided to press on with what they knew would be a hard struggle. Among the 60 SAP delegates in Dresden was Willy Brandt: Herbert Frahm had decided to adopt a pseudonym, that of Mr Everyman. Like his comrades, he had to become secretive in order to escape the notice of the authorities.[28] It was decided: the SAP would resist illegally and would open branches abroad. Walcher would go to Paris and Frölich to Oslo, to put pressure on the Norwegian Labour Party, which leaned further to the left than the SPD. Perhaps their Norwegian comrades would be willing to finance the little German party?[29] Brandt was entrusted with preparing for Frölich's departure for the north of Germany. On 21 March, Frölich was recognised by an officer of the Sturmabteilung (SA), the paramilitary wing of the Nazi Party, and arrested on Fehmarn, an island in the Baltic that was a stopover on his route to Norway. Lübeck's SAP group, thinking Frölich would not withstand questioning and torture, expected the Gestapo at any moment. When it became clear that Frölich had not given them away, Brandt was chosen to travel to Oslo as the SAP emissary to their Norwegian comrades. With this political mission he left Germany, although later he tried to downplay this motive and instead emphasised the threat hanging over his life at the time.[30]

Scandinavia was not a completely unknown quantity for him. He had been there for the first time on a school trip in 1928, and he had also travelled through Denmark, Sweden and Norway with a friend in the summer of 1931.[31] This time, though, it was a different sort of journey. On one of the first nights of April 1933, Brandt left Germany. He had with him 100 marks in his pocket, given to him by his grandfather, who had withdrawn them from his savings account, a few shirts in a small suitcase and, half as a talisman and half as reading material, the first volume of Marx's *Das Kapital*.[32] A fisherman, Paul Stooss, agreed to take him by boat from Travemünde, in Lübeck, to the Danish port of Rødbyhavn, a crossing of a few hours. He went on from there to Oslo via Copenhagen. And there he was in a foreign country, equipped only with his youth. Luckily he already spoke the language well. He left behind him his mother, whom he saw once more in 1935, and then not for another ten years, his grandfather, who committed suicide in 1935, and Gertrud Meyer, his 'Trudel', who joined him again in the summer of 1933.

From Oslo to Paris and Barcelona

Almost 30 years later, in 1961, Franz Josef Strauss, the ultra-conservative head of the Bavarian Christian Social Union party and federal minister for defence, said maliciously: 'There is one thing we could still ask of Herr Brandt: what exactly were you doing during those 12 years away from Germany?'[33] His words reeked with the taint of betrayal and the reproach of having been, at heart, a bad German. Strauss added: 'We, we knew what we had done by staying in Germany.' Germany was divided after 1945 between those who had stayed, and had to confront their consciences after the war, and those who had chosen exile, including numerous opposition politicians, intellectuals and writers – like Thomas Mann and his family, Bertolt Brecht and Stefan Zweig. Brandt justified himself: 'I was a young man and I did not want anything more to do with a German state that was stamping on human rights and dignity.' And was it a national duty to get oneself murdered? At least, he added, the numerous exiles meant that the name of Germany was not solely associated with that of Hitler.[34] The desire to let the world know that there was 'another Germany', and that there were Germans opposed to Nazism, was what drove him to become an extremely prolific journalist in Scandinavia – and, moreover, it was what kept him alive. In a period of 12 years he wrote hundreds of articles and several books about Germany, the international situation and the future of socialism in Europe.

When he arrived in Oslo on 7 April 1933, he had no idea how long his exile was going to last. He expected three or four years at most. He spent seven years there, until the German attack on Norway in April 1940, and then five more in Sweden, before returning to Berlin after the end of the war, aged 32. He always said they were the most important and happiest years of his life.[35]

In Oslo, a small capital city of 250,000 inhabitants, Brandt was welcomed by the Norwegian Labour Party (DNA), and by journalists from the daily newspaper *Arbeiderbladet*. The editor in charge of foreign affairs, Finn Moe, was especially friendly, although in a northern fashion that made Brandt feel practically Mediterranean in contrast.[36] The editor-in-chief, Martin Tranmæl, helped Brandt find somewhere to stay and, as he was a socialist exile, the party gave him 30 kroner per week to live on, and 50 kroner per month to help him pay his rent. It was far from a fortune, but he topped it up by quickly being employed to write numerous freelance articles. He was in demand because he could supply fresh information about Nazi Germany. His first article, written in Norwegian, appeared four days after his arrival, in the 11 April 1933 edition of the *Arbeiderbladet*, with the title: 'What is Hitler's Germany Like?' His answer was unequivocal: fascism had won and the labour movement was failing.[37]

He was soon well settled in the Norwegian socialist milieu, which had an international outlook. His extremely harsh criticism of the SPD, namely that it had failed because of its own weakness and lack of effort, were timely in this country where the DNA, further to the left than the German SPD, was the opposition party. He soon felt completely at home in the Norwegian language. After a few weeks he could speak and write sufficiently well in Norwegian to be able to run youth groups or trade union meetings, to act as an interpreter and to give German lessons. He made the most of the demand for the latter in a country where German was commonly used as the language of academic study at university level. He published articles in various socialist organs, as well in publications intended for the population of German exiles, on Nazism, the reality of the dictatorship in Germany and the future of socialism. He signed them Felix, F. Franke or Martin. As he was paid per piece, he let his inspiration flow freely and wrote a lot, of varying quality: articles, a brochure on Hitler's Germany and commentaries on the Nazi regime that he wanted to unmask.[38]

Gertrud, his girlfriend in Lübeck, joined him in Oslo and they moved into a minute flat. Trudel was only 19, but she had already cut her teeth in the movement. She was a member of the clandestine SAP, like Willy, and had just spent five weeks in custody in Lübeck. When she was arrested, she swallowed a letter Brandt had written her so that it would not compromise his position.[39] She was a courageous woman, 'a true comrade', and he could depend on her for help. She assisted him in the various menial tasks involved with making false papers or preparing the invisible ink they used to send messages to Germany, usually slipped between the lines of mundane letters or written on Bible paper. An important part of their activity was sending information – using false-bottomed suitcases or fake books – to those who were still underground in Germany. Brandt introduced the blonde Trudel as his wife, and they were happy despite their frugal lifestyle. He liked Oslo, where society was very democratic, in a country that had never had a tradition of courtly aristocracy. It was governed by a peaceful monarchy, and there was a popular story of how, when in 1927 a conservative tried to warn him against letting the 'dangerous communists' gain power, King Haakon VII had replied: 'I don't see the problem; after all, I'm also the king of the communists.'[40]

Brandt wrote every day, started smoking a pipe and continued to enjoy drinking. He hosted meetings of the little SAP cell in Oslo at his flat, although they were attended by only a dozen of the 200 political exiles in Norway. Brandt's residence permit in Norway was granted on condition that he did not engage in any political activity. It was a difficult promise to keep: in truth, that was all he did, whether it was welcoming exiles, writing articles or engaging in any of his various conspiratorial SAP activities, from organising contacts to financing SAP cells in other countries. In order to obtain a residence permit, he had had to become a student and pass an entry exam for the University of Oslo, where he was to study history and philosophy. This was his only higher education, and he was not an assiduous student. He preferred spending his time with Mot Dag (Towards Day), a Marxist and rather exclusive group made up of around 100 intellectuals who saw themselves as an elite, avant-garde section of the working class. The group was welcoming. Its leader, Erling Falk, was a fascinating man, and the group published interesting material in which otherwise taboo subjects like sexuality and the revolution of the individual were discussed freely. This was all well and good, apart from the fact that there were not actually any workers in the group, and moreover the principal labour party, the DNA, viewed Mot Dag as a sectarian group and did not look kindly on the meetings. In April 1934 Brandt was called to order because of the DNA's view that the two groups had been incompatible since 1925, but it took another year before he finally left the radical circle he liked so much. In the end, it was too important to maintain a good relationship with the Norwegian Labour Party. Indeed, after it had left Comintern, the DNA had become the biggest party in the International Bureau of Revolutionary Socialist Unity, also known as the London Bureau, which gathered together left-leaning socialists during the 1930s.[41] Brandt eventually saw the wisdom of staying on good terms with the party that could continue to support him through its networks.

In Oslo his life was never completely carefree. Despite his numerous pseudonyms, the German embassy in Norway was aware of him, probably because he had been reported by someone associated with the Norwegian Nazi Vidkun Quisling, who spied on exiles. A misspelt memo from 9 August 1933 mentions a 'communist agitator named Frahn', and under the name Willi Braun, Brandt had been noted as one of the 'agents' whom the Conservatives and the Farmers' Party wanted to expel. Until the DNA gained power in 1935, the exiles lived in fear of the Conservative government, which cooperated with the German authorities over exiles.[42] For Brandt, who regularly travelled between Oslo and many other European cities, this was especially true. On his way back from a trip to Brussels in February 1934, he went to the Netherlands to attend a conference of young socialists in Laren. Normally such meetings would be safely clandestine, but this time, when the debate was well underway, the police burst in, taking the meeting by surprise, after having been tipped off by the fascist, pro-Nazi, Catholic mayor of the town. Four Germans were arrested, and the non-Germans were sent to Belgium. Willy Brandy managed to trick them into believing he was Norwegian and escape arrest by handing over his plastic-wrapped residence permit instead of his passport and talking loudly in Norwegian with his DNA friends Finn Moe and Aake Ording.

The solidarity he experienced with his Scandinavian friends made a great impression on him, as did the way numerous Norwegians were prepared to break the law to help him. In 1936 a student agreed to a marriage of convenience with Gertrud, Willy's girlfriend, which would give her Norwegian citizenship and let her send information to Germany more easily. The student was called Gunnar Gaasland, and neither did he hesitate to lend Brandt his passport which, once it had been modified slightly, could be used for Brandt's mission to Berlin. He learned the details of Gunnar's life by heart so that he could take on his persona convincingly. For her part Gertrud, by 'bringing home the bacon', was a great support to her partner and political ally. Employed as a secretary, she became a psychoanalyst's assistant and was soon working for the famous doctor Wilhelm Reich, who regularly hosted the couple socially. Reich was later a favourite of the 1968 youth movement, which saw him as the great forefather of sexual liberation. Mixing psychoanalysis with Marxism, his 1933 book *The Mass Psychology of Fascism* had linked social behaviour under authoritarian regimes to economic inequality, sexual oppression in education and obedience in the family. Once more, Brandt was fascinated by a peerless personality and became one of a number of Reich's enthusiastic disciples.

During his first few months in Oslo, Brandt was torn between his exile's homesickness and his excitement at discovering freedom in all its forms. He was worried about his status as an immigrant, but he was reassured by the tolerance he found in the political culture of his new country and its uninhibited attitude to sensual pleasure. Nevertheless, he was aware of Reich's pseudo-scientific excesses as well as the slightly irrational extent of his interest in paranormal phenomena.[43]

Just before his mission to Berlin, in May 1936, Brandt went to Paris with the same enthusiasm of all anti-Nazi emigrés. Paris was, with Prague, one of the principal centres of German emigration, not just in terms of the numbers of exiles but also because of its symbolic significance. It was the capital of the French Revolution, and had always welcomed prestigious German refugees, like Heinrich Heine in the 1830s and Karl Marx ten years later. As on his first visit to the French capital in February 1934, in 1936 Brandt was going to meet Jacob Walcher, the head of the SAP. Later, while Brandt chose the moderation of reformism in postwar West Germany, Walcher opted for the East and the German Democratic Republic (GDR), but he was quickly banned by the East German Communist Party because of his readiness to criticise. In the middle of the 1930s the various exiled members of the SAP were still very left-leaning and invested their hopes in the USSR as the force to resist Nazism. Seduced by Paris like all the Germans who lived there, Brandt relished the city and enjoyed the white bread, cheese and red wine. Later he would say he had been captivated by the energy of the French left.

On his first visit in 1934 he had arrived at the Gare du Nord on 12 February, the day of the general strike. The strike had been organised in response to the dramatic events of 6 February, when an anti-parliamentary protest held by the far-right leagues had turned into a riot, provoking a political crisis. In his letters Brandt was quite critical of the way the French Socialist Youth was organised, although what really bothered him was his lack of proper contacts in Paris. Although he moderated his judgement of the French Popular Front in later accounts and in his memoirs, at the time he was very depressed by what he saw of the exiled anti-Nazis, whose main activity seemed to be passionately discussing the idea of forming a German Popular Front that would unite the social democrats of the SPD, the communists of the KPD and the various socialist groups like the SAP. It was not a completely hopeless utopian dream: the Comintern did have plans at the time to start cooperating with former 'social traitors', and the German communists were less hostile than they had been.

About 50 exiles met regularly at the Hotel Lutétia, a gathering point for the German left in Paris which became, four years later, the headquarters of Admiral Canaris's Abwehr (the German military intelligence service) and remained so for the rest of the Occupation. In 1935–6, the push to create a German Popular Front centred on the writer Heinrich Mann, who had fled to the South of France after Hitler gained power. Heinrich was the older, more republican and more politically active brother of Thomas Mann, and he put the German exiles – whom he called 'the voice of a people who have become silent' – in contact with French intellectuals like Henri Barbusse and André Malraux.

A formal petition on behalf of the Lutétia committee was drawn up in February 1936, with almost 120 signatures; among them was Willy Brandt's for the SAP. His was a rather absurd addition, as he had never been to any of the committee's meetings and was only at the Hotel Lutétia as an SAP observer.[44] However, his future detractors in the Federal Republic of Germany (FRG) in the 1960s and 1970s would never forget that he had signed the petition, and suspected him of closer links to the communists than he admitted. Even though Brandt did not meet Walter Ulbricht, the future leader of the GDR, until 1949, their signatures appear together at the bottom of another petition for unity against Hitler created in May 1936, which was also signed by the heads of the KPD in exile in Moscow. In his writing Brandt supported the idea of a popular front, in particular for the socialist youth,[45] although he found the discussions at the Lutétia much too abstract compared with those of the Nordic Conference for the Popular

Front, held in Gothenburg in October 1938. The project for a German Popular Front was short-lived; the agreement between communists and socialists was temporary and artificial. The SPD leadership, under the name Sopade, at that time based in Prague (they moved to Paris in 1938, and then London in 1940), was particularly circumspect about the project.

At the end of 1936, after his mission to Berlin, Brandt went via Prague, the city of Kafka, to Mährisch-Ostrau, in northern Moravia, to attend the SAP's 'family gathering'. Although there were comrades from several different regions in attendance, with only 16 delegates the little political party did not look in good shape. The mood was gloomy on the journey home – by train from the Sudetes to Copenhagen via Poland, and by boat from Copenhagen to Oslo.

Brandt's only real success at that time was the triumph of the campaign for the German pacifist Carl von Ossietzky to receive the Nobel Peace Prize, a campaign in which he was energetically involved. Ossietzky had succeeded the famous political writer Kurt Tucholsky at the head of the weekly democratic magazine *Weltbühne*. He was arrested by the Nazis after the Reichstag Fire in February 1933 and interned at the Sonnenburg concentration camp. Although he was suffering from tuberculosis he was condemned to hard labour on a project to dry out a swamp at the Papenburg-Esterwegen camp, and he became a martyr of the anti-military cause. Brandt had not been involved in setting up the campaign for the Nobel Prize, but he promoted it actively among the Norwegian left. The task was somehow to convince the members of the Nobel Committee to withstand international pressure and to support Ossietzky. After two failed attempts in 1934 and 1935, Ossietzky was nominated again in 1936 by the Labour members of the Norwegian parliament, and he received the support of several former Nobel winners, including Romain Rolland, winner of the Literature Prize in 1915, and intellectuals around the world, including Albert Einstein and Thomas Mann. Ossietzky was under guard in hospital when the prize was finally awarded to him on 23 November 1936. Hitler was furious. Göring summoned Ossietzky to a meeting, and the German press, under orders from the regime, mocked the Nobel Committee. Ossietzky died, in large part because of his mistreatment by the Nazis, in May 1938. For Brandt, the prize was a small personal success. In 1971, when he received the same prize for his engagement with Ostpolitik, he paid tribute to Ossietzky as a pacifist and to the courage of the Nobel Committee for this 'victory over barbarity'.[46]

Internationally, the situation in Spain since Franco's coup in July 1936 had polarised Europeans. The more dramatic the Civil War became, the more the SAP socialists grew anxious about the in-fighting among the Spanish, and Moscow's attitude towards Spain. The SAP decided to send Brandt to Barcelona at the beginning of 1937, where he was to act as an observer for the party as well as a correspondent for the Norwegian press. For Brandt, it was a brilliant opportunity, although he had good reason not to let his freedom of movement go to his head. His numerous journeys had not gone unnoticed in Oslo and he was interrogated by the police about his political activities abroad before he could discreetly start his trip to Catalonia, via Paris.[47]

There are several versions of Brandt's time in Barcelona and his 'participation' in the Spanish Civil War, differing according to the teller's desire to praise or discredit him. What is certain is that the time he spent in the Catalonian capital made him aware of the full extent of the crimes of his compatriots in the Condor Legion – a unit of volunteers from the German Luftwaffe who helped Franco militarily – especially after the notorious massacre at Guernica on 26 April 1937. He had already had the reality of war brought home to him in March, when he witnessed the fighting around Huesca. But he did not participate directly in the fighting and he was not wounded, unlike George Orwell, whom he met while he was there. Confusingly, there is another Willy Brandt, from Hesse, who did fight in Spain, as part of the Thälmann Centuria, a communist international militia group named after the leader of the German KPD, Ernst Thälmann. Arrested in Brussels, handed over to the Gestapo and imprisoned at Dachau, which he survived, Brandt's communist namesake was interrogated and tortured by the Nazis, who believed him responsible for our Brandt's activities in Norway as well as his own crime of fighting with the communists against the Germans in the Spanish Civil War[48] – an act which would in turn be attributed incorrectly to the Social Democrat Willy Brandt by West German conservatives.

In reality, Brandt's main activity while at the Hotel Falcon in Barcelona in 1937 was writing letters to the leaders of his party, and penning articles that he never managed to type up or send, being without either a typewriter or a trustworthy courier. Frustrated by his isolation and the impotence his material circumstances forced upon him, he even considered cutting his mission short. Anyway, what exactly was this mission? Acting as something between observer and intermediary, he maintained contact with the Spanish socialists of the anti-Stalinist Workers' Party of Marxist Unification, POUM, which like the Norwegian DNA was a member of the London Bureau. He observed the political situation closely, especially the way the Stalinists managed to take charge of the Republican government and eliminate their enemies from the labour movement, socialists and anarchists both. In the written reports he sent to the SAP leadership, Brandt was quite critical of the POUM; he felt the Spanish socialists were letting themselves be blinded by Moscow, and that their national policy was too inconsistent.[49]

One of the ways the Soviets contrived to control the Spanish left was by giving material and logistical aid in return for a guarantee that the communists would have the dominant position. Their direct attacks on the POUM, which they tried to ban in June 1937, followed the same logic as the trials against supposed internal enemies in the USSR, where the Stalinists used the accusation of Trotskyism as a way to get rid of their critics. Members of the SAP were also the victims of these attacks when they tried to defend the POUM socialists. Brandt formed a very accurate idea of Stalinist practices while he was in Spain. He was aware of the elimination of activists and was very affected by the disappearance of his friend Mark Rein, kidnapped from his hotel room in Barcelona in April 1937. The son of the Menshevik politician Rafael Abramowitch, who had fled Lenin's Russia, Rein had been brought up in Berlin and, apparently, was too obvious an emblem of the social democratic orientation of those on the left who were fighting alongside the Spanish Republicans. When he disappeared, Brandt helped search for him and questioned the Comintern communists in Spain in particular. One of them, his compatriot Karl Mewis, agreed to meet him but responded to his concerns with a shrug of the shoulders. Mewis was later part of the leadership of the East German Communist Party in Berlin, when in 1948 he suggested publicly that Mark Rein had been liquidated by Trotskyists 'after having passed his last evening with Willy Brandt'.[50] In July 1937, in his final report from his mission, Brandt described the Stalinists and their methods in detail. In the same report he promised that the German revolutionary socialists would learn much from the experience of their Spanish comrades in their fight for liberation. He finished his report with the words, 'Long live the Spanish Revolution! Long live the victory over Fascism!'[51] Even so, the unsavoury atmosphere of unfounded accusations left a bitter aftertaste when, at a meeting of the London Bureau in August 1937, he was accused of having been somehow implicated in the communists' arrests of his friends from the POUM.[52]

The outcome of 'his' war in Spain was not altogether positive. On his return to Oslo, however, he began to realise that he had learned a great deal in his few weeks there, and that his experiences would prove useful for his ongoing political activities. He felt less and less Marxist and – perhaps because of what he had learned in the field in Barcelona, perhaps because of the reformist influence of the Norwegian Labour Party – he gradually started rebuilding his relationship with the SPD. He met an exiled member of the SPD, Erich Ollenhauer, in Paris and then again in Oslo. Twenty-five years later, Brandt succeeded him as head of the party in West Germany.

'Frahm, Herbert Ernst Karl, born on 18 December 1913 in Lübeck, is hereby deprived of his German nationality, with effect from 1 September 1938.' On 5 September 1938 the Reich's official publication released the fifty-first list of traitors disowned by Nazi Germany. Brandt only learned the news a month later, because that September he was in Paris, where the German Popular Front was in its final throes. Heinrich Mann had asked to be introduced to Brandt, now 25 years old, about whom he had heard but who never attended the Front's meetings because the KPD communists refused to admit 'SAP Trotskyists'. They met at the Hotel Lutétia a few days after the Munich Conference, where Daladier and Chamberlain had appeased Hitler and allowed him to annex the Sudetenland without reprisal. They had responded in a similarly passive way to the Anschluss of Austria in March. 'We will never see the seven towers of Lübeck again,' Heinrich Mann said tearfully to his equally homesick young compatriot. For a brief moment, the ageing son of a grand patrician family and the fatherless man with his whole life before him were united by the shared experience of exile.[53]

Now stateless, Brandt needed to apply for Norwegian nationality, but he only fulfilled one of the two necessary conditions. Although he had lived in Norway for more than five years, he was not a regular taxpayer. He was told to reapply in a year. During this transitional period, with the international situation growing ever tenser, his private affairs began to get complicated. In 1939, his girlfriend Gertrud decided to follow Wilhelm Reich to the United States, but meanwhile a new woman had come into Willy's life. Anna Carlota Thorkildsen, almost ten years older than him, was a small, lively brunette with dark eyes.[54] Her father was

Norwegian, her mother half-German and half-American. She worked in Oslo as a secretary at the Institute of Comparative Cultural Studies, but Willy met her for the first time in the Mot Dag movement. At Carlota's side, Brandt now entered into a completely Norwegian world, and the flat saw fewer and fewer German guests.

He still wrote numerous articles for the Norwegian press, especially about the situation in Germany, which was deteriorating, but where he was sure that 'Nazis would be in the minority if you could hold a secret, truly democratic vote', and that 'the German people have not actively helped with the persecution of the Jews.' In his view, the pogroms of 1938 had been above all an instrument of terror used by the Nazis to 'intimidate the German people'.[55] The political landscape had changed significantly when Stalin signed the Nazi–Soviet pact with Hitler during the night of 23 August 1939. Certainly, it was theoretically possible that the pact was merely a tactic to gain time and prepare the USSR for conflict with Germany, but after seeing Moscow's role in Spain and the attitudes of the German communists in Paris, it seemed to Brandt that the Russians had finally shown their true colours. Brandt wrote to Walcher on 26 August, warning that 'we should now see the USSR as a leading reactionary force, alongside Hitler.' The Soviet attack on Finland at the end of November 1939 threw old friendships and enmities into disarray and completely altered 'our position regarding Russia'. Brandt was now moving firmly away from revolutionary socialism and formulating what would be his new creed: 'Socialism must be based upon liberty and democracy in order to be worthy of its name.'[56] It was an early outline of the Western sense of 'democratic socialism' that would reach maturity 20 years later in the SPD's Godesberg Programme: 'Socialism can only be achieved through democracy, and democracy through socialism.'

On 8 April 1940, Brandt had three important pieces of news that brought his personal life into close contact with history: he received the first copy of his first book, *The Military Goals of the Great Powers and the New Europe*; Carlota told him she was expecting a child; and in the early hours of 9 April, the rumour of a German attack on Denmark and Norway was confirmed. Brandt had to leave the capital, along with the flood of Norwegians fleeing the Luftwaffe planes. There was no doubt that he would soon be sought by the German authorities, who were received with open arms by the Norwegian politician Vidkun Quisling. On 9 April Brandt left Oslo and headed north with Tranmæl and other members of the DNA leadership, with the initial intention of going to Sweden, but ultimately he decided to hide out in the rural villages of northern Norway. He left Carlota behind. British troops soon arrived to try and halt the German advance but, badly equipped, they fell back after a few weeks in the middle of May 1940, at the same time as the Germans were beginning their invasion of Belgium, Luxembourg, the Netherlands and France.

On the same day in May, Brandt was hiding in a valley north of Åndalsnes. There was only one route out of the dead-end valley, and the advancing Wehrmacht forces had cut it off. He decided to try his luck and get captured posing as a Norwegian. If it worked, and they did not realise he was German, he could count on being freed quickly; to the Nazis, Scandinavians were Aryans *par excellence*. He happened to meet a friend from his time in Barcelona who was with a group of volunteer fighters based not far from where he was hidden. The friend was Paul Gauguin Junior, the painter's grandson, who said he would prefer to stay in hiding there and gave Brandt his Norwegian uniform. Brandt put on the clothes, which were a little tight but otherwise a reasonable fit, and destroyed his own papers. It was a good decision: Brandt was taken to the prisoner-of-war camp at Dovre, and, along with all the other Norwegian prisoners, was released in the middle of June.[57]

That uniform saved Willy Brandt's live. He never imagined the trouble it would cause him when, in Bonn and in Berlin, he was accused of treason for being 'the stateless man who dared to wear a foreign uniform'.

Stockholm, the Resistance and the Secret Services

Brandt was now a foreigner, stateless, uprooted once more. In Europe in 1940 traditional loyalties were being shaken, and one's friends became one's only family. On his arrival in Stockholm, Brandt was welcomed by a group of Norwegians who were hostile to Quisling's collaborationist regime. The Norwegian minister of trade, Anders Frihagen, had also fled Oslo for the Swedish capital but remained in contact with the rest of the Norwegian government, who were in exile in London. Thanks to him, Brandt received his Norwegian identity papers on 2 August 1940: having been a German exiled in Norway, he was now a Norwegian exiled in Sweden. For a while he toyed with the idea of travelling even further, to the United States, like Walcher and Gertrud, who tried to persuade him to join her in New York.[58] He was reasonably well informed about America from his émigré friends, although his perception of the great power was still strongly influenced by his own socialist ideas, as well as those of his contacts across the Atlantic.

He registered with the Swedish government as a journalist employed by the Overseas News Agency (ONA), which had close links to the American and British secret services. He allowed doubt to circulate about whether he would remain in Sweden – it was one way of keeping out of the authorities' way. Sweden was cooperating with Nazi Germany, albeit as little as possible, in order to avoid the same fate as its neighbours Denmark and Norway.[59] Nevertheless, Brandt was arrested multiple times and threatened with deportation. Sweden was trying to protect its neutral status, which in practice meant trying hard not to provoke Berlin, and indeed turning a blind eye to the content of certain commercial exchanges. After spending a few months considering his situation, Brandt decided to stay in Stockholm, where he was well integrated into the resistance network, along with other Norwegian exiles and social democrats from 14 different countries. The

Norwegian press office became a hub of external resistance, second in importance only to the London office.

Brandt was not as calm or happy as he had once been. He was now 27 years old, and father to a baby girl, Ninja, born on 30 October 1940. Carlota and the baby had stayed in Oslo. Just before Christmas he decided to travel to see them. Mixing business with pleasure, he also made use of the trip to renew his contacts with the internal resistance network. Even though he tried to travel discreetly, he had to pass through border controls between Sweden and Norway twice, and on his return to Stockholm he was being watched by the Swedish secret police. His flat was searched.[60] He was able to relax slightly when Carlota and the baby joined him in Stockholm in the spring of 1941, and he and Carlota were married on 28 May. Carlota found work in the press department of the Norwegian diplomatic mission. The Frahm family seem to have been happy; photos from the time show a healthy baby, a good-looking young couple and groups of friends.

He was very busy with work. Between writing articles and books, his political activities and his involvement with the secret services, he barely had any time to spend with his family. His relationship with Carlota was still harmonious, although only for another couple of years. They always remained close, however, perhaps because of little Ninja, or because their lives, friends and political activities were so deeply intertwined. There is a photograph of them at a parade on 1 May 1944: Brandt is smiling, with Ninja perched on his shoulders, and Carlota stands at his side with a jaunty hat perched on her wavy hair.

Brandt was more prolific than ever in Stockholm. His articles were becoming more professional, and he wrote hundreds of them for 70 different newspapers, as well as chapters for edited volumes and several books of his own. These dealt mainly with the question of how to imagine peace: *The Military Goals of the Great Powers and the New Europe* and even *After Victory: The Goals of War and Peace*.[61] His major concern, which he shared with the International Group of Democratic Socialists which gathered together comrades from neutral and occupied countries, was the fate that awaited Germany once Hitler was defeated and the war was over. Brandt was the secretary of this 'Little International'.[62] They discussed how to go about the democratisation that was so necessary in Germany, as well as the question of any territorial losses. On this latter point, Brandt disagreed with his socialist friend Bruno Kreisky, the future Austrian chancellor, who insisted that in future Austria should be a separate nation from Germany. Brandt had two guiding principles at that time: national unity and 'the integration of German interests with the interests of the community of Europe' in the 'United States of Europe'.[63] The idea that it would be possible to organise a peace based on equality between all European countries, Germany included, was an unusual one at a time of almost unanimous hatred towards Germany and Germans.

When his book *After Victory* appeared in 1944, he was already known to the American secret services, who wrote positive reports about him, considered him to be one of the trustworthy European socialists, and studied his suggestions for the Old World's future with interest. Brandt was anxious that European democrats should win America's trust: 'America will be of decisive importance after the war,' he wrote to Walcher in June 1942, 'and Europe will not be able to solve the problem of reconstruction without help from across the Atlantic. The Americans' choice will be decisive: whether they go back to isolationism, or whether they invest their immeasurable resources in aiding progress in Europe.'[64]

The fact that Sweden was a neutral country meant that all the various secret services could be found there: American, British, and of course the Soviet NKVD. Brandt was not actually employed as a spy for any of these foreign powers but, as an emigré and a journalist, he had no qualms about talking to everyone, especially once Hitler's breaking of the Nazi–Soviet pact and his Operation Barbarossa – invasion of the

USSR – had changed the game once more on 22 June 1941. From that point onwards all those in the resistance, including the conservative group led by Goerdeler and Stauffenberg, considered cooperation with the Soviet Union to be a useful way to harm the Nazi regime. Brandt passed on sporadic information, such as what he had seen of the state of German troops in Norway. At the Soviet embassy he met ambassador Alexandra Kollontai, who was well known in the diplomatic world. A former fellow traveller of Lenin, she had been a people's commissar in 1917–18, and then a women's rights activist, following the example of the German Clara Zetkin.

Traces of Brandt, going by the name Polyarnik, can be found in the NKVD dossiers of the time. It was through his contact with the Soviet embassy that he was introduced, one day in June 1944, to a German who wanted to meet the famous Kollontai, and brought him 'greetings from Julius Leber'. The German was Adam von Trott zu Solz, an aristocratic diplomat who was a member of the Kreisau circle, a conservative resistance group that met secretly inside Germany. Several of the group were preparing to form a government once Hitler had been deposed and his regime overthrown by a coup. Among them were Claus von Stauffenberg, who tried to set off a bomb at Hitler's feet a few weeks later on 20 July 1944, and Julius Leber, Frahm's mentor and role model from Lübeck. Leber's name was the magic word for Brandt, because he still saw Leber as the incarnation of the principle that democracy should be able to defend itself, the idea 'that you must only commit yourself to your country if you are decided to make it a country of love and justice'.[65] Von Trott explained the planned coup to Brandt and probed him about his readiness to aid a future German government. He wanted Brandt to set up an interview for him with Kollontai so he could find out about Moscow's intentions once Hitler had been eliminated. In the end, von Trott decided not to go ahead with the meeting in case the Soviet embassy was being watched by the Gestapo.[66] Brandt never saw him or Leber again: after their attempt on Hitler's life failed, von

Trott was arrested at the end of July and executed at the end of August, and Leber was condemned to death in October and executed on 5 January 1945.

Leber knew nothing of the last phase of Frahm-Brandt's journey back from SAP radicalism to the SPD. On 9 October 1944, the Stockholm SAP cell announced its support for the exiled SPD. After plenty of setbacks, the rebellious young socialist rejoined the party which, in the end, was his true home. His experience of radicalism and his contact with communists had repelled him and pushed him towards an even closer adherence to the principles set out by the Social Democrat Otto Wels, when he had justified the SPD's refusal to vote to give Hitler full powers in the Reichstag on 23 March 1933: 'We, the Social Democrats of Germany, declare at this grave hour our faithfulness to the principles of humanity and justice, to freedom and socialism.'

Far from being a hollow phrase, Wels's words went to the heart of social democratic thought, from its roots in the revolution of 1848–9. Brandt would defend democratic socialism over the coming decades, notably during the Godesberg Programme of 1959, which saw a rightward shift in SPD policy, and also against attacks coming from the extreme left, Maoists, extra-parliamentary opposition and pacifists during the 1980s. His own detour through radicalism may have been a 'sectarian impasse', but by forcing him to justify himself, it allowed him to become the Willy Brandt of the reformed SPD.[67] Above all, it is clear that his experience of Scandinavian socialism profoundly influenced his attachment to democratic socialism, a term which the social democrats would have to defend against the communists' usurpation of the world 'socialism' as a screen for their slide towards totalitarianism.

By the spring of 1945, Nazism was nearly finished. Liberated from their concentration camps through Count Folke Bernadotte's intervention, the Norwegian deportees arrived in Stockholm and, famished as they were, took part in an emotional May Day parade. That evening, during a meeting, Brandt rushed to the microphone to announce the news of Hitler's suicide. One week later, on 8 May, Nazi Germany surrendered unconditionally. Brandt had difficulty deciding what to do next – should he return to Germany? At 31 years old, he had hardly anything to return to. What could he do there? Meanwhile, he had plenty going for him in Scandinavia, not least the relationship that was beginning to take shape with Rut Hansen, a Norwegian resistance fighter who had escaped to Stockholm, where she had married her friend from the Norwegian resistance, 'Brum' Ole Olstad Bergaust, in 1942. She was six years younger than Brandt, but they had much in common. Like him, Rut came from a humble background. Her father had died when she was very young, and she had been raised by her mother, who worked in a milk factory. Also like Willy, she had joined the socialist party when she was 16. They started to grow closer, although in 1945 both of them were still married to other people. In fact, they met for the first time on Rut's wedding day: 'He was surrounded by women and apparently very happy to be so,' she remembered. Soon she too fell victim to the charm of this Scandinavian-seeming German.[68] Rut's husband died unexpectedly in 1946, and when Carlota finally agreed to a divorce in 1948, Willy and Rut made their relationship official. Their marriage was to last 30 years.

The Nuremberg Trials

In November 1945, torn between Norway, where he had a good career as a journalist, and Germany, whose future obsessed him, Brandt travelled as the Norwegian press correspondent to the International Military Tribunal at Nuremberg, where the Nazi war criminals were to be tried. He used the opportunity to make a detour to Lübeck and see his mother for the first time in ten years. His ancient hometown was so utterly ruined that he was unable to find his way around. The same devastation awaited him in Nuremberg, in Bavaria. The British bombardment on 2 January 1945 had destroyed the medieval town, one of the great free cities of the Holy Roman Empire and the site of the proclamation of the 1356 Golden Bull which fixed the rules for electing new emperors and made Nuremberg the location of the first Imperial Diet of every emperor's reign. The Nazis had tried to capitalise on its aura of importance and its connection to German tradition by holding their party congresses there. It was at Nuremberg, at one of the vast rallies held to celebrate the new, supposedly millenarian Reich, that the race laws of 1935 were announced. The incendiary bombs raining down in their hundreds of thousands were just one part of the retribution Germany had to endure in 1945. The international tribunal revealed the full extent of the crimes committed by the Nazi regime and showed how deeply implicated the administration and the military high command had been. Brandt stayed in Nuremberg covering the trials until February 1946 and returned again in May. His official papers from that time, with photographs of him in the Norwegian uniform he was made to wear by order of the military government, were circulated in the press 15 years later when people wanted to denounce him as 'the traitor'.

Who were the traitors and who were the criminals in 1945? For Brandt, there was no doubt, and he believed Germany should have to face up to what had happened to it, and what it had done to Europe. His new book, which was published in Oslo in 1946, was titled *Criminals and Other Germans*, and in it he tackled the question of culpability. The philosopher Karl Jaspers had given a series of lectures at Heidelberg University over the winter of 1945, dealing with the same problem; his *The Question of German Guilt* was published at about the same time as Brandt's book.[69] Both men were convinced that the theory dominant in the United States at the time, according to which the whole German population was guilty, was futile. Brandt found the idea of collective guilt unhelpful and damaging, because it played down personal guilt just at a time when those who were most guilty wanted to escape it. He believed the only collective guilt was that shared by the war criminals themselves, and that they should be punished. For the rest of the German people, rather than guilt he preferred to talk of responsibility and its consequence, the obligation to make financial as well as moral reparations.[70]

At Nuremberg, Brandt discovered the true horror of the concentration camps. Even in Sweden, where people had been very well informed, and where information about the use of Zyklon B gas had been circulated, people had believed it was a rumour, a resurgence of World War I propaganda. Admittedly, in his book *After Victory*, Brandt had denounced the Vichy regime's participation in the Holocaust, as well as the support the Nazis had received all over Europe, but these aspects only served to make him more certain that it was unthinkable to try to excuse Nazi Germany. The defeated Germans had to face their responsibility head on.

In Germany, the hour of reckoning had come. On 5 June 1945, the generals of the four victorious powers – Eisenhower of the United States, Zhukov of the USSR, Montgomery of Great Britain and de Lattre de Tassigny of France – signed the Berlin Declaration, announcing the assumption of supreme authority in Germany by the Allies, and setting out regulations for the disarmament of the German armed forces. Brandt, who had written that 'the Soviet Union and Great Britain will by and large take the reins, but the Americans have also decided to exercise their influence in Europe, rather than retreating into isolationism,'[71] saw this declaration as confirmation of his analysis. The Berlin Declaration restricted Germany to its borders as they had been on 31 December 1937, before the project of German expansion had begun with the Anschluss of Austria in March 1938.

Germany's new status was confirmed in the Potsdam Agreement, published on 2 August 1945: the defeated Germany was to be demilitarised, de-Nazified, decentralised and democratised without delay, and this process was to be carried out jointly by the four powers, who would each exercise control in their respective occupation zones. The four Allies were all, therefore, both collectively and separately responsible for Germany's fate. This meant imposing penalties, removing Nazis from positions of power, taking control of the economy and of production, and overseeing material as well as political reconstruction. Berlin played a central role in this immense enterprise, which was already starting to crack as the first signs of disagreement between the Soviet Union and the Western Allies were visible. Seen as the heart of Nazi power, and a symbol of the evil to be eradicated, the Reich's former capital was coveted by everyone.

While the war was still going on, in February 1945, the Allies of the anti-Hitler coalition had gathered in Yalta and discussed the future division of Berlin into four sectors. The United States even withdrew its army – which had advanced east all the way to Thuringia, in what was to become the Soviet zone – over 100km westwards so as to ensure the Soviets would give them a sector in Berlin, which was right in the middle of the territory controlled by the Red Army. Stalin capitalised on the Western powers' desire for control over the German capital by demanding a larger Soviet occupation zone in the eastern part of Germany, in return for allowing them a slice of Berlin. The city was divided into four sectors, under the control of the four-power Allied Control Council (ACC). The ACC was supposed to act as a unanimous group, but it was soon split by differences of opinion and conflicts of interest between the Western powers and the Soviets. The two sides were unable to reconcile their radically different conceptions of the sort of democracy that should be installed in Germany.

Berlin was one possible option for Brandt's next move, although he hesitated until the autumn of 1946 before making his decision. By now he was fully integrated into the Norwegian labour movement, but he still felt German. Above all, what had motivated him to go into exile no longer existed. The time had come, it seemed, to be consistent and to put his democratic principles into action in the reconstruction of his country. In the spring of 1945 his letters to his friends in exile in the United States mentioned his fear of not being welcome in Germany, of being seen as a stranger, or even a traitor. On the other hand, he talked of his desire to be useful by returning home, even if the prospect of a move to Germany did not make his relationship with Carlota any easier.[72] There were also legal obstacles: he could not return without authorisation from the Allies, who were currently trying to manage a catastrophic lack of supplies in Germany at the same time as dealing with the hundreds of thousands of refugees still flooding in from the eastern zone. Anyway, he was officially Norwegian and did not yet know how to go about having his German nationality, stripped from him by the Nazis, restored.[73] After a few weeks in Nuremberg he returned to Scandinavia and officially re-established his links with the SPD when he attended a party congress in May 1946. He was certain that it was the party he belonged to – although he felt strongly that it did not expect him back.

Paris was also a possibility. The Norwegian foreign minister, Halvard Lange, had recently offered him a position as press attaché at the Norwegian embassy in France. 'Paris tempts me, certainly,' he wrote to his friend Stefan Szende. The job would put him in a good position to move on to an international organisation and participate in the construction of a new Europe. The problem with the idea was clear, however: 'If I accept, it will mean renouncing any active political role in Germany.'[74] When Lange unexpectedly offered him another position, this time as a press officer at the Norwegian Military Mission in Berlin, he leapt at the opportunity. Although his duties were primarily civil rather than military, he was given the rank of commander. He moved to Berlin on 17 January 1947. Once more he had to wear the Norwegian uniform that he would be reproached for in the near future. Rut joined him in Berlin at Easter. After 12 years abroad, looking at his country from afar, his exile was finally at an end.

2

In Berlin, at the Heart of the Cold War

1947, Berlin in Ruins

'Germany was no longer a state, it was no more than a geographical notion. Its government and its transport and supply systems were all in ruins. The Nazis left behind nothing but heaps of rubble, destroyed towns and factories, uprooted and desperate people [...] and motorways.'[1] The people, and their dreams of power, were as ruined as the cities. After the surrender of 1945 the Allied Powers were faced with an unprecedented task of reconstruction. All volunteers were welcome, although any Germans wanting to help had to be deemed 'reliable': free from any Nazi taint or suspicion of involvement in the crimes of the war. Men like Brandt were welcomed by the Western Allies because they could be certain they had not been corrupted by the Nazis and because, having lived outside Germany, their minds had not been poisoned by 12 years without democracy: 'In Scandinavia I absorbed a huge amount: a sense of reality, of the values of a liberal and social democracy, and of the advantages of being open-minded. I was able to draw from those experiences to help me assume my later responsibilities in Bonn and Berlin.'[2] For the moment his work consisted of keeping up to date with the news, reporting back to Norway about what he saw and heard from the Allied and German politicians he met, and analysing the development of East–West relations.

When Brandt arrived in January 1947, Berlin was already experiencing difficulties with the quadripartite division of Germany, and its own division. The policies being implemented in the Soviet zone and the eastern sector of Berlin belied the promise that all the zones would be treated equally, and strengthened the West's fears about Moscow's real intentions. Under the administration of the Soviet military, the transition had been very rapid. Thanks to the Soviets' support, German communists exiled in Moscow started returning home in April and May 1945. The de-Nazification process was being conducted through two vast programmes of confiscation and nationalisation, one agrarian and the other industrial, and the Soviets had placed German communists in all the important newly created positions. Nevertheless, the SPD still had a strong support base in the Soviet zone. To avoid any competition from the SPD, the KPD leadership, centred on Wilhelm Pieck and Walter Ulbricht, managed to force the SPD's Otto Grotewohl to 'unite the forces of the left'. The two parties, the KPD and the Soviet zone SPD, joined together on 22 April 1946 to form the Socialist Unity Party of Germany (SED). Pieck and Grotewohl's handshake on that occasion became, in a stylised image in front of a red flag, the symbol of the party that would govern the GDR for the next 40 years.

In the West, the formation of this new party – in which very few people had had any say – had an electrifying effect. The Social Democrats could not deny that a considerable number of East German workers were celebrating the fusion of the two parties, whether out of genuine conviction or opportunism. There was a sense of relief, too, that the sort of trench warfare the two parties had waged against each other for decades was a thing of the past. In West Berlin, however, where SPD members could be consulted, 82 per cent of Social Democrats opposed such a fusion; a majority only envisaged 'cooperation' with the communists.

The episode reinforced anti-communist feeling among the socialists of the western zones and, because they were right on the front line, especially in West Berlin. Brandt's return to social democracy was complete, and he had to bid farewell to his dream of doing away with class altogether. On 30 April 1946, he wrote bitterly to Walcher that there was undeniably 'joy at the move towards a more progressive structure in the eastern zone. But the joy is heavily counteracted by the fact that this "new democracy" has little in common with fundamental democratic rights.'[3] It was a pity, because now the war was over he would very much have liked to see the workers' movement united at last.[4] Even so, there was a certain naivety in his inability to predict what direction things were going, despite having seen the communists at work in Spain.

On 12 March 1947, in Fulton, Missouri, US President Truman announced what would come to be known as the Truman Doctrine. He offered American 'economic and financial aid' to the 'free peoples who are resisting attempted subjugation by armed minorities or by outside pressures'. Everything pointed towards a cold war that had already begun between East and West. In Moscow, in April 1947, a new Council of Foreign Ministers had ended in stalemate once again. The four powers, really only ever united by their shared hostility to Hitler, were more and more incapable of agreeing on how to govern occupied Germany. The United States and the United Kingdom decided to go ahead with their own idea of how to rebuild the economy by fusing their two zones into a 'bizone' which would be better suited to the task of reconstruction. In August 1948, the French joined them.

For Brandt in Berlin, the priority was to find his place again in the SPD. Since Germany's defeat, the oldest party in the country had re-formed itself around the charismatic figure of Kurt Schumacher. Schumacher had opposed the Nazis – he had publicly called them swine in 1932 – and he embodied the idea of 'the other Germany', challenging the communists' monopoly on resistance to Hitler.[5] Severely injured in World War I and mistreated in Nazi prisons, his disfigured body was the image of the German people whose dignity he wanted to rebuild. Schumacher was a difficult man; some said this was the fault of his Prussian origins, but to others it was because of what he had suffered. He was brusque and could be cutting, and he was uncompromising in his stance towards the Western occupying forces. They, in their turn, vastly preferred dealing with Konrad Adenauer, Schumacher's Christian Democrat rival and a much more flexible man. The Americans, British and French distrusted Schumacher and called him as a 'red-painted fascist'. He certainly made a powerful impression on the young Brandt, although the two men disagreed about almost everything. In particular, Brandt disapproved of Schumacher's hostile attitude towards the project of integrating the western zones into the new structures of the Western world. He told Schumacher that he reserved the right to discuss 'certain turns of phrase and formulations that come right from the party leader'. In the same letter, however, he assured him of his loyalty to the SPD; he knew he needed to counter the rumours spread by his rivals that he was a communist agent.[6]

Brandt dealt directly not with Schumacher but with his right-hand man, Franz Neumann. Neumann had also been an important opponent of the Nazi regime and had been sent to prison and then placed under house arrest for years. After the war, he joined the SPD leadership again and fully intended to stay there despite his fear that Brandt, the young and ambitious 'remigrant', coveted his position. Many of these 'remigrants' – those who had come back from exile – were quite put out at not receiving a warm welcome on their return. The first few months at the SPD were hard for Brandt, and his life was not altogether comfortable, although his position at the Norwegian Military Mission came with considerable benefits. There was a shortage of good-quality accommodation in Berlin, as well as coal and fuel; there were always people in the Tiergarten, the huge park in the city centre, cutting down their own firewood. Willy and his wife Rut were given a flat in Charlottenburg, in the British sector in the centre of West Berlin. Their situation improved slightly in 1948 when the

West German party leadership paid for them to have a house and a car in Wilmersdorf, complete with maid and chauffeur. It was privilege verging on luxury.

Life was harsh for everyone in Berlin; the first few postwar months, an icy winter in the ruins, were terrible. In his first weeks in Berlin, before Rut joined him, Willy wrote her dozens of letters in which he sounds completely overwhelmed by the situation there, describing the lack of electricity and the people who were found frozen to death in their beds: 'I don't usually pray, and I don't believe it does much good. But if I did I would throw myself on my knees and say: Dear God, give these starving people in their ruined homes at least a bit of heat!'[7] When Rut arrived, appointed by the Norwegian Mission as his secretary, he was depressed and not far from giving it all up. Fortunately, their status as foreigners attached to the occupation forces gave them access to better food – and, above all, to large quantities of one of the black market's most important commodities: cigarettes. In an economy ravaged by Nazi policies and then the war, American cigarettes became a medium of exchange, much more valuable than the completely devalued Reichsmark. Even after the monetary reform in the spring of 1948 which improved Germany's finances and re-established a supply-and-demand market system, Berlin would experience more shortage due to the USSR's blockade of the city. Rut liked to tell the story of how after the birth of their son Peter, on 4 October 1948, they paid the hospital doctors in margarine, sugar, flour and cheese.[8]

Despite their slightly straitened circumstances, Willy and Rut were happy, and his career seemed to be on the right track. On 1 February 1948, Schumacher had appointed him to mediate between the SPD leadership and the Allied Powers in Berlin. This was a significant promotion, as he was now the representative of his party's management committee; he was instructed to try to persuade the Allies to follow policies that would be favourable to Germany. He and Rut were married on 4 September, just one month before the birth of their first child. Earlier that summer, on 1 July, Willy had regained his German nationality, although without becoming Herbert Frahm again. 'I associated that name almost solely with my difficult childhood; my mother no longer used it and my father never had.'[9] He still had to go through the bureaucratic process to get Brandt recognised as his and his family's surname. His request was finally granted on 11 August 1949.[10] His years of resistance in exile were now part of his life story, not just as a memory but as the foundation on which he built the rest of his career. Despite all his loyalty to his rediscovered homeland, Norway would always remain his second country, as well as that of the women in his life: Carlota, his daughter Ninja and Rut. Throughout his life he spoke Norwegian to all three of them.[11]

The Blockade: Throwing Down the Gauntlet

In 1948, Berlin was one of a kind, its special status having been defined by the Potsdam Agreement. Although most of historic Berlin, the capital of the former state of Prussia, was in the Soviet sector, the three sectors of West Berlin formed a unique area. It was a little provincial island, a long way to the east of its natural political and ideological home in the western zones between the Rhine and the Elbe. It had a hierarchical system of authority, in which the German elite and local government were subordinate to the three Western powers. In practice, that meant that any law passed by the city's parliament had to be ratified by the Allies before coming into force, and that the mayor of Berlin could not govern without their agreement. Despite the partition of the city into sectors, from a legal point of view it was effectively under collective management.

In the spring of 1948, the ACC finally failed definitively: after having pursued a politics of obstruction for months, the Soviets left the Allied Kommandantur (the Berlin department of the ACC). They started putting pressure on West Berlin, which, it was now clear, they saw as an intolerable foreign body in the middle of their Soviet zone. At the beginning of April they claimed control over trains coming from the western zones, which had to cross the Soviet zone on their way to West Berlin. They began interfering with trade between their sector and the Western part of the city. On 7 April, a collision between a Soviet fighter plane and a British transport plane raised tensions between the Allies even further – according to the agreement, the Soviets were not supposed to fly above West Berlin. The anxiety in the city was palpable: there were fears of a new, perhaps global conflict, and there would certainly be difficulties at home, on the little Western raft of West Berlin, adrift in a sea that looked more and more menacing.

In the end it was the monetary reform of West Germany, which took effect in West Berlin as well, that gave Moscow the excuse to cut all access to West Berlin. Borrowing tactics from the siege warfare of the Middle Ages, the Soviets imposed a total blockade on the city. The monetary reform was a windfall for the Russians, because the replacement of the old, depreciated Reichsmark by the Deutschmark, and the significant reduction in Germany's money supply, were unilateral decisions taken by the Western Allies without Russia's consent. The new notes were printed in the United States and transported secretly to West Germany which, theoretically, should have been treated together with East Germany by all four of the Allies, including Russia. Even though, as Brandt emphasised, the Russians' policies had all been aimed at separation rather than unification from the beginning, the Soviets seized the opportunity to object. They believed they would be triumphant if it came to the use of force in Berlin. Overnight, they severed all routes linking Berlin to the western zones – roads as well as railways. They also cut any access from the city to its Soviet zone surroundings, which was where it obtained most of its food and fuel. In the tiny island of West Berlin there was suddenly no coal being delivered: 'Without coal, there is no heat, no gas, and no electricity, and so no trams, no trains and no work.'[12]

In response, the Western Allies decided to airlift in anything West Berlin lacked – food, coal, machines – so that the city would hold out. This extraordinary aerial bridge was put in place on 24 June 1948. Nobody at the time had any idea how long it would be needed. In fact, it lasted 11 months and had several decisive effects. On the ground, the airlift meant hardship for the besieged city, with electricity only available for four hours a day, and public transport shut down at 6 p.m. Watching from afar, the rest of West Germany, as well as Berlin, felt immense gratitude towards the Americans, who were in charge of the airlift. The British also contributed aeroplanes, and the French, who did not have many planes, built an airport at Tegel in just 90 days to relieve some of the pressure at Tempelhof airport. It was the magnanimity of American power that left the strongest impression, however. In the new global confrontation that became the Cold War, the United States did not simply represent the pole of liberalism facing communism, and the Americans were no longer seen as occupiers: they had become the liberators of West Berlin, without whom the city would have been swallowed up by the seemingly unstoppable Communist tide.

It was a long time since Brandt had had any illusions about the communists, but there were still plenty of Germans who were tempted by the promise of a better world under the auspices of the hammer and sickle; the Berlin blockade did much to disabuse them of that idea. For the Americans, the aerial bridge was always also a propaganda opportunity. In a few days, the blockade had worked a miracle around the free world, transforming the Germans from accomplices in the Nazis' crimes to victims of the communists' aggression. The former capital of the despised Reich had become a martyr city. Berlin was suddenly very visible, and its political figures started to be known in the wider world. On 9 September, Ernst Reuter, the mayor of Berlin, made a famous speech outside the ruined Reichstag:

> People of the world! […] Look upon this city and see that this city and this people must not, cannot be abandoned! There is only one thing for us all to do: to stand together for as long as it takes until the battle is won, until the battle is finally won, and we have victory over our enemies, victory over the forces of darkness.

Reuter and Brandt were friends, despite the 24 years that separated them. They first met in 1947 at the house of Annedore Leber, Julius Leber's widow, who lived in Berlin. They had much in common, besides a shared engagement in social democracy and the fact that both had lived in exile. When Herbert Frahm left for Scandinavia in the early 1930s, Reuter, the former mayor of Magdeburg, fled to Turkey, where he stayed until the end of the war, teaching administrative law at the University of Ankara. In contrast to the younger Brandt, he had already had a long political career, having been taken prisoner by the Russians during the Great War, converted to Bolshevism and named people's commissar for German affairs in the Volga German Autonomous Soviet Socialist Republic. On his return to Germany he was present at the 1919 founding of the KPD. There was a genuine understanding between the two men, and Brandt and Rut often visited Reuter and his wife. People even took Brandt for Reuter's political heir. He was still searching for a father …

They shared the same conviction, opposed by Schumacher and Neumann, that the links between West Berlin and the rest of West Germany should be kept open at all cost, even if it meant collaborating with the conservatives. West Germany was in the process of developing the institutions and structures worthy of a state.[13] Admittedly, its constitution, called the Basic Law, was only intended to be effectual temporarily, until Germany was reunited; but for the democrats of West Berlin a connection to the Federal Republic of Germany (FRG) was the only one that bore thinking about. Brandt made his choice explicitly: 'Nowadays one cannot be a democrat without being anti-communist.'[14]

When the Soviets relaxed the blockade on 12 May 1949, Brandt gave up his position as intermediary between the SPD and the military governments of the three Western Allies. He wanted to be involved in active politics. He rejected Reuter's offer of a job managing the city's public transport, preferring a seat in the Berlin city parliament. Despite its special status as a quadripartite city, Berlin was effectively a city-state, like Bremen or Hamburg in West Germany. It was a city council at the same time as being a *Land*, or state, with its own legislative, executive and judiciary institutions. The Allied Powers were insistent that Berlin must remain a separate *Land*. It would be represented at the Bundestag, for which elections would be held in Bonn before the end of the summer, but its representatives would not be elected in the same way as elsewhere in West Germany. They would be appointed by the city parliament, and they would only have a deliberative vote – they would not enjoy full voting rights, only an advisory vote. Although the three western sectors of the city would not officially be part of the new Federal Republic of Germany, founded on 23 May 1949, Berlin would be able to use the FRG's laws. To make things clear, the Kommandantur reminded Ernst Reuter that Berlin would not be able to participate in the first Bundestag elections on an equal footing with the other regions of Germany.

In the middle of August, Brandt, at 35 years old, was appointed one of Berlin's eight representatives at the Bundestag. From then on he was constantly on the move between Berlin and Bonn, the FRG's capital city on the banks of the Rhine.[15] For the first time Rut started to feel the loneliness of a politician's wife. At the same time, Brandt was the victim of intense defamatory attacks, focusing on his 'ignoble past' and calling him a traitor; Rut regularly received anonymous hate mail.[16] Berlin managed to be both closely involved in and removed from the political life of the new Germany in the West. In Bonn, its tiny, temporary capital, the Bundestag had elected the first chancellor of the Federal Republic, the Christian Democrat Konrad Adenauer, at the head of a centre-right government. Brandt was a member of the opposition and was active on committees whose subjects interested him: foreign affairs and Berlin, where he thought the Allies' presence was vital to keep West Berlin safe.

In Berlin's city parliament he was a member of the majority party, but he still had some fighting to do: the SPD was riven by a bitter internal struggle. Brandt was head of the local SPD branch in the Wilmersdorf district of Berlin, and his conflict with his rival Franz Neumann, Schumacher's man, was becoming more and more open. He particularly objected to the idea that the members of Berlin's city parliament could pick and choose which federal laws to accept.[17] In Brandt's view, everything should be done to maintain links with Bonn, and that meant accepting all its laws, even those coming from the conservative group around Adenauer, who was not a popular figure in the SPD. On more than one occasion, Brandt stood against Neumann in the elections for the party's Berlin presidency. He lost in 1952, and again in May 1954, although by only two votes. His consolation was that losing so closely was more satisfying than winning by such a tiny margin.[18]

In the summer of 1952 Neumann lost his mentor Schumacher, whose ravaged body finally gave up at 56 years old. Reuter's and Brandt's moderate wing hoped that the intransigence Schumacher had encouraged, which had been so damaging to the socialists' image, would die with him. Schumacher had said no to everything, and especially to the suggestion that West Germany should cooperate with the Allies and their other European neighbours, on the pretext that the collective structures and integrative measures they proposed were a dangerous way of controlling Germany, of exploiting German resources and delivering them to the powers of capitalism, and of making the division of the country permanent. The uncompromising Schumacher had dismissed the Schuman Plan, published on 9 May 1950 as 'capitalist, conservative, clerical and cartelised'. The Schuman Plan proposed a greater level of cooperation between Western

European countries, including transferring control of the coal and steel industries to a common authority, the European Steel and Coal Community.

Schumacher's virulence is slightly surprising, because at heart he shared Adenauer's desire to reconcile all Germany's democrats and see them united in their opposition to communism. However, their ideas about how to go about this were very different. The more Adenauer pushed for cooperation with the West in order to achieve equal rights, and to maintain strong links with democrats there with a view to eventual reunification, the more Schumacher condemned his betrayal of his homeland and vilified the structures of the new Europe. For Brandt, there was no doubt: Schumacher's ideas were wrong in form as well as content. He believed the future would necessitate a combination of socialism and the 'United States of Europe'. 'Fundamentally, that is what I want to fight for in the years to come,' he wrote to Rut in 1947.[19] He said the same thing publicly at the party congress in 1948, insisting on the integration of Germany with democratic Western Europe. Two years later, the newspaper where he was now editor – the former *Sozialdemokrat*, which was now renamed the *Berliner Stadtblatt* – openly approved the Schuman Plan, against the view of Schumacher's SPD.

In Berlin, even more than elsewhere, a united Europe seemed to be a utopian idea. The clash between the two systems was part of daily life, as movement between the two halves of the city was still permitted and relatively easy. From the GDR's point of view, West Berlin was a provocation, a showcase for capitalism right in the heart of the country. Meanwhile, the inhabitants of West Berlin had front-row seats at the unfolding spectacle of East German socialism, as it had been formalised at the founding of the GDR on 7 October 1949. The SPD established an office in West Berlin, called the Ostbüro, with the aim of maintaining contact between the inhabitants of the new republic of workers and farmers, and the SPD in the West. The goal of eventual reunification had not been abandoned, and so it was necessary to keep the East Germans supplied with information from the 'free world'. The SPD made an alliance with the radio station Rias, which the Americans had set up in their sector in Berlin to broadcast to the GDR.

It is hardly surprising that the Ostbüro were accused of being 'provocateurs' and 'saboteurs' by the GDR when, on 17 June 1953, workers descended on the streets of East Berlin and other East German cities to protest at their production quotas being increased without giving them a better salary. The protests quickly escalated into a rebellion against the regime, and the rioters demanded free elections. On the other side of the Brandenburg Gate, which marked the boundary between the two sectors, the people of West Berlin witnessed the protest being repressed by the GDR police, and then crushed completely by Soviet tanks, with thousands of arrests and several dead.

The intervention of Russian tanks caused stupefaction in the West. The uprising was, quite logically, seen as tangible proof of the dissatisfaction felt by those on the other side of the demarcation line, and a sign of their desire to rejoin the truly democratic FRG. The East German regime was genuinely shaken by the events of 17 June, which the party elite saw as the greatest trauma in the history of their country so far, and in the West that date became the symbol of the shackled nation. The government of West Berlin renamed the great avenue between the Brandenburg Gate and the Victory Column 'Strasse des 17 Juni', 17 June Street. The Bundestag decided that from 1954 onwards 17 June would be a national holiday, the Day of German Unity. The decision to fix this national holiday on the day when unity became a distant dream was a perfect example of the schizophrenia affecting the FRG, which refused to accept the country's division.

Willy Brandt's position was in line with that of all the West German parties – except the KPD Communists. On 20 September 1949, in his first speech as chancellor of the Bundestag, Konrad Adenauer had announced that the eventual goal of all policies would be 'reunification with our brothers and sisters in the eastern zone and in East Berlin'. Any contact with the illegitimate communists who claimed to represent the citizens of East Germany was out of the question. According to the preamble to the West German Constitution, the communists had prevented their citizens taking part in the establishment of democracy.[20] Reuter, the Social Democrat mayor of Berlin, was in agreement with Adenauer when, on 27 October, he confirmed his ongoing 'firm desire to maintain close links with our Eastern brothers and sisters', without, however, 'having any links with Messrs Pieck, Grotewohl et al.'[21] Willy Brandt said the same thing in May 1956 when he declared that encouraging as close a relationship as possible between the two populations was 'a matter concerning the very existence of our nation'.[22] He was unequivocal, however, along with all the other non-communist parties, about refusing to give the GDR any recognition.

He was still not thinking along the lines of his colleague, the former communist Herbert Wehner, who in 1955 suggested initiating conversations with the GDR authorities as a possible way of starting to work towards reunification. One year later, Wehner drew up what would form the basis of the SPD's strategy regarding its East German neighbour: holding talks with the SED communists 'in order to exercise some influence over the GDR and guide it towards a more democratic future'.[23] Brandt was still very sceptical and wanted to limit any contact to what was essential for technical reasons, and for it to take place under the aegis of the four powers.[24] As proof of his hostility towards communism, he took part ungrudgingly in the fight over the occupation of public space, taking every opportunity to assert the irreplaceable value of freedom and justice in a democracy. He reminded the Social Democrats, who hardly needed reminding, that a communist regime could not satisfy those basic needs.[25]

In June 1950 he attended the Congress for Cultural Freedom, which gathered together over 100 writers, artists, scientists and politicians in response to the 1949 Scientific and Cultural Conference for World Peace, presided over by Frédéric Joliot-Curie and organised by the communist parties of Western Europe. The first years of the Cold War were a clash of propaganda. The question on everybody's lips was whether it would come to actual armed conflict, as had happened in Korea. Brandt was not among those who believed no German should ever wear a soldier's uniform again. His Germany was, and had to remain, anchored to the West because, as he said in 1951, 'if the choice is between freedom and slavery, one cannot remain neutral.' In his view, German soldiers should help to defend the West, within the framework of the North Atlantic Treaty Organisation (NATO) rather than as part of that strange structure, the European Defence Community, which was abandoned when the French parliament refused to ratify it on 30 August 1954.[26]

Rise to Power, at Last

Although for a while Brandt was a rather marginal socialist in Berlin, his efforts eventually paid off. When Reuter died in 1953, control of the city hall passed briefly to the Christian Democratic Union (CDU), but quickly returned to the Social Democrats. In December 1954 Otto Suhr, the president of the Berlin city parliament, was elected mayor, and Brandt succeeded him to the now-vacant presidency. The local press welcomed his appointment. Rut cried, and not from happiness; her husband was now an extremely well-known figure, and she was not sure if that was what she wanted. The Brandts were seen more and more frequently at society events, cocktail parties and theatre evenings. They were an attractive couple. On their first appearance at a major event of Berlin social life, the Journalists' Association ball, they stole the show: Willy in a dinner jacket with his characteristic smile, and Rut in an ultra-fashionable white silk dress, a black ribbon around her waist. The bourgeois occasion was not to everyone's taste, and Brandt's critics among the older pillars of the SPD exclaimed: 'And he calls himself a social democrat!'[27] The 5-foot 11-inch Brandt, although perhaps a little on the bulky side, was a handsome man, with his long face, high cheekbones and square jaw, softened by a slight curve. He was easily recognisable by his wavy hair, cut short and swept backwards, and the slightly receding hairline that caused a tuft to stand up on top of his head. His blue eyes and natural smile, as well as his taste for stylish hats, coats and gloves, added to his appeal.

Everyone knew that, like many other politicians spending time in Bonn, when Willy was in the federal capital attending the Bundestag he 'Bonnified' himself. That was not to say that he lost contact with his own constituency, but simply that he led a double life. From the beginning of the 1950s he was having an affair with a vivacious dark-haired journalist, who sometimes accompanied him publicly, and who made him laugh. She held lively parties in her flat, where she invited politicians of all persuasions to riotous carnival dances, disguised and decked out in red noses. The Bavarian Franz Josef Strauss could be seen celebrating along with the others,[28] including of course Brandt. He wrote almost as many letters to the tall, slim Susanne as to his wife Rut, but he signed his letters to Susanne 'your bear'. The allusion to the symbol of Berlin was endearing, but hardly prudent. Susanne Sievers was also known as Johanna – in the dossiers of the East German secret service, the Stasi, who had recruited her at the Leipzig trade fair in September 1951.

Was she really a scandalous Mata Hari, or just one of the countless Western spinster secretaries manipulated by the false promises of happiness the Stasi dangled before them? Intriguingly, there is reason to believe Susanne was a double agent; at least, the documents she sent to her 'contact' in Berlin woke the Stasi's suspicions, and they arrested her in July 1952. They interrogated her about what she had found out in Bonn and were dissatisfied when it seemed that she really had fallen in love with Brandt and was not spying on him as she should have been. She was sentenced to eight years' imprisonment in a Stasi cell, although she was released after four. Brandt, who had known nothing of her secret life, was generous when she reappeared in 1956. He gave her money and helped her find somewhere to live, although assuring her that their romance was a thing of the past. His certainty did not last long, however. Their relationship began again, but this time Susanne felt Willy was too cautious of being found out, partly because of his wife and partly because of his career. He did not know that Susanne had been released early in exchange for agreeing to rejoin the Stasi, this time under the pseudonym Lydia. Susanne-Lydia hosted social events at what was known as her 'salon', where she continued to entertain various politicians in Bonn. By 1958 Susanne and Willy were no longer lovers, but he still attended her 'salon' parties, where he regularly met Strauss, who had found Susanne a new job. What nobody knew was that these parties were paid for by Markus Wolf, the head of the GDR's intelligence service.[29]

Meanwhile, as Nikita Khrushchev announced at the twentieth Congress of the Communist Party of the Soviet Union in February 1956, the era of peaceful coexistence had begun. The Cold War was turning into an economic and ideological competition rather than a military one. The various powers kept to the status quo on the German question. The Geneva Summit in July 1955, where the leaders of the 'Big Four' met, sent a clear message in that regard to the Germans. For Moscow, that meant they each had free rein within their own zones. Emotions ran high again in Berlin when, in a repeat of what had happened in 1953 in the GDR, Russian tanks crushed an insurrection in Hungary at the beginning of November 1956. Amidst all the fear of a nuclear escalation, it was vital to try and keep West Berlin calm, despite the regular spontaneous protests in the city. Some way had to be found of stopping the German protesters marching on the Brandenburg Gate in anger. 'If you cross the border to the other side, you will face many unpleasant hours with the East German police and army. It won't help the Hungarians in the slightest, but it could provoke a war!' Brandt thundered through a police megaphone, standing on top of a car in order to be heard. Before him, Otto Suhr, the SPD's Franz Neumann and the CDU's Ernst Lemmer had all failed to change the crowd's mind. Brandt's hoarse voice struck up the national anthem: 'Unity and Justice and Freedom!'[30] The people of Berlin recalled Ernst Reuter's voice calling to a besieged Berlin in 1948 and realised they had found a worthy successor.

After the death of Otto Suhr less than a year later, the city parliament voted to elect Brandt as the mayor of West Berlin, by a margin of 86 to 32 votes, on 3 October 1957. The position of mayor meant governing the city, but also becoming leader of the government of the city-state. At 43 years old, Brandt was the youngest ever minister-president of a Federal German *Land*. His position in the city gave him greater national visibility. During his first year as mayor, he was also president of the Bundesrat in Bonn (the Bundesrat, the legislative body where the representatives of all the *Länder* draw up federal laws, has an annually rotating presidency). Smiling contentedly, he posed for photographs outside the city hall in Schöneberg. Berlin's traditional city hall, the Rotes Rathaus, had ended up in the Soviet sector after the division, and the city hall was moved to an imposing but rather stark building, in the cold architectural style of the early twentieth century, in the south of the city. After all the difficulties he had had imposing himself at the local level in the SPD, Brandt finally felt satisfied. He had even managed to become head of the local branch. As the SPD's Berlin representative, as well as being mayor of the city, he had at last proved his detractors wrong.

Unable to devote enough time to both roles, he soon gave up his seat in the Bundestag, but committing himself fully to Berlin did not mean confining himself to local politics. In divided Germany, Berlin was a matter of state. Brandt wanted to transform the little enclave, surrounded by hostile forces, into a bridge between East and West. It was a huge undertaking, and a rather presumptuous one in view of the ongoing petrification of the Eastern Bloc. In his first mayoral declaration, on 19 October 1957, he claimed:

> If we succeed in making a capital city of Berlin, we will reinforce our Soviet zone compatriots' sense of belonging to a shared community, we will rebuild the entire country's belief in the possibility of reuniting the nation, and we will let the whole world know that we do not and will never accept this unnatural division. Berlin must be a living bridge between people in the East and the West.[31]

Nevertheless, local problems – accommodation, employment, the refugees flooding in from the East – were already enough to occupy his team full time. He also had to manage relationships with the occupying powers, who still had control over Berlin even after the creation of the FRG. The three commanders – American, British and French – may have been well meaning, but they were very particular about the city's special status; their approval was necessary before any law voted in by the city parliament could be passed, and the hierarchical system placed them above the local government in all areas, especially in matters of security and the maintenance of order. There was no question of the Allies agreeing to the Mayor's request to make Berlin the capital of the new Federal Republic. Berlin remained separate, nothing more than a theoretical capital waiting for the day when Germany would be reunited. Meanwhile, the prospect of reunification was growing ever more distant in the new crisis which suddenly propelled Brandt to the forefront of international politics and made him a sort of second minister of foreign affairs.

In the eyes of Nikita Khrushchev, the leader of the Soviet Union, West Berlin was an intruder that could no longer be tolerated. He gave the three Western powers an ultimatum on

27 November 1958, demanding that they leave West Berlin within six months. The message was clear: if Washington, London and Paris would not agree to make West Berlin a free city, demilitarised and placed under the control of the United Nations (UN), Moscow would give the GDR full control over access to Berlin. The people of West Berlin had no say in the matter. Regardless, Brandt spoke up and declared in the Bundestag, well aware that his words would be heard in the East and elsewhere in the world, 'We are not the sort of people to be blown over by a gust of wind. The people of Berlin have been through too much already for that. We have no weapons. But we do have the right to live, and we have nerves of steel.'[32] Even so, there was a danger that his fellow citizens would succumb to the Soviet sirens promising them a demilitarised 'free' city. It was a war of words. Brandt's SPD, with a campaign slogan of 'Berlin stays free', won an absolute majority in the city elections on 7 December. For those who still believed that West Berliners would prefer their city to join the GDR, the result was shocking: the East German SED, which had been allowed to run in the West Berlin elections, received only 2 per cent of the vote.

The Social Democrats could now govern Berlin unchallenged, but they decided to renew their coalition with the CDU anyway, to present a united front. There were worrying signals coming from Washington that the Americans might be ready to negotiate with the Russians about Berlin. The French were the only ones who stood firm. General de Gaulle, whose new Constitution for the Fifth Republic had recently been adopted, and who had been elected president a few days afterwards, had several good reasons to resist the Soviets over Berlin. France's status as a great power rested on the rights it had been granted in 1945, and so the French, de Gaulle in particular, were determined to uphold these. It also seemed to be a good occasion to make France's voice heard, both as a key member of the Western camp and as an autonomous party capable of holding its own against the two great powers whose confrontation had reorganised the world, and in whose shadow all other nations moved. Moreover, de Gaulle saw the FRG as an important part of his plan to build a more independent Europe. In the middle of September 1958, he received Chancellor Adenauer at his residence in Colombey-les-deux-Églises, which, in his own words, was the most suitable location for 'the historic encounter between this old Frenchman and this very old German in the name of their two peoples'.[33] Two months later, Brandt went to Paris and met the three Western powers' ministers of foreign affairs. His journey was made with Adenauer's blessing; Adenauer recognised his value to the German cause.

Brandt put extraordinary energy into fighting for this cause: from January 1959 onwards, he visited various capital cities and international organisations, from Europe to the United States, Canada, India, Pakistan and Japan. He was intoxicated by his newfound international fame, which he basked in for almost two years. Famous at last! What a pleasure to read the French press praising his 'mischievous smile', his 'athlete's stature, square jaw, youthful head of hair and blue eyes', calling him 'handsome Willy' and talking of him as a future chancellor![34] In February 1959 he received a hero's welcome in the United States, and he was struck by how much his image had improved there even since his first visit a year earlier, when he had met President Eisenhower, Vice-President Nixon and Secretary of State John Foster Dulles. This time, in New York, as he stood in a convertible car, showered with confetti falling from skyscrapers, he was amazed at the size of the parade held in his honour, and very moved by the crowd chanting his name: 'Willy! Willy!' The cover of *Time* magazine on 25 May 1959 showed a close-up of his face with the caption 'Berlin's Willy Brandt'.

Willy must have wondered if he would have received the same reception if he had gone back to Lübeck instead of Berlin. Perhaps, but it would have been in some other form. Nowhere but Berlin could have guided his conception of politics and his understanding of the challenges of the time in quite the same way. Berlin was the prism through which he saw the world, the fulcrum between East and West, and it forged his analytical understanding.[35] If the Soviets insisted on thinking in terms of power ratios, then – faced with Khrushchev's ultimatum – it was vital not to compromise, and to reinforce the Western front. Brandt was emerging as a key figure in that enterprise. He was seen with the press magnate Axel Springer, owner of the conservative daily broadsheet *Die Welt* and the powerful tabloid *Bild Zeitung*, and one of the most fervent anti-communists in the West German press world. On 25 May 1959 the two men stood side by side and posed for photographers as they placed the first stone of the new Springer Group offices in Kochstrasse, right on the edge of the Soviet sector. There was a message embedded in the stone, signed by both of them: 'We place this stone today, directly on the border between the sectors, and will not just wait apprehensively until the negotiations between the great powers bear fruit. This stone is proof of our unbreakable faith in the historical unity of this city, and the historical unity of Germany.'[36]

Brandt had become one of the most uncompromising hawks in West Germany, and the Springer press was seen as the mouthpiece of the Senate of Berlin (the government of Hanseatic city-states was traditionally called the senate). The two men saw each other often and contributed to each other's growing prestige. For Brandt, there was no question of aligning himself with Herbert Wehner, who had recently published a plan for Germany which conceded too much to the other side. Wehner had proposed the idea of forming a joint council where the representatives of the two halves of Germany would discuss a shared constitution. In Brandt's view, this would be to admit the legitimacy of the East German communist authorities, whereas they had none because they had not been freely elected and did not express the will of the people. A joint council would give too much credit to Moscow's puppets, who were proclaiming the decline of capitalism. The SED could proclaim all it wanted, as it did at its fifth party congress in 1958, that the GDR would not only match the FRG's economic progress, but even overtake it; the claim was difficult to believe when the West German economy was thriving as it was.

The economy grew so quickly, after the difficulties of the first postwar years, that West Germany's sudden affluence was seen as a miracle. The SPD had little to offer beside a CDU government that most Germans credited with this remarkable recovery. Behind closed doors, it was clear that their sensible policies had been helped along by favourable circumstances. Their policies included structural reforms which, since 1948, had created an environment that was conducive to business and to the flourishing of a moderate market economy, and the CDU had also carried out crucial monetary reform. Admittedly, once more, German savers had lost their money because of monetary reform, but the move had restored the currency's health and established a banking system that valued stability.[37] As for the favourable circumstances, the Korean War had provided timely external demand that helped sustain German industry, employment and investments. The CDU were also lucky in that the work ethic was given high priority in a society recovering from political intoxication. After years of constant mobilisation under the Nazis, it was unsurprising that many of Brandt's compatriots shunned ideology and approved of the CDU's slogan: 'No more experiments!' In the legislative elections of 1957, the conservatives' posters showed the lined face of their octogenarian patriarch, the Catholic Adenauer, who had been head of the federal government for eight years. This time, the CDU acquired an absolute majority in the Bundestag.

The SPD were not making much headway on a national level, in part because their image as part of the labour movement deterred the largely anti-communist electorate. This was slightly unfair, considering the Social Democrats' openly hostile attitude to the GDR regime, but it was one effect of the extreme polarisation of this phase of the Cold War. All the anti-communist propaganda played on the motif of the hidden enemy, and on the ambiguity of the word 'socialism'; the communists in the Eastern Bloc used it of themselves, which interfered with the Social Democrats' message. 'We have to define ourselves more clearly,' thought the younger members of the SPD like Brandt and Helmut Schmidt. 'We need to make people understand that our commitment to pluralism and freedom is compatible with democratic order and a social market economy.'

Adenauer was very popular in 1955 when he negotiated the repatriation of 10,000 German prisoners of war released from Soviet camps after ten years' imprisonment, but even so he was a man of the past. There were social transformations taking place that could not be ignored: the rise of the middle classes, and a widely held desire for a quiet, peaceful life. Like the CDU, the SPD was hindered in this respect by the fact that it was the oldest and most sectarian party members who set the tone; moreover, their leader, Erich Ollenhauer, was somewhat lacking in charisma. Brandt was in an awkward position within the party. He supported Adenauer's foreign policy, especially his desire to integrate with the West, and he was convinced that the SPD's traditional Marxist message was outdated and no longer appealed to the left's voters. Unless it expanded its electoral base, he believed the SPD would never gain power at a national level, and he was determined for this to happen.

When a new programme was announced that set out to achieve that goal, Brandt was sceptical at first, but he was soon persuaded. He was joined by Herbert Wehner, Fritz Erler and the even younger Helmut Schmidt, who was one of the more right-leaning SPD members. The young liberals, taking on the older, more orthodox members of the party, pushed through a programme of reform that culminated in the Godesberg Programme, ratified on 15 November 1959 at the party conference in Bad Godesberg. In it, the SPD officially turned away from Marxist doctrine and from its traditional role as the workers' party and set out its goal of a liberal and democratic socialism, which was similar to West Germany's current social market economy. Six months later, the shift was complete when, in a memorable speech at the Bundestag, Wehner announced the party's decision to adopt a policy of integration with the West and its institutions, such as NATO.

It was Wehner, too, who suggested that Brandt should head the campaign against Adenauer in the 1961 elections. The SPD's message was clear: dynamism and forward-thinking belonged to the young, elegant and already popular new candidate for federal chancellor. It was a pragmatic move, too. The party would not be able to win the election without a moderate leader who had discarded the utopian dreams of an earlier age, and whose anti-communism fitted seamlessly alongside his political and social aims as well as his image of youthful energy. But youth is always relative. While the men like Brandt in their forties and early fifties were pushing their elders out of the SPD, in their turn they were distancing themselves from the party's more left-wing younger members, especially the noisily protesting students. When the party decreed, in 1961, that members of the Socialist German Student League (SDS) were automatically excluded from the SPD, Brandt could not help but think of his own rupture from the party 30 years earlier, and his conflict with Julius Leber.

13 August 1961: A Wall in Berlin

At 3 a.m. on Sunday 13 August Brandt was woken in the sleeper carriage in which he was travelling from Nuremberg to Kiel, where he was to open his election campaign. A telegram had come for him from the head of the Berlin Senate Chancellery, Heinrich Albertz, announcing that 'the others, on the other side, are cutting the city in half', and that he should return immediately.[38]

'Operation Chinese Wall' had begun. At 1 a.m. East German engineering units, transported from all corners of Berlin, had started to lay out kilometres of barbed wire and spiked *chevaux-de-frise* (portable barriers of spikes) along the border between the Soviet and western sectors. Builders had been requisitioned, and were setting up concrete posts, hanging barbed wire between them and filling in the gaps with breeze blocks, all under the watchful eye of more than 10,000 policemen, border guards and militia combat groups. The passages between East and West Berlin were closed; the U-Bahn and S-Bahn were no longer allowed to cross between the two halves of the city. It was so simple, and yet so utterly absurd. Thirty train stations were made inaccessible, so that trains leaving the north of the city in the French sector had to pass through empty stations in the Soviet sector before rejoining the West in the British sector.

At 5 a.m. Brandt left the train at Hanover and took the first available flight to Berlin. He was driven from Tempelhof airport straight to Potsdamer Platz at the Brandenburg Gate, where a crowd of onlookers had gathered on both sides of the barbed wire, wavering between disbelief and indignation. Before he had even reached the city hall and looked at a map of the city, he understood that West Berlin was being surrounded. To prevent their citizens crossing over to the little Western island in the heart of communist Germany, the East German authorities were in the process of building a wall which extended for more than 45 kilometres right through the centre of the city, running between houses, as well as for 160 kilometres around the edge of West Berlin, where the city met the countryside and the GDR. West Berlin was being walled in, so that East Germans could no longer seek refuge there.

The brutality and the extent of the project were shocking, even though it could have been foreseen that the Russians would act soon. The Western secret services were well aware that something was going on, and in fact Khrushchev had warned the Americans on 27 July that he would soon have to close the border. This information had been passed on to Brandt by Reinhard Gehlen, the head of the West German intelligence service. The East German authorities had given signals that they would not tolerate the little capitalist island much longer. It functioned as a funnel through which 'traitors to the cause' could sneak out and join West Germany by train, road or air, following routes which were carefully established and controlled by the Allies. During the summer, the flood of fugitives heading for West Berlin had grown significantly: 30,000 people in July and 20,000 in the first fortnight of August alone. Many had taken the decision to flee after hearing Walter Ulbricht, leader of the GDR, say at a press conference on 15 June: 'Nobody has any intention of building a wall in Berlin.' A journalist had asked him whether, if Berlin became a free city, a national border would pass through the Brandenburg Gate. His reply was not a slip of the tongue. Brandt understood now that Ulbricht had wanted to throw oil on the fire, to provoke a panicked reaction and increase the number of refugees fleeing East Germany, so as to spur Moscow into giving him the go-ahead for Operation Chinese Wall.[39]

For years East Germany had been asking the Kremlin to take effective steps to halt the exodus, which was weakening the GDR considerably. Since 1945, no fewer than 3.5 million Germans had left the Soviet zone for the West; since the foundation of the GDR in 1949, the figure was 2.5 million, or one in six people! Half those fleeing were under 25, and three-quarters under 45 – a young, qualified and educated population abandoning ship for a more promising future. From East Germany's point of view, the sight of the country's vital force, the most productive members of society in whom they had already invested much, leaving in such numbers was insupportable, especially as the only people left were the elderly, who were a drain on state finances. Up until that point, however, Khrushchev had wanted to avoid disproportionate moves in his power struggle with the West. He wanted to use Berlin as a lever to help resolve the German question but did not want actual conflict.

The situation had become dramatic in May 1960 when an American U-2 aeroplane was shot down in Soviet airspace, and Khrushchev had clashed violently with President Kennedy at the Vienna Summit on 3 and 4 June 1961. Kennedy wanted to maintain the Western presence in Berlin, but Khrushchev saw West Berlin as an tumour that needed to be removed. Ulbricht took matters into his own hands and, by increasing the number of people fleeing, convinced Moscow that the situation was urgent. The Soviet embassy in Berlin finally informed him that the Kremlin had given him the green light on 6 July. On 5 August, the Warsaw Pact was officially ratified, supporting Ulbricht in his fight against the 'capitalists and their plots to harm the GDR'. The builders started work on 13 August, several weeks after Erich Honecker, the head of security in the SED political bureau and the logistical director of the wall operation, had begun transporting almost 500 tons of barbed wire, concrete posts and construction materials to Berlin.

On 13 August, the image of the Iron Curtain that Churchill had been using since 1946 became reality. In East Berlin the Soviets deployed tanks in the streets next to the wall, but otherwise they left the East German authorities in control. This alone constituted a breach of the quadripartite status of Berlin, because according to international law the GDR's army had no business to be in what was still the Soviet sector. It was overly provocative, and Khrushchev decided to adopt a more cautious approach. He ordered that the wall should not encroach one single centimetre into the other sectors, and that it should at first be a provisional structure, and only be filled in with concrete later, if the West failed to react to his ultimatum.

The West did not react. In vain Brandt went to the Allies at the Kommandantur to ask for at least a few jeeps in the streets to reassure the population. In Paris Minister of Foreign Affairs Maurice Couve de Murville said in private: 'we write memos, and that's it.'[40] This deafening silence was denounced three days later in the daily newspaper *Bild*, which at that time had a circulation of more than 3 million. Its front-page headline on 16 August was 'The West Does Nothing!' surrounded by a border of barbed wire. Below the headline it went on: 'Kennedy is silent [...] Macmillan goes hunting [...] and Adenauer insults Willy Brandt.' The Chancellor had decided not to interrupt his summer holiday and, thinking only of the election campaign which was in full swing, had made some remarks criticising Brandt. Adenauer only went to Berlin a week later, on the 22nd, and the two rivals had to appear side by side for the journalists, with the same solemnity, the same overcoats and the same bowler hats.

Since 16 August, the world had looked on impotently at the panicked flight of those whose horizons were being hemmed round with barbed wire. In the centre of the city Bernauer Strasse was in the strange position of having its houses in the East and its pavement in the West. Its residents fled through their windows, carrying a few hastily gathered possessions. Brandt called the Senate to a special session and gave a sombre speech, part of which was reproduced in a press release denouncing the 'closure of the Soviet sector by a concentration camp wall'. The call for help was clear: 'The government and the population of Berlin are waiting for the Western powers to intercede with the Soviet government in the strongest terms.' According to his colleagues, Brandt grew more and more disappointed by the day. He later described how he spent those days counting the hours while his supposed friends in the West did nothing.[41]

What exactly was he waiting for? An armed intervention from the Americans? Such a move would have been mad and might have caused all-out war, given how fraught the East–West relationship had become. The tension had been almost palpable when Kennedy and Khrushchev came face to face at the Vienna Summit. At the very least, Brandt might have hoped that the Western powers would try and negotiate with Moscow to demand that the Russians respect the quadripartite status of the city, and to insist on the destruction of the wall which had been built by the East Germans – who were not supposed to have any authority in the Soviet sector. In other words, he wanted the West to remind the Soviets of their responsibilities according to the Potsdam Agreement of 1945.

As time went on, however, it became evident that in Washington the main concern was to avoid incurring significant expenses, while leaving the Soviets free to act as they chose in their own sector as long as they did not touch West Berlin. It was a question of perspective. Brandt now realised that all the West's recent posturing over Berlin went no further than that: posturing. The fact that the young new American president, Kennedy, had been less affected than his predecessors by the Berlin crisis of 1948–9 was surely partly to blame.[42] In Kennedy's first great foreign policy speech, broadcast on radio and television on 25 July 1961, the President restated the 'three essentials' regarding Berlin, formulated at the NATO summit in Oslo the previous April. These three essentials, over which there would be no backing down, were: 1) maintaining a presence of Allied troops in Berlin; 2) guaranteeing freedom of access to the city; and 3) ensuring material survival of the city. The White House made clear that these demands, originally intended to apply to the whole city, now referred to West Berlin alone. As long as the Soviets did not stop the Western powers accessing, supplying and garrisoning troops in their own sectors, the West would be satisfied and would turn a blind eye to what was going on in the Soviet sector. In fact, Brandt concluded, the Soviets could do whatever they wanted in, and with, East Berlin.[43]

The FRG government in Bonn also confined itself to sending messages of reassurance. The minister of foreign affairs, Heinrich von Brentano, told Brandt on the telephone that 'there must be cooperation between Berlin and Bonn.' None of the federal ministers went to Berlin, however. The only visitors from West Germany were some MPs and the president of the Bundestag, who arrived on the 14th. Brandt took the little delegation to the Brandenburg Gate, a place full of symbolism in the city's history, so they could judge for themselves how real the closure was. Opposite them, on the other side of the wall, some East Berliners had gathered together behind soldiers and policemen, known as the Vopos.[44] The two sides looked at each other, and a few civilians on the Eastern side dared to wave at the envoys until the policemen pushed them back unceremoniously. Suddenly, a man detached himself from the crowd, jumped over the barrier and sprinted towards the President of the Bundestag and the Mayor of Berlin, hoping that the police would not dare to shoot in their direction. 'I will never forget the scene, or the man's expression, a mixture of excitement and sang-froid,' Brandt wrote later.[45] Dozens of people jumped the barriers in the first few hours of the wall, several East German soldiers among them. On 14 August there were thousands of refugees in West Berlin's Marienfelde camp. As time went on, the flood of fugitives decreased and eventually dried up.

What could the West Berlin Senate do, what could the Mayor do, to attract the world's attention and give the city courage without provoking conflict or endangering its inhabitants? Faced with an apparently insoluble problem, Brandt called for peaceful protests. On 16 August, almost 300,000 people gathered in front of the city hall in Schöneberg to protest against the GDR's violence and the West's inactivity. People carried banners reading 'Munich 1938 = Berlin 1961?' Among the protesters were employees of Siemens, Borsig, Osram and AEG who had been allowed to leave work early so they could attend the protest and express their anger. The previous evening, encouraged by the trade unions, they had signed a petition and observed a two-minute silence at work. They were protesting against their own impotence. Brandt's loud hoarse voice was heard over the microphone, and he was hoping it would be audible on the other side of the wall: 'You, supporters of the regime in the Soviet zone, police officers and soldiers, do not become murderers! Do not shoot at your compatriots!' The Rias radio station broadcast his speech over a wide area in the East. Brandt announced to the assembled crowd that he had written a letter to President Kennedy. A few hours earlier, he had telegraphed Kennedy to ask him for 'more than words: action' for 'this city which wants peace but will not surrender [...] but watch out: weakness has never helped create peace before'.[46] He was trying to put the West under pressure, and was reproached for it a few days later by Minister Brentano. His fear was that maintaining their presence in the city was not enough of a priority for the Western powers, and that they would refuse to help develop connections between West Berlin and the FRG. The West Berliners were expected to bear the cost of the quadripartite system being downscaled to a low-budget tripartite one. 'The curtain went up and what a surprise! The stage was empty,' Brandt said to anyone who would listen.[47] Where were the great powers now, the supposed protectors of Berlin?

Kennedy's response finally arrived on 19 August, in the person of Vice-President Lyndon B. Johnson, who brought a letter addressed to the Mayor of Berlin. Kennedy's tone was reassuring. Brandt wanted to be encouraged, but the facts were the facts: the only possible course of action was to increase the number of Western troops in Berlin. He had to content himself with welcoming a supplementary battalion of 1,500 American soldiers, conspicuously transported along the motorway linking the American zone to West Berlin. Johnson and Brandt visited the Marienfelde refugee camp together and drove round Berlin in a convertible car. There was something slightly ridiculous about the enthusiastic Vice-President waving at the crowds as if he was on an election campaign, while absolutely nothing was done about the daily rising wall. The next day, 20 August, was a Sunday, but Johnson had set his heart on buying a pair of shoes like those Brandt wore. Next he asked a porcelain factory to open so he could buy a dinner set of the same model as one he had just been given, as well as some small, inexpensive ashtrays which caught his eye.[48]

The closure of all crossing points between East and West Berlin meant about 500,000 daily journeys could no longer take place. Some 90,000 people found themselves living in a different half of the city from their workplace, 53,000 of them were residents of the East who worked in the West.[49] Overnight, everything came to a halt. Life had to be reorganised, on both sides of the wall, without contact between the two halves. Supply networks had to be redesigned, especially the gas and electricity grids, and cultural life was transformed. On a larger scale, according to Brandt, the wall 'forced me to reconsider the future of Germany and of Europe'.[50]

The SED political bureau updated a 1960 ruling on the use of arms and gave its East German troops the order to fire on escapees. 'The use of firearms is authorised against traitors and anyone who attempts to violate the border.'[51] It seemed unlikely that the wall would ever become a calm border, uninterrupted by gunfire. The first few weeks were certainly noisy, with a propaganda battle raging. On the Western side, television cameras had gathered to show the world the 'wall of shame', which Springer called an 'attack on the culture of Europe'. The East responded by throwing smoke grenades to stop the camera crews filming. The West set up loudspeakers and established the 'Studio at the Barbed Wire', which broadcast information and messages for the East … which, in turn, installed its own loudspeakers. In the Soviet sector and the wider GDR, the Communist Party needed to convince the population that the 'Anti-Fascist Protection Rampart' was justified, and necessary for the GDR's survival. On 14 August 1961 the SED party newspaper, *Neues Deutschland*, described the 13th as a 'day of mourning for the warmongers', those vengeful capitalists.[52] In East Germany as in the West, it was all a matter of conviction. Erich Honecker wrote in his memoirs that the wall had been a show of force and the proof of the socialist regime's superiority: 'It was […] not only our military strength which was expressed during those days in August but also the strength of our socialist order, the superiority of our political system.'[53] Seen from this point of view, things were easy to explain to children: 'The important question is not whether Uncle Max can visit Aunt Gertrude, but if we can ensure peace, for without peace Uncle Max and Aunt Gertrude will never meet again alive or on a healthy earth, but rather in a mass atomic grave.'[54]

In West Berlin, people were trying to stop disappointment turning into resignation. Admittedly, Kennedy had sent General Clay, the hero of the Berlin Airlift, to Berlin, but ultimately the Americans restricted themselves to protecting their own right as Allies to access the Soviet sector. On 25 October 1961, Berlin witnessed a disheartening scene, as American and Soviet tanks faced off against other for a few hours at the Allies' crossing-point between the sectors, dubbed 'Checkpoint Charlie'. Three days earlier, the second-in-command of the American mission, E. Allan Lightner, had been stopped by the East German police and had refused to show his official papers, as he was on his way to see a play in East Berlin, accompanied by his wife and in a civil car. The East German authorities were not authorised to impose such a control. According to the rule that representatives of the four Allied Powers had freedom of movement around Berlin, only the Soviets had the right to so much as speak to the Americans, British or French. On the 25th, General Clay decided to respond with a show of force and ordered a dozen American tanks to advance to Checkpoint Charlie, guns pointing towards to the East. British and French tanks were also posted at the border between the sectors near the Tiergarten. The Soviet commander of the city, Soloviev, reacted with tanks of his own, guns trained on the Westerners. It was only after long negotiations that both sides withdrew their tanks. Another world war had never felt so close.[55]

During these weeks Brandt kept trying to free himself from the Allies' straitjacket and was regularly called back into line, notably by France, which of all the Allied Powers was the most stubbornly attached to the special status of Berlin as defined in the Potsdam Agreement, and to its own rights and prerogatives therein.[56] The Mayor's initiatives, like his new project of discussions with Khrushchev, were met with firm objections. The French commander of the city, General Toulouse, complained to Paris that Brandt 'is actually seeking, discreetly but with perseverance, to give himself a bit of elbow room independently of the Allies'.[57] Paris objected and opposed the Berlin Senate's plan to use the UN Commission of Human Rights to denounce the GDR's crimes at the Berlin Wall, while the whole world looked on, helpless, at what began to seem like political assassinations.

On 17 August 1962, the television cameras filmed the agonising final hour of young Peter Fechter, a builder from East Berlin who had tried to climb over the wall and was shot by the border guards. Unfortunately, he fell on the East German side and nobody on the West side was willing, or perhaps able, to help him. It was very bad publicity for Walter Ulbricht's GDR regime. It was also a public admission that the West would not move, as long as the East did not impinge upon West Berlin. In the Western half of the city, the first anti-American demonstrations took place.

'And finally President Kennedy has come to Berlin. We waited for him on the runway as the plane came towards us. When the door opened he appeared, exactly as we had seen him countless times on the television: young, in a grey flannel suit, with a wide smile.'[58] Like most of her compatriots, Rut Brandt was charmed by the President, who combined the power of the leader who had faced up to Khrushchev during the Cuban Missile Crisis with the seduction of the man who had been publicly serenaded by Marilyn Monroe. On 26 June 1963, Kennedy, on official business in the FRG, landed in Berlin to show that, yes, the Americans were there, 'in the front lines', as he said. On his first trip through the city he travelled along the wall and visited the Brandenburg Gate. To stop the people of East Berlin seeing the despised hero of the capitalist world, the SED hung black drapes between the pillars of the Gate. Brandt and Kennedy had already met when Brandt had visited the United States, and they had seen each other the previous evening in Bonn. 'Can you give me some advice for my speech tomorrow?' the President had asked. Brandt had replied, 'I think it essential that you address yourself to the Berliners' pride and that, above all, you emphasise the human dimension.'[59] Crowds had gathered in the streets to see the President go past. Adenauer had come to Berlin too, but Brandt made sure to let him know that it was he who was Mayor of Berlin. In the convertible car that transported them through the town to the sound of cheering, Brandt was in the middle, with the elderly Adenauer on his left and Kennedy, hair blowing in the wind and smiling as always, on his right. In front of the city hall in Schöneberg, where the Berliners had previously gathered to protest against the wall, several hundred thousand people were waiting for Kennedy. His slightly nasal American accent rang out over the crowd: 'Two thousand years ago, the proudest boast was, "*civis Romanus sum!*" Today in the world of freedom, the proudest boast is, "*Ich bin ein Berliner!*"' Judging by the crowd's reaction, this phrase, which he had practised a little earlier, laughing, in Brandt's office, had struck a chord, and he repeated it at the end of his speech: 'All free men, wherever they live, are citizens of Berlin. And therefore, as a free man, I take pride in the words, "*Ich bin ein Berliner!*"'[60] A few hours later, Kennedy was taken to the Free University of Berlin, where he gave a speech to the students. He sketched out the contours of an idea that Brandt, anxious to improve the lives of people on the other side of the wall, had already been considering. 'The winds of change are blowing across the curtain,' Kennedy told them, and suggested that contact between East and West could help to ease the tension. 'This American President sees the world on a grand scale,' thought Brandt, 'and he is certainly an extraordinary personality with exceptional influence – even if what he is proposing are only words.'

The Berliners' enthusiastic welcome of Kennedy was a measure of their gratitude towards their American saviours. The dramatic potential of the situation had also been well harnessed by Kennedy, who, as he confided to Brandt, was becoming irritated by de Gaulle's new plans. There was an obvious one-upmanship between Kennedy and de Gaulle over who could gain the Germans' favour: that '*Ich bin ein Berliner*' had outdone the great French appeal to the '*großes deutsches Volk*', the 'great German people', made by de Gaulle in Ludwigsburg in September 1962.

In the months before June 1963, when Kennedy spoke of two equal pillars in the transatlantic community, one European, the other North American, the European Allies had been finding him a little too assertive, especially in Paris. De Gaulle thought Europe should free itself of American domination in which America claimed hegemony over the Western world and wanted to install nuclear weapons in Europe while reserving the right to decide when to use them. The nuclear multilateral force arrangement which Washington had proposed in 1962, with the help of its 'Trojan horse', Great Britain, was one of the factors leading to the rapprochement of Adenauer and General de Gaulle, and the signing of the Franco-German Élysée Treaty on 22 January 1963.

After the failure of the Fouchet Plan, which had aimed to organise Europe as an intergovernmental 'Union of States' rather than subordinating states to the supranational, federal European Communities, de Gaulle suggested to Adenauer that they should have an ongoing agreement to consult each other bilaterally 'with a view to reaching as far as possible an analogous position' on 'all important questions of foreign policy'. Clearly, General de Gaulle wanted to counteract what he saw as Washington's excessive influence over Bonn. De Gaulle saw France as the natural leader of a liberated Europe, capable of talking to the two superpowers as equal to equal, but he needed to attract the West Germans to the French cause. The elderly Adenauer, for his part, wanted to ensure his successors would cooperate with Paris, against the advice of those at home who were alarmed by such audacity and feared that America would soon lose interest in an ungrateful Germany. The disagreement between 'Atlanticists' and 'Gaullists' affected the whole political spectrum. Brandt was torn between his natural affection for France and his conviction that Europe would never make any progress without a Franco-German agreement, and his certainty that American protection was invaluable and irreplaceable, for Germany as much as for Berlin. When the Élysée Treaty came to be ratified at the Bundestag on 15 June, he sided with those who voted for the addition of a preamble which moderated the bilateral project, at the same time as reiterating that the treaty did not in any way alter the FRG's major goals: the consolidation of the close relationship between the United States and Europe, the pursuit of collective defence within the NATO framework, the unification of Europe, including Great Britain, and, of course, the strengthening of the European Communities.

At the end of April, Brandt was in Paris as part of a tour of France, where he had been welcomed as a future chancellor. Internal reports at the Ministry of Foreign Affairs described him in complimentary terms, although at the same time noting that he was 'the Americans' man'.[61] From Paris's point of view, Brandt was a good alternative to Adenauer's expected CDU successor, Ludwig Erhard, who was one of the most avid Atlanticists, determined to defend the interests and the security of the FRG in the face of the lure of the French. On 24 April the Mayor of Berlin was received by President de Gaulle, whom he had met for the first time four years earlier, accompanied by his wife Rut. That first time, the 40 minutes Brandt spent alone with de Gaulle at the Élysée were a real rite of passage for Brandt. The conversation was carried on half in French and half in German, as each of them understood the other's language well enough to render an interpreter unnecessary. De Gaulle had asked to see Brandt again on his official trip to the FRG in September 1962, but the General had refused to go to Berlin as long as the wall was in place.[62]

This time, de Gaulle sent a helicopter to collect Brandt from Paris and take him to Saint-Dizier, where the Frenchman was staying. They discussed Europe and the transatlantic relationship. Brandt justified the preamble to the Élysée Treaty: 'We should not push the German people into pointless confrontations, especially with the United States, who have had and still have an enormous importance for Europe's progress since the war.'[63] As Brandt's adviser Egon Bahr told him in no uncertain terms in a note: 'Anything that strengthens our relationship with France is good, but anything that strengthens our relationship with the United States is better. We must be aware of that hierarchy, while hoping that we are never placed in a position of having to choose between our two friends.'[64]

3

From Party Chairman to Foreign Minister

Once Kennedy had left Berlin, what remained of his visit? His few hours in the city had caused great excitement, and images of him there had been broadcast well beyond the little encircled island's borders. The crowds had cheered the young American President and his legendary promise of solidarity, '*Ich bin ein Berliner*', but the details of how the United States actually planned to deal with the situation in Berlin remained vague. Brandt's only real cause for satisfaction was the clear and widely noted contrast between the two Germans sitting with Kennedy in the convertible car: Brandt, the promising young social democrat, and Adenauer, who was known as 'the Old Man'. Thirty-seven years separated the Mayor of Berlin, who would be 50 at Christmas, and the 87-year-old Chancellor.

Brandt was appropriately respectful towards Adenauer, but he certainly did not complain when the photos highlighted the similarity between him and Kennedy. The stage was set to his advantage: Adenauer, a Catholic Rhinelander, felt out of place in Berlin, the capital of Protestant former Prussia. Undoubtedly, from a geostrategic point of view, Brandt was absolutely in agreement with Adenauer's choice to ally West Germany with what he saw as a Western European culture; indeed, he had long been opposed to the SPD majority on that point. On a personal level, however, he enjoyed his new role as the symbol of the future, and he was delighted when the media called him the 'German Kennedy' because of his energy and stylish appearance. His advisers had perfected new ways for him to make his mark on the four-yearly election campaigns, using modern tactics such as whistle-stop tours or the extensive use of publicity material and opinion polls.[1]

For Brandt, his popularity was a sort of retribution for his rival's numerous attempts to tarnish his image. Adenauer had been calling him a former communist since the 1957 election campaign; three years later, when Brandt was decorated with the Norwegian Order of St Olav, the Chancellor's team had methodically combed through his time as an exile in Scandinavia, dissecting his writings and speeches in order to try and prove what would surely be an indelible double crime: communist and traitor.[2] This campaign against Brandt, orchestrated by Adenauer's team and by the Bavarian Christian Social Union (CSU), lasted several years and seized every opportunity to discredit him, taking quotes and photographs out of context and churning out defamatory and demagogic publications. Why not go as far as to claim that the construction of the Berlin Wall was a publicity stunt organised by Moscow to give 'Willy Brandt, alias Frahm' a boost in his election campaign? This phrase of Adenauer's, which he used in the 1961 campaign,[3] was more revealing than the members of the CDU and CSU wanted to admit. Franz Josef Strauss wrote later that the Chancellor 'did not mean to say what the left deliberately misinterpreted',[4] which was that the choice of words suggested the indignity of Brandt's illegitimate birth, as if he was a criminal whose real identity was being revealed. Even among the Christian Democrats, people were shocked by it. Helmut Kohl, the leader of the CDU in the Rhine-Palatinate state parliament, wrote to Brandt that he was confused by his own party's tactics.

Outwardly, the Christian Democrats knew how to engage with conservative values such as politeness and honesty, values which provided a life-raft for those German citizens struggling to retain a sense of honour as they faced up to the recent past of their nation. In the political sphere, however, they were clever insinuators. They returned again and again to Brandt's invented name, playing on the motif of the enemy in disguise which had been used regularly in the 1930s and 1940s to denounce internal enemies, from Bolsheviks to converted Jews, who were suspected of threatening the integrity of the nation. The subtle implication of dishonesty evoked the image of a traitor endangering a recovering society. Brandt saw it as an attack on his moral and political integrity, since he was accused of being a deserter when in fact he had been part of the resistance. The founder of the weekly newspaper *Der Spiegel*, Rudolf Augstein, thought that when Strauss asked his spurious question about what exactly Herr Brandt had been doing away from Germany for so many years, he was aiming his rhetoric at 'the manure piles hidden in the corners of the German soul'.[5]

Brandt was outraged, although privately at first, writing, 'What have things come to, that we have to defend and justify ourselves for having fought against a criminal regime?'[6] Later, he pressed charges against each new attack. There were 80 proceedings in all, lasting months, and all the time Brandt flipped back and forth between belligerence and gloom. There were even melancholic episodes when he considered moving back to Norway. Even though he won each case, the damage done to his image was permanent. The CSU's posters during the 1965 election campaign placed Ludwig Erhard, with his title 'Professor Doktor', side by side with a photograph of Willy Brandt in uniform with the caption 'as a Norwegian commander'. Underneath, the front covers of both men's books were shown with the description: 'Professor Ludwig Erhard's books: *Well-being for All*, *The Collective Effort of the Germans* and *German Economic Policy*. The Norwegian Willy Brandt's books: *Criminals and Other Germans* and *Guerrilla Warfare*. If you vote SPD, you are voting for Willy Brandt. So vote CSU!'[7]

Had Brandt chosen the title of his book badly in 1946? The electorate took it as an accusation that all Germans were criminals, which was the opposite of the book's argument. Brandt had written that of course there were Germans who were not Nazis, and that a successful future depended on the just punishment of those who really had been criminals, but that the German people needed to understand that they shared a collective responsibility – not guilt, but responsibility – and that as a nation they needed to face up to that responsibility. There is some similarity between his argument and the ideas of the first federal president, Theodor Heuss of the Free Democratic Party (FDP), who discussed the notion of collective shame, although Brandt had gone even further, and as soon after the war as 1946. His approach was notably different from that of the Allies, who constantly told the Germans: 'You are to blame for this,' while forcing them to see the reality of the camps at Buchenwald and Dachau first-hand. Brandt would have said instead, 'You allowed this to become possible.' *Der Spiegel* came to his rescue, defending the respectability of his career and his writings, and launching counter-attacks in the electoral battle. Rudolf Augstein, a liberal, asked ironically: 'Would Brandt have had to fight with the Condor Legion to be a respectable candidate for the centre right?'[8]

Successive elections revealed a steady erosion of the CDU's position. After having lost their absolute majority in 1961, the Christian Democrats governed with the support of the FDP liberals. In the SPD camp, the effects of the Godesberg Programme were beginning to show. In 1961, there was already celebration that the SPD had won their highest share of the vote since the election of the Weimar National Assembly in 1919. Brandt knew that if the SPD were doing well, it was partly because Adenauer's government's image had suffered during the *Spiegel* affair in 1962, when the magazine's offices had been raided and searched, and its editors arrested for having published information about the condition of the German army. Nevertheless, the liberal-conservative majority held onto the Bundestag, and the SPD had to remain in opposition.

Brandt, for his part, governed Berlin and benefited from the visibility that Kennedy's visit had given him after the construction of the wall. He had very little time to devote to his family, which had grown with the birth of his third son, Matthias, in October 1961, joining Peter and Lars, who were already 15 and 12 years old. Aside from his family life, which he just about managed to keep going, he still had a good relationship with his first wife, Carlota, who became his literary agent in Scandinavia. Carlota and Rut also got on well, and Rut treated Brandt and Carlota's daughter, Ninja, like a fourth child.

Dealing with the Division

As mayor of Berlin, Brandt's most important job was the day-to-day management of the city-state, which stretched in a semi-circle from the north-west to the south of Berlin. There were local concerns like a lack of housing, and a project to improve public roads and the transport system. Construction work was constantly underway. In Berlin the water table is very high, and the earth has such high clay content that any new building requires a permanent system for pumping out the water which rises to the surface. Numerous pipes had to be installed in the streets, curving around junctions and over roads in metallic arches. The division of the city created a new modern centre near the Kurfürstendamm, in what had previously been suburbs. Despite its new configuration, the city was still huge, with forests and lakes around a vast circumference, drawn up in the Greater Berlin Act of 1920. It was at one and the same time a city and a little state, and the mayor, as the leader of the executive body, had the same concerns and priorities as other heads of regional government: housing, welfare and modernising a city which had been a latecomer to the 'economic miracle' of Federal Germany. After 1958 the city's growth rate increased, and its very high unemployment levels finally began to drop.[9]

Berlin was also in a unique geographic and geopolitical situation. From the outside, West Berlin was a dramatic yet almost absurd little island at the heart of the GDR, following a course that was all its own. It was clear that Brandt's leadership of Berlin would have to take the way the wall had changed the city into account. The curtain of barbed wire and concrete had interrupted traffic between the two halves of Berlin, and the two halves of Germany, but it had also brutally eliminated the prospect – or illusion – of any possible reunification in the short or medium term. Up until that point, Federal Germany's official position was that its was the legitimate, because democratically elected, government, whereas the GDR regime was a puppet of the Soviets and their German communist acolytes. The GDR, like the Nazi regime, served as a useful foil against which the FRG could define itself as the anti-totalitarian government. Brandt and the West German government had long counted on the lure of democracy and freedom, hoping that eventually the house of cards that was East Germany would simply collapse, unable to compete.

This was the logic behind Bonn's adoption in 1955 of the Hallstein Doctrine, which was intended to isolate the GDR and damage its international prospects by persuading non-aligned countries, often the recipients of development aid, to sever links with the East German regime. Federal Germany threatened to break diplomatic relations with any country that recognised a second German state, and it carried out the threat on a small number of occasions. The official name of the country with no right to exist was generally avoided. Instead, people talked of their 'brothers and sisters' who were 'on the other side' or 'in the zone'; the furthest anyone would go was to call it 'the so-called GDR'. But the construction of the wall in 1961 gave the division immediate material reality. It may have been built to prevent the East Germans leaving their country, but it also forced the West to come face to face with the division, and to acknowledge the failure of its policies towards the Eastern Bloc.

When Brandt saw the Allies' lack of active response to the construction of the wall, he understood that the situation was unlikely to change, and indeed that it was in all the other parties' interests for the current situation, which was ultimately quite convenient for them, to stay the same. It was up to the Germans themselves to try and change things. The priority was to aim to reduce the impact of the wall, both for the Berliners who were directly affected by the division of their city, and for the East Germans, who were expected to watch their regime carry on in peace behind the shelter of the 'anti-capitalist rampart'. The first step was to act at the local level, in Berlin, because to have any influence at the global level, Brandt would need to be powerful at home. Even so, there was nothing stopping him suggesting and designing policies that departed radically from those in place at the time; by now they seemed like tunnels, with the hope of reunification shining like a tiny, inaccessible light at the other end.

Brandt governed his city-state while constantly aware of the great wind blowing around the world. He chose the theme of peaceful coexistence for the speeches he gave at Harvard University in October 1962, which were published soon afterwards under the title *The Ordeal of Coexistence*.[10] 'The balance of terror must retreat before rational efforts to find a peaceful solution to these problems. That is the strategy of peace.'[11] This was the outline of the nascent concept of Ostpolitik, which Brandt had been piecing together bit by bit in his public pronouncements. On 15 July 1963 he was due to give a speech to the political society of the Tutzing Christian Academy. He knew that his suggestions risked having the audience up in arms and had decided to be cautious and to embed his idea about needing a change of tactics vis-à-vis the East in a larger reflection on the history of Germany and the importance of not losing their neighbours' trust. He was listed as the first speaker, to be followed by his adviser Egon Bahr, who would revisit and develop some of Brandt's points. Brandt was late, however, and Bahr spoke first – and gave a speech that would go down in the history of postwar Germany. 'He stole my thunder,' commented Brandt, 'but luckily, he also attracted some of my criticism.'[12]

Egon Bahr and Brandt were very close, although Bahr was nine years Brandt's junior. Bahr was born in 1922 in Thuringia, a region that became part of the GDR after the war. He had grown up in Torgau, in Saxony, where the American and Soviet troops had met on 25 April 1945. He was denied permission to study music by the Nazis because of his Jewish ancestry, and he ended up studying industrial management. After the war, he became a journalist in Hamburg, Bonn and finally Berlin, where he worked for the Rias radio station. Originally created by the Americans to challenge the Russians' monopoly of the airwaves, in a few years Rias had become the home of free speech in Berlin, and the place where young people could listen to new music.

In 1960, Brandt hired Bahr to manage Berlin's press office. Bahr was not content with organising mayoral communications, however, and pushed Brandt to think bigger, starting with the idea of acknowledging the reality of the division in order to be able to fight it more effectively. The result of their long discussions became clear in the two men's speeches at Tutzing, when Brandt declared that the situation had to be stabilised from a military standpoint before it could be dealt with from a political one, and that there was no hope for Germany unless there was a change of policy. The idea of a change of policy violated a dogmatic taboo and was sure to provoke outcry. Brandt manoeuvred his pawns cautiously around the complex chessboard of the German question. 'We need to stop saying "no" to any proposal from the East, just because it comes from the East.' Bahr's speech, intended to give practical examples of the new approach, made things even clearer, starting with its title: 'Change through Rapprochement'. In his office in the city hall, Brandt had spent long hours with his adviser formulating their analysis, which was directly opposed to the prevailing doctrine: they believed that reunification was a foreign policy issue, that the key to the problem was to be found in Moscow, and that no progress could be made either against or without the Soviet Union. 'It will be a succession of small steps, taking the situation as it stands as a starting point,' Brandt announced calmly, surrounded by smoke from the cigarettes he chain-smoked when he was thinking.

He meant that the aim should not be to topple the other Germany's government directly, but on the contrary, to accept the idea that cooperation with the hated regime was the only way to effect change. 'The construction of the wall is a show of weakness and fear, not force,' he said:

> The East German people are the ones worst affected by the GDR's financial policies, which are aimed at defending the GDR against us. If we want to make life better for our brothers and sisters, we need to relax the tension and convince the East German leaders to trust us. By undermining the communist regime's need for defence, we can 'soften' it gradually, and allow the GDR to prosper economically, rather than staying in its current impoverished state.

And if it was a case of 'the more you eat, the bigger your appetite', mused Bahr, then the population would get a taste for prosperity and reject ideology.[13] The two men understood each other well: there was undeniably a subversive element to what they were suggesting. The East German minister of foreign affairs, Otto Winzer, was certainly aware of it when he called the first outline of the new policy 'aggression in felt slippers'.

In 1963, though, they were still at the ideas stage, and Brandt thought Bahr had moved a bit too quickly. For him, the phrase 'change through rapprochement' was too extravagant, and likely to meet resistance from those who would see it as an unacceptable collaboration with the hated communists. He did see a way of testing the idea of cooperation, however, by putting it into practice at the local level. In Berlin itself, he thought, even if they could not pull the wall down altogether, it should be possible to make it slightly more permeable, and it was his responsibility to try and do so. He wanted to persuade the communist authorities to open up a temporary crossing-point so that Berliners could visit their families for Christmas. Brandt put Bahr in charge of the project, aware that it would be a difficult balancing act. Contact with the East German government somehow had to be initiated without making the deal seem like an agreement between two states. It had to be conducted at the lowest possible level, without rushing the government in Bonn or the Allies, and in language carefully calculated so as not to give any impression that it implied recognition of the GDR. They also had to be prepared for the possibility that the GDR would claim the approach meant recognition, either of the division of the country as permanent, or of the GDR's own existence as a sovereign state.

'Policy of Small Steps' and a Border-crossing Agreement

Brandt's team started by refusing to talk of 'West Berlin' in the documents they exchanged with the GDR. The term itself would be a kind of validation of the division of the city, whereas they wanted to emphasise its unity. The addition of parentheses may seem like a small detail, but it was a victory: 'Berlin (West)'. In public, it was impossible to speak of the 'GDR', because it would be tantamount to recognising its existence, but the alternative term 'the zone' was deemed to be discriminatory to the East. 'Over on the other side they don't have these difficulties,'[14] Bahr complained – and so created the term that was neutral enough to be acceptable to all concerned: 'the other side'. The way the negotiations were carried out reflected how both sides saw the agreement: the East Germans held their meetings at the seat of the GDR's government, while the Berlin Senate held theirs at the Ministry of Transport. And, gradually, an agreement was reached, known as the *Passierscheinabkommen*, or 'border-crossing agreement'. It was signed on 18 December 1963 and authorised inhabitants of Berlin (West) to visit relatives during the holiday and spend the day in Berlin (East), although not the other way round. Between 19 December 1963 and 5 January 1964, more than 800,000 West Berliners crossed the border. Brandt appeared on television praising the value of taking action rather than 'making ourselves comfortable in the trenches of this war of words we have been waging for the last few years'.[15] The humanitarian benefit of the operation was undeniable, but the question of language was not yet completely settled. A particular problem was that the East Germans insisted on calling Berlin (East) 'the capital of the GDR', which was a usurpation that violated the city's quadripartite status according to the Potsdam Agreement.

Brandt's friend Axel Springer, the press magnate who owned 80 per cent of Berlin's newspapers, was suspicious of the initiative, although Brandt tried to convince him that the border-crossing agreement would bring the two halves of the city together and would surely lead to marriages. From the end of 1963 onwards, the relationship between the two men began to deteriorate rapidly. The more Brandt tried to tackle the problem of division another way, by talking to the East German authorities, the more he irritated Springer. Springer even started to target Brandt in his newspapers,[16] and so it is all the more striking that Brandt's popularity as mayor was at an all-time high, a well-deserved reward for his fiscal policies which had made the city more attractive to businesses and young couples.[17] Nor was Brandt spared in Bonn, where his decision to take matters into his own hands was not looked on kindly. As well as being mayor of Berlin, he was the leader of the opposition at a federal level, and he was gradually developing a sort of parallel diplomacy.

On 25 November 1963, a melancholy Brandt sipped whisky on a flight from New York to Washington. He was on his way to the funeral of John F. Kennedy, assassinated in Dallas three days previously. He was there as a representative of the city Kennedy had claimed as his own, but also to pay tribute to a man who could have become his friend if they had had more time. Brandt was also emotional to be travelling with Jean Monnet, a man who was already widely honoured as 'the father of Europe'. He had been part of General de Gaulle's Free France government in Algeria during the war, and since then had been at the head of various different initiatives in the ongoing construction of a united Europe. It was the first time the two men had met.[18] Monnet was a reserved but fascinating man, whose life's great project was the creation of the United States of Europe. Since the 1940s the scheme had inspired Brandt, and he was impressed by the mixture of pragmatism and daring with which Monnet had introduced, with Robert Schuman, the idea of achieving real, concrete cohesion by creating structures that would be common to all European states. Monnet had heard people speak highly of the Mayor of Berlin, who in the spring of 1963 had become a member of the Action Committee for the United States of Europe, which Monnet had founded in 1956.[19] The committee members, several Frenchmen among them, were in favour of Europe taking charge of its own destiny.

Brandt had met French delegates in Berlin, and he knew they were very keen to protect their prerogatives as one of the powers jointly responsible for the city. Even more than the British or the Americans, the French military government were hostile to the Berlin Senate's attempts to strengthen links between West Berlin and the FRG. There was no question of them agreeing to the proposal that the Bundestag could meet in Berlin, or that the federal president could be elected there. The German position might be that Berlin was part of the FRG, but the French insisted on preserving its special status. They refused courteously, but firmly. When French Minister of Foreign Affairs Couve de Murville asked Brandt 'not to create problems', Prime Minister Georges Pompidou again expressed France's desire to see the Western Allies' rights properly upheld. Brandt angered him by wanting to change Berlin's status; in Paris the preservation of the Potsdam four-power arrangement was seen as crucial, partly to protect France's rights (although this was not said openly) and partly because the quadripartite city was a thorn in the side of the Eastern Bloc, keeping the possibility of reunification open. In May 1964 Pompidou told Brandt: 'It is our best chance of opposing the Russians' plan to make the division of Germany and Berlin permanent.'[20]

Within the SPD, Brandt struggled against his party's hostility towards the French. In particular, criticism was directed at the behaviour and policies of General de Gaulle, who had come out of retirement in 1958 and then been elected as the first president of the Fifth Republic. Many of the German Social Democrats feared de Gaulle would establish a form of dictatorship in France. Brandt was certainly not one of them. He was on reasonably good terms with the General, and he appreciated his plans to start making changes in Europe and to improve relationships with the two great powers. However, he did have some reservations. Was de Gaulle really giving Germany's problems the attention and care they deserved? Admittedly, he had announced in 1959 that 'the reunification of the two halves of Germany into one whole, completely free nation, seems to us to be the aim and normal destiny of the German people.' By doing so, he had granted the Germans the right which, in his view, all populations should have to live in a united nation. But in Germany he had irritated people by going on to specify that this fundamental right could only be exercised on condition that the German people 'do not question their current frontiers to the west, east, north or south, and that they move towards eventual, contractually arranged integration with Europe, for the sake of cooperation, freedom and peace'.[21]

Everyone understood that this reservation referred to the Oder–Neisse line, which since the Potsdam Agreement of August 1945 had demarcated the border between East Germany and Poland. Disagreements between the signatories, and the Western Allies' desire to keep the discussion peaceful, meant that the final decision on the border had been, rather carelessly, postponed for consideration at a future peace conference – which then never took place. The only document that referred to the current border as definitive was a treaty signed at Görlitz by the East German communists in July 1950. The line, bearing the names of the Oder and Neisse rivers, became one of the most famous borders of the Cold War. In Federal Germany, insistence upon the temporary nature of the Oder–Neisse line was for show. Politicians in all the parties knew that in the end they would have to accept it as the definitive border between Germany and Poland, but all felt an obligation to protest publicly against being pressured into the decision.[22] They were especially concerned by the reaction of the former refugees and repatriates who had been forced to leave the areas of East Germany that had been lost to Poland. Numbering around 8 million people, they formed an important electoral group, and it was feared they might be attracted by the extreme right, which denounced the abandonment of ancient German territory to their Slavic, communist neighbour. Contrary to the stereotype of these refugees from eastern regions, a significant number of them were SPD voters because of the labour tradition in the mining and industrial regions they were leaving behind, especially in Silesia. The subject of the eastern border was, therefore, a difficult one for the SPD as well.

It was not the only issue where de Gaulle's stance caused problems. More Francophile than others in his party, even Brandt had an ambivalent relationship with the French President. He had real admiration for the great resister, the man who had said no to Hitler and who, like Brandt, had left his country in order to continue fighting the Nazis from abroad. But Brandt disagreed with whole swathes of the General's policies, on both the construction of Europe and his relationships with the United States and NATO, although he knew things were more complex than they seemed. The two men shared the same idea of Europe, which included the countries in the Eastern Bloc as a natural part. This great Europe, stretching from the Atlantic to the Urals, was one which Brandt had been writing about since he was a young man in 1940. And, although he was annoyed by France's insistence on its rights as one of the Allies, he could see that maintenance of the quadripartite status was useful when dealing with the Soviet Union. In person, Brandt addressed de Gaulle as '*mon général*'. He disapproved strongly when de Gaulle vetoed Britain's application to join the Common Market, but on the other hand he liked that de Gaulle dared to think differently about the equilibrium of the European continent, and that he tried to find a way to alter the balance of terror – as the posturing and arms race was known.

On 15 May 1964, Brandt gave a speech to the Foreign Policy Association in New York. Faced with an American audience who were getting annoyed with the French leader's show of independence, Brandt explained that de Gaulle was right to want to explore all possible lines of action and to 'think the unthinkable', because the balance of terror was not fixed, and it might be possible to move the fulcrum. He paid tribute to de Gaulle and then said, obliquely, 'sometimes, I wonder why Germany is alone in having started to explore this route.' In case his words had not reached as far as Germany, he restated his position a month later at the German Council on Foreign Relations in Bad Godesberg, near Bonn. On 11 June he announced calmly: 'The potential for mutual destruction is self-paralysing, which means that the use of military force is out of the question. De Gaulle knows how to exploit that fact, and so do other countries. Meanwhile, what are we doing?'[23] Eyebrow raised, he let the silence linger.

Günter Grass, the writer and self-declared moral conscience of post-Nazi Germany, declared that is was now time to form a new government that would at last be able to reform the country. He was one of many intellectuals who gave Brandt their support when he was elected leader of the SPD in February 1964, after the death of Erich Ollenhauer. After a long struggle to impose himself in the Berlin SPD, Brandt's handling of the Berlin Wall crisis had increased his standing, and propelled him to leadership at the federal level. He had become indispensable. Brandt would remain the face of his party for the next quarter of a century, until 1987. To complete the SPD's generational shift and reap the benefits of the Godesberg Programme, he wanted to open the party, the oldest in Germany, up to new social groups and to enlarge its electoral base to include white-collar workers and middle managers. The result of the 1965 elections attested to the wisdom of this strategy to lift the SPD out of the ghetto of the labour movement and make it a party with widespread appeal, centred on the middle classes.

However, even though the SPD received 39.3 per cent of the vote, an improvement on the previous election's result of 36.2 per cent, it was still not enough to win. The good economic progress made by the governing party, and the reassuring figure of the chancellor, Ludwig Erhard, proved too popular. More time was needed before the SPD could impose its new strategy. Besides, this strategy was not yet strong enough to count as an alternative to the current state of affairs, which those on the left denounced as a restoration, a continuation of Germany's past in the Adenauer era. Strikingly, Brandt made the connection between his new strategy and the need for 'our people to make peace with themselves'.[24] But his eloquent and yet somehow vague speeches disconcerted people. Was it perhaps a convenient way of refusing to commit, of simply sketching imprecise outlines which could be fleshed out to fit the expectations of each listener? As a framework, it had the advantage of being able to accommodate the idea of domestic reform just as well as changes in foreign policy, without worrying the Allies unduly. The day he received his honorary doctorate from the New School for Social Research in 1965, Brandt chose the words of his acceptance speech carefully: 'German politicians need to help the German population find a balanced national consciousness.'[25] After the excesses of nationalism under the Nazis, and its suppression since the end of the war, somehow the right mix had to be found: without arrogance, and friendly to other people and other countries. 'Success in this is crucial for the future of democracy in Germany.'

The strategy was not particularly well defined, it has to be said. It had just a little bit more flexibility than Adenauer's and then Erhard's governments had shown. Admittedly, the Christian Democrat Gerhard Schröder,[26] who was minister of foreign affairs between 1961 and 1966, had talked of implementing new policies regarding the East, but these were limited to the opening of trade missions in Warsaw Pact countries, such as Poland, which were thought to be less strictly controlled by the Soviets. The CDU government in Bonn still refused to countenance the idea of negotiating with the GDR, because it would mean recognising its existence. A few CDU members were convinced of the necessity of a new Eastern Bloc policy, but they were few and isolated. One of them was Richard von Weizsäcker, who in the 1980s would become mayor of Berlin, and then president of the FRG. He represented the Christian lobby, especially Protestants in the Evangelical Churches of Germany (EKD), who had witnessed the GDR's attacks on evangelical churches in East Germany; the West German Protestants feared they would not be able to maintain their links to their co-religionists, who were being systematically harassed by the SED.

The Economy in Trouble, and the Grand Coalition

Over the course of a few months in 1966, West Germany was plunged into a state of uneasiness. Opinion polls revealed a sudden crisis of confidence. After more than a decade of impressive economic results, Federal Germany was experiencing its first recession. For the first time since the inflationary episodes of the early postwar years, prices rose, growth stalled and unemployment went above 2.5 per cent. This was an unheard-of figure after years of full employment, when German industry had had to employ immigrant workers in massive numbers just to be able to meet demand. Miners' strikes in the Ruhr were the final confirmation of the failure of the Erhard government's economic policy, despite Erhard being known as 'the father of the economic miracle'. The ghosts of the Weimar and the 1930s reared their heads again, after a period in which growth had been the new norm. The extreme right-wing National Democratic Party (NPD) won enough votes to cross the 5 per cent threshold and gain representation in several state parliaments. In the autumn of 1966, the Erhard coalition government was in crisis; on 27 October, the little liberal FDP party left the government, and new negotiations between the three main parties had to be held in order to form another coalition. For some at the SPD, the best solution was to form a grand coalition uniting the two major parliamentary wings, right and left. After the *Spiegel* affair of 1962, Herbert Wehner had already started working towards such a possibility.[27] Brandt preferred the idea of forming a coalition with the liberals, with whom he was now cooperating in Berlin, but he allowed himself to be convinced in the end, and indeed a coalition with the CDU was not a completely unknown entity to him, as the SPD and CDU had already formed a coalition in the Berlin state parliament in 1963, before the CDU had objected to his border-crossing agreement. An undeniable advantage of such an alliance between the two big parties would be that it would enable the passing of social reforms that required a two-thirds majority, because they affected the Constitution. On 25 November, the SPD agreed to a partnership with the CDU/CSU, and the new coalition government was created on 1 December 1966.

Did Brandt want to become a minister and relinquish his position as mayor of West Berlin? He had not taken part in the scrambling for federal ministerial positions because he had been ill with a lung problem since October. This lung problem was merely the official story, however; in reality he had been suffering a breakdown which left him unable to engage in any political activity. In later interviews, he discreetly referred to a bout of depression brought on by new accusations of desertion during the 1965 election campaign, as well as a more general midlife loss of energy.[28] Despite his illness, his party made his choice for him. The SPD wanted a key post for their leader in the unusual coalition between the CDU and SPD, especially as the rank and file of the SPD were beginning to grumble.

Once more, Wehner was the driving force, handling the party so skilfully that eventually Brandt gave in and agreed. He would be reproached later for his indecision, for letting himself be guided by the shadowy figure of Wehner, and indeed for having been the most easily manipulated of the troika he formed with Wehner and Schmidt. Slightly against his own better instincts, Brandt accepted Wehner's offer. He left the city hall in Schöneberg behind[29] and took charge of the FRG's foreign affairs, becoming the second most powerful man in the government, with the title of deputy chancellor. He took Klaus Schütz, one of his closest allies in Berlin, with him. Schütz had been in charge of the technical aspects of Berlin's relationship to the FRG. Brandt's appointment as head of West German diplomacy was welcomed by the Allies and in particular by Paris. Brandt had acted as the FRG's spokesman abroad for some time, so in a certain sense his appointment just made what was already the de facto situation official.

German Foreign Minister

'We have not become part of a CDU government; we have formed a new government! We have not adopted the CDU's policies; we have made our demands heard and are following our own new policies!' To make sure the party's reasoning and aims were clear to everyone, the SPD's organ *Vorwärts* (*Forwards*) published Brandt's letter to the party's 730,000 members on 7 December 1966. In it, he tried to justify the direction the Social Democrats were taking, and to calm the first signs of rebellion within the ranks against the grand coalition.[30] It was certainly an unlikely partnership – between Brandt, the former exile, and Kurt Georg Kiesinger, the former Nazi Party member. Brandt compensated at some symbolic level for the new CDU chancellor's delicate past. He saw the coalition as a multicoloured compromise, each party appointing ministers who would be difficult for the other party to deal with: if the CSU's Franz Josef Strauss, whose image had been severely tarnished by the *Spiegel* affair, was minister of finance, then Brandt appointed the former communist Herbert Wehner as the SPD's minister of all-German affairs, handling the problem of the division. Compared to some of his more intransigent colleagues, Brandt was pragmatic when it came to his compatriots' pasts, as long as they had not committed any crimes. Unlike Schmidt, he tended to prefer a conciliatory approach. He certainly did understand the people who cried foul, and who applauded the young Beate Klarsfeld when she publicly slapped Kiesinger on 7 November 1968,[31] but he respected the way Adenauer had managed to reintegrate former Nazis into a parliamentary democracy. As the intellectual Eugen Kogon wrote in 1949, when the questions of reintegration and of amnesty for smaller crimes were being debated, either we have to reintegrate former Nazis, or kill them. And we can't kill them.[32]

In the name of reconciliation Brandt was willing to have his name next to that of Kiesinger, who had been, at worst, an averagely zealous functionary working under Ribbentrop in the Nazi Foreign Ministry, where his work between 1940 and 1945 had involved radio surveillance and propaganda. Next, the SPD appointed an unexpected candidate as federal minister of economic affairs: Karl Schiller, a former Nazi Party member who had become a Social Democrat and was professor of economy at Hamburg University. He followed Keynes in advocating a counter-cyclical policy of economic stabilisation. The wide range of backgrounds and political orientation in the government reflected the reality of the country as it was 20 years after the war. Brandt seized the opportunity to win some political territory and to present the outside world with an image of a diverse and constantly changing Germany. He told the party members that the unlikely coalition between the SPD and CDU could only end up benefiting the SPD, even if only by proving that the party was capable of assuming the highest levels of responsibility. The Social Democrats already held power in many of the *Länder*, but the final test of federal government still awaited them: it was an opportunity not to be missed. It was still a difficult pill to swallow for a significant number of the militant wing of the party, especially for the younger members, who protested against what they saw as collaboration.

Those demonstrating in the streets saw themselves as the voice of opposition that the grand coalition had erased from parliament. Among them was the young Peter Brandt. He was now 18 years old and in his final year of school, and had stayed in Berlin when the rest of the Brandt family moved to Bonn. He had protested against American policies in Vietnam in 1966 and was now active among the Marxist youth who were critical of the SPD's decision to form a coalition with the CDU. He was close to Rudi Dutschke, figurehead and leader of the protesters in the West German version of the 1968 movement. Berlin was, along with Frankfurt, one of the most active centres of protest, especially since a confrontation with the police had taken a dramatic turn with the death of a student, murdered by a policeman in Berlin on 2 June 1967. Heinrich Albertz, who had succeeded Brandt as mayor of Berlin, resigned in September 1967 following revelations about police conduct; it was Brandt's close friend and ally Klaus Schütz who took his place. The fact that the policeman responsible for the death of student Benno Ohnesorg had been an SED activist in East Germany was only discovered several decades later; at the time the young protesters were as convinced as those in the French 1968 movement that the police were just another method of repressive, inherently fascist state control.

At Easter 1967, Brandt was confronted simultaneously by family problems and the wider generational conflict of the left: his son Peter was fined after having been arrested at a demonstration.[33] The young people were protesting after a failed attempt on Rudi Dutschke's life, carried out by a young idealist whom the Springer press had fired up against the 'long-haired hippies' who were a threat that needed to be 'incapacitated'. As the years went by, Berlin continued to be the West's shop window, a lighthouse of freedom and a tiny encircled island of resistance. But the city had also become a hotbed of alternative resistance, a refuge for young people who wanted to avoid military service (residents of Berlin were exempt) and a convenient focal point for the protest movements that were gradually taking shape.

The grand coalition was committed to reforming the budget and finding a solution for the economic problems Germany was going through, but they also benefited from being in a situation where they could resolve questions that had been unanswered for years. With two parliamentary groups in the Bundestag, in the capable hands of their respective leaders Helmut Schmidt (SPD) and Rainer Barzel (CDU/CSU), the grand coalition occupied 90 per cent of the parliamentary seats. It is not surprising that both the extreme left wing and extreme right wing expanded in West Germany in response. In particular, the coalition's overwhelming majority allowed them to pass laws requiring a two-thirds majority. Such was the case for the controversial dossier of 'emergency acts', which had been proposed since the 1950s. These acts aimed to adjust the Basic Law in order to reclaim control from the occupying powers, in particular over the response to national emergencies.

Since 1949, and despite the Paris Agreements of 1954 which put an end to the Allied occupation of West Germany, there had been no German legislation on internal security. The Western Allies had retained their right to declare a state of emergency in case of attack, revolution or natural disaster in the FRG. In Bonn, providing West Germany with legislation that would allow it to take measures similar to those of neighbouring states in such cases was seen as a regaining of sovereignty and a sign of normalisation. The coalition's fortunate position in the Bundestag, where parliamentary opposition was reduced to one small liberal party, the FDP, allowed them to pass the new laws authorising intervention in case of natural disaster or public disorder, as well as in case of external threat, by which was meant the East. The laws authorised the restriction or suspension of fundamental rights, such as postal confidentiality or freedom of movement. It was enough to provoke comparisons to Weimar and to the emergency powers of the Reichspräsident (the head of state during that era), and to raise fears about the danger of a coup. Hints of a rebirth of fascism in West Germany began to grow stronger, giving grist to the mill of the 'extra-parliamentary' opposition which was making its voice heard in university lecture halls and in the streets. Apart from the great mobilisation against rearmament and nuclear weapons in the 1950s, West Germany was experiencing its strongest social agitation since the war.

Brandt's position on the emergency acts was at the moderate end of the scale. He could understand the youthful fervour of those like his son, without supporting their excesses of language or their violence; he could understand the need for the legislation without being as inflexible as Schmidt, the leader of the parliamentary group, who could not bear the intransigence or idealism of the younger generation: anyone with a vision, according to Schmidt, should go and see a doctor. Fortunately for his image as a party chairman who tended towards reconciliation, Brandt was not seriously involved in the explosive question of the emergency acts. He was focused on the concerns of his Ministry of Foreign Affairs, with the small team he had brought with him from Berlin: the key figures were Klaus Schütz, who only stayed ten months in Bonn before going back to Berlin to take over as mayor when Albertz resigned, and Egon Bahr, whom Brandt appointed head of policy planning. Brandt's first act as minister was to go to Paris to repair the damage done by the Atlanticist previous government, Erhard and his foreign minister, Schröder. Brandt was counting on his reputation in France to help smooth things over. He was also popular in Washington, where he was seen as a solid ally in the fight against communism. He embodied a dynamic, non-Nazi Germany a little over 20 years after the fall of the Nazi regime, and this image helped him gain the trust of those with whom he worked. Moreover, his ministry was not a particularly polarising one, and the two coalition parties agreed on the fundamental features of German foreign policy: integration with the West, moderation, seeking balance between the various parties and paying special attention to the protecting Allies.

He also managed to avoid criticism in domestic debates, and he could continue laying the foundations of his 'policy of small steps' in peace. This policy had begun with the border-crossing agreement in Berlin, which he implemented while he was waiting until he had won real power and could act more freely. The goal now was still the same as the one he had set out at Tutzing: to find a *modus vivendi* with the East and 'to transform the other side' by building trust and seeking a détente. In private, he talked of accepting reality and, in veiled terms, of stable coexistence with the GDR. All Brandt's colleagues understood the need to abandon the ineffective Hallstein Doctrine of isolating the GDR internationally. After all, Nasser's Egypt had received the East German leader Walter Ulbricht as a true head of state in February 1965. Brandt and his department began to tone the doctrine down, starting by re-establishing diplomatic relations with Yugoslavia on 31 January 1968. The plan was to gradually normalise the idea that Germany would have relationships with its eastern neighbours by starting with those furthest away – and those that had been least affected by the horrors of Nazism.

Before Brandt made his first advances to the Romanian capital, Bucharest, in the winter of 1966–7, he had made sure to inform his Western counterparts, in particular Couve de Murville in Paris. One day, it would be necessary to gain Prague's trust as well, and to convince the Czechs that Germany did not pose any new threat and simply wanted to be on good terms with its neighbours. It was far from a simple task, especially in Czechoslovakia and Poland, which were still full of resentment towards Germany. Their sense that they were once more victims of external oppression, this time from the communist regime, only added to the wounds Hitler had left behind. 'Reconciliation' on the Franco-German model was very hard to translate to the East. Brandt was very aware that one of the major sticking points was the question of whether Germany would accept its postwar territorial borders. He remembered de Gaulle's words in 1965 well: 'France supports reunification, even though we have never had a good experience with united Germany. But the Germans should know that reunification will not be possible unless they accept their borders with Czechoslovakia and Poland.'[34]

Negotiations with the East met another obstacle in February 1967, when the GDR launched its 'Ulbricht Doctrine', which declared that until West Germany recognised the GDR, states in the Eastern Bloc should refrain from signing any agreements with Bonn. And, for anyone who had still not understood, during the summer of 1968 the Russians showed that nothing could happen without their agreement and that the USSR had its world under control. The crushing of the Prague Spring on 21 August put an end to Dubček's idea that it would be possible to develop socialism with a human face, and showed how serious Moscow was about the theory of limited sovereignty in the satellite states, which were being warned to submit peacefully to Russian control.[35] Progress was still a distant possibility, and it made sense to try and ensure Germany was supported by its European neighbours. In the middle of July 1967, Chancellor Kiesinger delightedly reported to Brandt that de Gaulle had reassured him that they had Paris's support: 'We would rather have German reunification than American domination,' de Gaulle had said.[36] It was crudely put, but there were many in

Bonn who felt the same way about the United States. The only problem was that the French President's conditions remained the same, as he reminded them on 9 September 1967 during a visit to Poland. Significantly, he visited Silesia, the former German province which had been given to Poland in 1945 and was also on the edge of the notorious 1937 borders. In a speech, de Gaulle said that Silesia had always been Polish and praised its industrial centre, Zabrze, formerly Hindenburg, as 'the most Polish of all Polish cities'. His message was heard loud and clear in Germany. The SPD congress at Nuremberg in 1968 ended with a discussion of the fact that one day they would have to recognise the Oder–Neisse line.

This was not the only area where there was friction with France. In 1968 and 1969, tensions were running high. This was in part because of disagreement about the exchange rate between the Deutschmark, which was attracting investment, and the franc, which de Gaulle had had to devalue in November 1968 because for the first time Federal Germany had refused to submit to pressure from the Western powers and revalue its currency to suit the others. It was a psychological conflict, out of which grew France's obsession with German economic success. Two visions of Europe and how it should relate to the Allies were hanging in the balance: 'De Gaulle wanted a French Europe in which France would be only a partial member of NATO, but Brandt wanted an Atlantic Europe in which his country would be a full member of NATO.'[37] It was a hard balance to find for Brandt. He tried to keep a good relationship with the French without provoking the Americans, who at the time were deeply engaged in Vietnam, to reduce their military presence in Europe. Messages from President Nixon and Secretary of State Kissinger had given Brandt cause to fear that they might do just that. American withdrawal from Europe was one of Brandt's biggest fears. He had always supported his great ally, and had not joined in the chorus of voices criticising American 'colonial' policy in Vietnam. In private, though, and as time went on, he had become more and more critical of the way Nixon had put his European friends in an awkward position. But he said nothing, and in the end decided not to send Nixon a letter he had written complaining about his strategy in Vietnam and his lack of respect for his European allies' opinions.[38] It was vital to remain tactful, on all sides. In Paris, the French and Germans were still at odds over the question of whether Great Britain should join the Common Market, which France vetoed. Brandt floated the idea of staggered entry for Britain, but he did not press the point. He had learned to equivocate.

On 5 March 1969, the two German television channels broadcast coverage of an event that was unprecedented for two reasons. It was the election of the new federal president, a largely ceremonial role intended to represent and inspire the German people rather than to hold any political power. The Federal Convention gathered to elect him – in West Berlin, which provoked vehement protest on the other side of the wall. For the first time since the creation of Federal Germany, moreover, it was a Social Democrat, Gustav Heinemann, who won. In fact, the Christian and pacifist Heinemann had left the CDU in 1950 to protest against the Adenauer government's rearmament plans. He had founded a neutralist party, the GVP (All-German People's Party), before joining the SPD. He was the sort of man around whom people congregate. At the party's headquarters, there was jubilation that his candidacy had been supported by the liberal party, the FDP. It was without doubt a sign of a change of direction for the FDP, a former ally of the conservative CDU and possible future ally of the SPD – and perhaps a precursor of change altogether.

The legislative elections, held every four years, were due to be held in 1969. The grand coalition had been formed between general elections; why not keep it in place? Having overseen a turnround from unemployment of half a million to full employment, and reinstated social harmony thanks to its new techniques of indicative planning and 'concerted action', the coalition had fulfilled its promises. However, the SPD wanted to follow its own policies, without being constrained by permanent compromise with the CDU. There were disagreements over how relations with the East should be initiated, and if the CDU/CSU accepted the need to improve relationships with their neighbours, they did not approve of the means used, or the moral dimension Brandt imposed on the project. When Cambodia recognised the GDR on 10 May 1969, followed 12 days later by Iraq, Kiesinger still wanted to employ the Hallstein Doctrine, while Brandt was ready to abandon it.[39] Without Brandt's agreement, on 4 June the government decided to 'freeze' relations with Cambodia, which, in response, broke all diplomatic relations with Bonn. When this was followed over the rest of the summer of 1969 by the Yemen, the Sudan, Syria and Egypt, the list of countries who recognised the GDR made West Germany's position untenable.[40]

Becoming Chancellor

In the 1969 election campaign logic dictated that Brandt, the party chairman, would be named the SPD's chancellor candidate if the party was in a position to form a government. The practice of nominating a chancellor candidate before the elections had the advantage of giving a possible future chancellor exposure in a set of general elections in which only parliamentary members were elected – and in which a majority government could only emerge from the final balance of power. The SPD's internal opinion polls gave the economist Karl Schiller the lead over Brandt,[41] but Brandt was accommodating enough to be sure of winning plenty of votes even if, as often happened, he had to endure the reproaches of his two colleagues, Wehner and Schmidt, who thought he did not have the party under tight enough control.[42] And why, out of the Wehner–Schmidt–Brandt troika, was Brandt the one the party wanted as chancellor candidate? Of the three, Wehner was not an option because of his communist past and rough character; Schmidt had to make way for Brandt, five years his senior and the more impressive of the two in terms of career and stature. And so it was Brandt's smiling, weathered face which adorned the posters announcing that the SPD was going to build a modern Germany, and that it had the right man for job. He had already proved himself in the outgoing coalition, making it harder for his rivals to question his competence.[43] Above all, he had a large support base among artists, intellectuals and academics, who, to an even greater extent than during previous campaigns, launched 'social democratic initiatives' all over the country, flooding the public arena with favourable opinions and helping to write his speeches.[44] The figurehead was, as always, the author of *The Tin Drum*, Günter Grass.

Election day, 28 September 1969, was full of surprises. The first estimates gave a clear majority to the Christian Democrats of the CDU and CSU, who together still formed the largest parliamentary group, but soon it was announced that the SPD had won 14 million votes, making up 42.7 per cent of the electorate, and so had beaten their previous seemingly unassailable record of 40 per cent. Wehner quickly made the case for renewing the grand coalition, but Brandt, whose memories of his cooperation with Kiesinger were not wholly positive, thought otherwise. He calculated that by adding the liberal FDP's seats to those of the SPD, they would have a majority in the new Bundestag – a small one, but a majority nonetheless.

In the early years of the FRG, the liberal party had not been particularly progressive, and it had even been seen as a haunt of former Nazis. Wehner and Schmidt were, therefore, wary of its members.[45] Brandt, though, felt that the FDP had changed a lot since then, and it had recently gained a more progressive wing centred on Ralf Dahrendorf and Hildegard Hamm-Brücher. Most importantly, he respected their leader, Walter Scheel, who had helped Heinemann win the presidential elections the previous spring. This time, unexpectedly, Brandt took matters into his own hands. While the Christian Democrat parties were celebrating their results, he contacted Scheel and immediately announced on television that he would try to form a coalition with the liberals. There were some who saw this move as a veritable coup against Wehner.[46] Brandt and his team were amused when the United States moved too quickly to congratulate Kiesinger, and the Secretary of State Henry Kissinger had to apologise to Brandt by telephone. Brandt observed, 'it's no bad thing that the leading power in the world made an error of judgement at the beginning of our term.'[47]

Once the Bundestag had been established and the agreement between the two new allied parties had been made behind closed doors, the chancellor still needed to be elected according to the rules of the parliamentary democracy. With the SPD and FDP, Brandt was a priori five votes in the lead. However, three liberal members announced suddenly that they would not vote for him. His two-vote lead was nevertheless enough, and on 21 October 1969, at 11:22 a.m., the Bundestag elected Brandt as the new chancellor. He needed 249 votes, and he won 251. He looked happy as he joked about his tiny majority: a two-vote lead was still 100 per cent more than Adenauer had in 1949, when he was elected with exactly half of the members' votes, plus one more, his own.[48] The first to congratulate Brandt was Helmut Schmidt, followed by Wehner. Facing the crowd of foreign journalists, Brandt announced his victory: 'Now Hitler has finally lost the war.'[49]

In the days after his election, headlines around the world were in agreement: all expressed approval and respect, and the general reaction was very positive. *The Times* emphasised the break with the past, the *New York Times* commented that his victory was the opposite of what one normally associated with Germany, while *L'Express* ran a picture of Brandt's face on the front page with the headline 'The New Germans'.[50]

Among the countless letters he received, there was one which genuinely flattered Brandt:

> Your leadership of Germany will reassure a troubled world. You have arrived at a moment when the world finds itself at an impasse, facing obstacles in every direction. We need to take constructive steps. […] You have arrived at a moment when Germany has regained her power. She must now rebuild her moral authority. For that, she needs you. […] We live at a critical time – there is an opportunity to make progress in the organisation of Europe and so in the quest for peace. I have no doubt that, if you march forwards, the people of Europe will follow you.

The letter was signed by Jean Monnet.[51]

4

The Chancellor of Ostpolitik

At the Chancellery

Willy Brandt did have experience of governing, but only on the much smaller scale of Berlin. Now he was the leader of the government of Federal Germany, and newly settled in the chancellor's residence, the Palais Schaumburg. Bahr said, 'Actually, it's just a matter of reading, writing, listening and talking. The only differences between being chancellor and normal activities are the scale of the subject matter, the importance of the speakers, the time it takes up, and the merciless spotlight pointed right at you.'[1] Despite his experience in Berlin, Brandt was soon to realise the truth of his friend Bahr's characteristically tongue-in-cheek description. On a daily basis, governing involved spending long hours crafting speeches and noting down ideas, always in green felt pen, and above all annotating and correcting the documents drafted by his team. In the Chancellery, his inner circle of state secretaries included Bahr, who dealt with matters relating to Ostpolitik, and the resolutely pro-European MP for Cologne, Katharina Focke, who handled European affairs and was the daughter of the intellectual Ernst Friedländer.[2] Internal reforms were monitored by the chief of staff of the Chancellery, Horst Ehmke, a long-standing loyal friend; he brought with him his expertise as a professor of public law at the University of Freiburg, and an excellent work ethic. Brandt's close advisers

– Bahr, Ehmke and Leo Bauer – accompanied him on a brief visit to Bad Münstereifel, a small town near Bonn where he prepared his inaugural address amidst an atmosphere of celebration. He could not have imagined that, at the same place a few years later, his government would officially come to an end.

Joy at his triumph helped Brandt's family forgive his ever more frequent absences, tied up as he was by work and travel. Outside the fashionable social life which his political position required, and where Rut assumed her official role as First Lady with elegance and charm, Brandt's home seemed to be no more than an intermittent refuge, especially during his regular bouts of depression, which even success had not managed to cure. After his busy days and the few minutes he found to play electric trains with his youngest son, Matthias, he would spend part of the night reading dossiers.

In the government, he may have been the leader, but he could do no more than guide his ministers who, in the German system, are responsible for their own areas. Compared to their French counterparts, German ministers are much more independent, especially in a coalition. The 12 ministers posed, smiling, for the official photograph taken on the steps of the presidential palace. Brandt is in the middle, flanked by the recently elected President Heinemann and the liberal Scheel, who was minister for foreign affairs as well as vice-chancellor. Beside Scheel is the talented Schiller, a social democrat economist of the Keynesian school. The round-faced liberal Hans-Dietrich Genscher, the new minister of the interior, is standing behind Brandt. A little further to the left is Helmut Schmidt, the new minister for defence, with his thick brown hair smoothed over to one side. Where is Herbert Wehner? He was not in the photo: rather than holding a ministerial position, he was in charge behind the scenes as the chairman of the SPD's parliamentary wing and deputy chairman of the party. In a country where every MP is free to vote as they choose, it takes a powerful personality to keep control of a

1 Two-year-old Herbert Frahm with his mother Martha Frahm in Lübeck, 1915

2 Willy Brandt, presumably Paris, 1937

3 Willy Brandt as Norwegian press correspondent on the press gallery at the International Military Tribunal (bottom section, third row from the front, fourth from the right), Nuremberg, 1946

4 Governing Mayor of West Berlin Willy Brandt in front of Rathaus Schöneberg, Berlin, 1957

5 President John F. Kennedy and Willy Brandt, Governing Mayor of West Berlin, in front of Rathaus Schöneberg, 26 June 1963

6 Federal Minister of Foreign Affairs Willy Brandt and Queen Elizabeth II at a meeting of the Council of Europe, Banqueting House, London, 5 May 1969

7 Appointment of the cabinet members of Federal Chancellor Willy Brandt by Federal President Gustav Heinemann at Villa Hammerschmidt, Bonn, 22 October 1969 (*first row, from left*: Gerhard Jahn, Käte Strobel, Gustav Heinemann, Willy Brandt, Walter Scheel, Karl Schiller, Georg Leber; *second row, from left*: Helmut Schmidt, Alex Möller, Erhard Eppler, Hans-Dietrich Genscher, Walter Arendt; *third row, from left*: Egon Franke, Lauritz Lauritzen, Hans Leussink, Horst Ehmke, Josef Ertl)

8 Federal Chancellor Willy Brandt on his knees in front of the Monument of the Ghetto Heroes, Warsaw, 7 December 1970

9 Chairman of the SPD parliamentary group Herbert Wehner, Federal Chancellor Willy Brandt and Federal Minister of Finance and Economic Affairs Helmut Schmidt at the convention of the Social Democratic Party (the so-called 'Troika'), Dortmund, 1972

10 Federal Chancellor Willy Brandt in dialogue with Vice-Chancellor and Minister of Foreign Affairs Walter Scheel, Fuerteventura, 1973

11 Federal Chancellor Willy Brandt, President Richard Nixon and Secretary of State Henry Kissinger at the Oval Office, Washington DC, 29 September 1973

12 Welcome for Willy Brandt and members of the North–South Commission after its inaugural meeting by Federal President Walter Scheel at Schloss Gymnich near Bonn, 9 December 1977

13 Willy Brandt and Shridath Ramphal handing over the ‘Brandt Report’ to President Jimmy Carter, Washington DC, 15 February 1980

14 Willy Brandt, Edward Heath and Federal Chancellor Helmut Schmidt at a reception at Schloss Charlottenburg during the meeting of the North–South Commission in Berlin, 29 May 1981

15 Official celebration of Willy Brandt's seventy-fifth birthday at the invitation of Federal President Richard von Weizsäcker at Villa Hammerschmidt, Bonn, 20 January 1989 (*back row, from left*: Björn Engholm, Peter Glotz, Holger Börner, Shepard Stone, Walter Scheel, Oskar Lafontaine, Bruno Kreisky, Ernst Breit, Karel van Miert, Kurt Scharf, Egon Bahr, Friedbert Pflüger, Basil Mathiopoulos, Hans Katzer; *middle row, from left*: Johannes Rau, Helmut Kohl, Layachi Yaker, Jacques Delors, Ingvar Carlsson, Hans-Jochen Vogel, Shridath S. Ramphal, Franz Vranitzky, Alan Boesek, Georg Leber, Valentin Falin, Rainer Barzel; *front row, from left*: Marianne von Weizsäcker, François Mitterrand, Gro Harlem Brundtland, Brigitte Seebacher-Brandt, Mieczslaw Rakowski, Willy Brandt, Richard von Weizsäcker, Mário Soares, Hans-Dietrich Genscher, Shimon Peres)

16 Willy Brandt at the Brandenburg Gate the day after the fall of the Berlin Wall, 10 November 1989

government with such a small majority as Brandt's. The more accommodating Brandt was, the stricter Wehner became, relying more on natural authority than on grand gestures to keep the party members in line.

As soon as Brandt was in office, his assistants presented him with three letters to sign, one for each of the Western powers, confirming that he was familiar with their special rights and the restrictions imposed on Federal Germany. Brandt shook his head, incredulous, thinking of his predecessors who must have signed the same letter. How many more of his successors would have to submit to this relic of an outdated and yet still valid supervisory arrangement?[3] Sitting in the office recently vacated by Adenauer, which Brandt had left unchanged, he knew the odd set-up was a guarantee of his country's freedom. It was crucial that the Allies in Washington, London and Paris stayed committed and did not withdraw their support because of nit-picking over the particulars of their prerogatives in Germany. On the whole, the Western governments were pleased with the new chancellor, even if his ideological journey seemed slightly dubious, especially his formerly close relationship with some communists, as well as Wehner's explicitly communist past.[4] The Allies were confident that Brandt was a reliable partner in the fight against communism. And yet he seemed to be taking an unexpectedly independent course when he announced that Federal Germany would contribute towards the détente.

His inaugural address at the Bundestag on 28 October 1969 included several phrases that caused surprise nationally as well as abroad. Had he not told his advisers that 'fortune favours the bold'?[5] His audacity was concealed in two grand, deceptively simple, themes: 'dare more democracy' and 'be good neighbours'. Being a good neighbour was not a new idea in Bonn when it came to the West, but this time Brandt announced that he would put into action a strategy he had already formulated by the end of 1945: 'Germans must encourage close cooperation with the Soviet Union, England and the United States, and with our close neighbours, France, Poland and Czechoslovakia.'[6]

There was to be cooperation with the West *and* the East, taking advantage of the improvement in American–Soviet relations during negotiations about disarmament.

Going to Moscow to Go to Warsaw

The Berlin border-crossing agreement of Christmas 1963 had been a humanitarian measure, allowing families separated by the wall to see each other once a year. But how could a feeling of shared identity be maintained in the long term without a more permanent arrangement for communication and exchange between the two sides? It did not take much imagination to see what the most likely scenario was: if reunification became possible in 50, 100 or 200 years, it would be too late, and completely pointless. Without contact, the two populations would have become estranged from each other. To stop things reaching that point, the 'reunification imperative' imposed by the Bonn Constitution on all German politicians had to be taken seriously.

Brandt had to negotiate a change in direction, by any means possible within the law, in order to introduce a new approach. 'If there are new objectives, we must admit that everything which has been taken for the absolute truth until now may not in fact be completely correct,' Brandt said in the Bundestag. He had spent hours refining his inaugural policy statement to make clear exactly how far this new Eastern policy should go, this Ostpolitik which would turn the Germans into 'good neighbours *at home* and abroad'.[7] Home included the Germany of the Soviet zone, although the Eastern Bloc wanted it to be recognised as part of Germany's 'abroad'. And what should be done about the GDR? Brandt continued: 'Even if two states exist in Germany, they are not foreign countries. Their relations with each other can only be of a special kind.' It was a well-chosen turn of phrase, which managed to please everyone. It insisted on the unity of Germany, but at the same time, as if in passing, referred to the GDR as a state. His words seemed peaceful, but they masked a breaking of Bonn's unconditional taboo: refusing to recognise the existence of the GDR and affirming that only Federal Germany had the authority to represent the German people.

Brandt's concession had a particular audience in mind: Moscow. Brandt and Scheel were convinced that the key to change lay with the Soviets, whose position was not definitively fixed, and who must somehow be movable. In Brandt, Leonid Brezhnev, the general secretary of the USSR Communist Party, saw an interesting man who did not correspond to the communists' image of a social democrat. If Brandt approached Moscow, Moscow might be open to discussion. The Chancellor judged that he had said enough in his inaugural policy statement, and that involving the whole government in the discussions would only end up complicating his plans. He decided to send Egon Bahr on a semi-secret mission to Moscow. He knew Bahr to be a fierce defender of the idea of Germany, so convinced of the West's superiority that he saw no danger that free Germany would be contaminated by contact with the East. Brandt could give him carte blanche to negotiate within the framework the two men had worked out together, through official channels but also thanks to unofficial contacts, such as a mysterious 'Leo'. Bahr would report back to Brandt on each journey, each stage of the negotiation. They had been working together for such a long time that Brandt had absolute confidence in him. Brandt was the motor, while the astute Bahr was the 'doer', although he did have a tendency to go slightly further than Brandt might have wanted when it came to offering concessions to the other side.

For more than 50 hours, spread over several weeks, Bahr met with the Russian minister for foreign affairs, Andrei Gromyko, known in the West as Mr Nyet. They were starting from positions that were hard to reconcile. Gromyko insisted that the FRG should recognise all existing borders in Europe and establish normal diplomatic relations with all states, including the GDR. This was unthinkable in Bonn. How could they recognise it as a state in international law at the same time as wanting it not to exist? Meanwhile, Bahr needed to make Moscow accept Bonn's attachment to German unity and remind the Russians of their quadripartite commitments. Step by step, the outline of a German–Soviet treaty was drawn up. The process was helped by Brandt's decision to renounce the use of force in dealing with East Germany, which implicitly meant recognising its territorial integrity and borders, although the word 'recognise' was never actually written down.

As for the borders, the Oder–Neisse line was still the stumbling block. Bahr told the Soviets that Bonn could not give up its territory east of the line while the peace treaty that had been announced but never finalised at Potsdam remained unsigned. Gromyko was annoyed:

> How is it a concession to give up something you don't have? Recognising reality is not a concession. The question of the border was definitively resolved by the Potsdam Agreement. Any future peace conference will only confirm what was decided at Potsdam. To think otherwise is to have your head in the clouds.[8]

On 22 May 1970 a preliminary agreement was reached, published as the Bahr Paper. It troubled the Allies because it failed to mention the Big Four's rights in Germany and Berlin. They knew that Bahr was the most vehement German nationalist. Was he following Brandt's policy, or was he the one pulling the strings? Were his manoeuvres perhaps even exceeding what would be in Germany's interest?

On 12 August 1970, it was Brandt's turn to travel to the Soviet capital, where he and Leonid Brezhnev would sign the Treaty of Moscow. The conversation lasted four hours, four long monologues in Brezhnev's dilapidated but still elegant offices. At last the tension eased, and they decided to stay in contact through a direct telephone connection, and through the 'back channel', a direct, personal and unofficial link between Bahr and the Russian emissaries. There was no doubt that the Kremlin trusted Brandt as much as the White House did.[9] The final content of the Treaty of Moscow is simple: an agreement between the two parties to accept the territorial status quo, a commitment to resolve conflicts exclusively by peaceful means, and so to refrain from force. The new friendly relationship would be developed 'in the mutual interests of both countries'. However, Germany did not yield to Moscow's pressure to give up the idea of reunification. Below the signatures, Walter Scheel, the German minister for foreign affairs, added a letter to the Soviet authorities noting that the signing of the treaty did not change the West German goal of 'working towards a state of peace in Europe, in which the German people regain their unity in free self-determination'.

Although the main points of contention had been resolved in Moscow, and although the first treaty provided a useful framework for those that would now be drawn up with Poland and the GDR, negotiations in Warsaw proved difficult. They were carried out at a more official diplomatic level this time, notably by the shrewd German diplomat Paul Frank, with Bahr again leading the talks. The main topic of discussion was the fate of the territories east of the Oder–Neisse line. The past weighed heavily on both sides. Poland's fear that Germany would try to claim part of its country again made it wary, while on the German side it was a struggle to get the population to accept the definitive loss of about one-quarter of Germany's prewar territory, made up of Silesia in south-west Poland, Pomerania and Masuria in the north, and former East Prussia, which lay between Poland and Lithuania.

Accepting reality meant acknowledging that time had passed, and that 40 per cent of the Polish inhabitants of the former German territories had been born there. Moreover, the refugees and repatriates were fairly well assimilated into Germany: the GDR had decided to overlook their special status in the spirit of harmony in the socialist family, and the

FRG had tried to integrate them materially and politically, at the same time as permitting them to practise and pass on their regional traditions. The majority of those who had been expelled and their descendants had no desire for revenge or to reclaim the territories, but for some, victimhood seemed more comfortable than the acceptation of loss. Countess Marion Dönhoff, whom Brandt asked to accompany him on his difficult journey to Warsaw, was one of those who focused on the future. A member of an old family of Prussian aristocrats, in her articles in the weekly newspaper *Die Zeit* she was a fervent supporter of reconciliation and liberal thought despite having lost everything in the expulsions. At the last minute she decided not to accompany Brandt, because even if signing the treaty renouncing the former territories was the right thing to do, she felt it was too much to ask her actually to celebrate it.[10]

Brandt arrived in a cold Warsaw on 6 December 1970. The visit began with a dinner hosted by Polish Prime Minister Jozef Cyrankiewicz, easily recognisable by his shaven head. He was about the same age as Brandt and had been interned at Auschwitz and Mauthausen during the war. There was an awkward silence when, during his toast, he greeted Brandt as the first German head of state since Hitler to visit Warsaw. The more optimistic members of the German delegation were pleased because his toast implied that the GDR's head of state, Walter Ulbricht, was irrelevant. The more realistic among them knew that, for Poland, Germany meant the FRG, the 'true Germany', and was detestable according to Marxist–Leninist ideology, which saw a continuity between Nazi Germany and the current country, a den of vengeful capitalists and imperialists. In the presidential palace on the following day, 7 December, Brandt and Cyrankiewicz signed the Treaty of Warsaw, which officially ratified the normalisation of relations and confirmed the current border, although still with the reservations contained in the Potsdam Agreement. The two parties would strengthen their economic and cultural links, as well as scientific and technical ones

– which would soon cause problems relating to the transfer of technology. The general atmosphere was positive; there was a sense of two peoples being reconciled, inspired by the new close relationship between Germany and France. However, Brandt's suggestion of creating a German–Polish youth office was not taken up by the Poles. It would be another two decades before it finally came into being. There was also the issue of the German minority wanting to leave Poland: in exchange for allowing 160,000 people to leave, Warsaw demanded half a billion marks in economic aid. As he signed the Treaty of Warsaw, Brandt declared: 'Germany accepts the consequences of history.' He had proved it that very morning.

On His Knees

The morning of 7 December 1970 was icy cold and gloomy. At about 10 a.m. Brandt was driven to the Monument of the Ghetto Heroes in Warsaw, where he was going to lay a wreath. The monument is a large grey wall, 15 metres high, with a bronze relief in the centre commemorating the Jewish population's uprising against the Nazis between January and May 1943. Brandt walked forward, Scheel half a step behind him, and behind them both came a wreath of white carnations carried by two Polish civilians, who set it down in front of the monument. Brandt straightened out the red, black and gold German banner, on which was written 'The Chancellor of the Federal Republic of Germany'. At that moment he was the symbol of his title, his position, his country. He took a step back and stood still, without saying a word. Suddenly, he dropped to his knees and crossed his hands in front of himself, his face immobile. He stayed a long time in that position, the only thing audible was the clicking of cameras and the stifled sobs of an old woman in the crowd.[11] No words were needed to understand that the Chancellor was begging forgiveness in the name of the German people for the crimes committed by their nation. As the *Spiegel* journalist Hermann Schreiber said, 'here is a man kneeling when he has no need to do so, in the name of all those who should kneel and do not.'[12] That the gesture came from a German who had done nothing to be reproached for, and who had even fought against the Nazis' barbarism, made clear what it meant to 'accept the past' for post-Hitler Germany.

Was it a premeditated gesture? When his wife asked him on his return, he replied by shrugging his shoulders: 'I had to do something.' He said to Bahr: 'I had the feeling that bowing my head was not enough.'[13] Günter Grass had sent him a letter a few days before the visit, advising him to ignore normal, banal protocol, and Brandt had underlined that sentence.[14] The public explanation was more solemn: 'I did what human beings do when speech fails them.'[15] Abroad, in the West, the gesture was praised as a symbol of repentance, but in Germany opinion was more divided about this chancellor who wanted to reconcile but who polarised people like nobody else. *Die Spiegel* published a survey a week later with the photograph of Brandt's genuflection on the cover under the question: 'Should he Have Knelt?' Of the people surveyed, 41 per cent thought that Brandt's action had been 'appropriate', but 48 per cent felt it was 'exaggerated', rising to 54 per cent among those aged 30–59. The newspaper commented: 'Apparently the wisdom of age and the innocence of youth help people understand a gesture that was as extraordinary as the acts to which it paid tribute.'[16]

In Poland the reaction was even more complex. The pictures were not published widely in the media, and among those who were aware of his gesture, there were some who thought it would have been better if he had honoured Polish martyrs rather than Jewish victims. It was also crucial to make sure the West was informed carefully about what was happening. Günter Grass and Siegfried Lenz helped Brandt prepare his televised speech, in which he declared that nothing had been abandoned in Warsaw that had not already been lost for a long time. To avoid the possibility that the Allies would disapprove of Brandt's show of independence, they had been regularly kept up to date with the negotiations.[17] In France, the consequences of Ostpolitik for the FRG's international position caused much interest, alternating between respect for the progress of peace and fear that Germany would want to be free of France's guidance and start to change the rules of the game. Everyone was watching closely to see what Bonn's next moves would be regarding East Berlin, which was the crux of the matter. The progress made in Moscow and Warsaw was crucial, but the most difficult part was still to come.

Normalising, and Making Changes

The normalisation of relations between the two German states was carried out in the same schizophrenic vein as the division. Somehow, West Germany needed to acknowledge that there was a second structure in Germany with the functions of an autonomous state, without recognising that it was a state in the full sense of the word – the inconsistent character of the division would be preserved. The GDR, on the other hand, wanted complete recognition and a legitimate international existence. The FRG wanted to avoid the two populations becoming estranged, and wanted to maintain a feeling of shared identity and the desire for reunification. In these circumstances, what Brandt was doing amounted to a small revolution. He agreed to say the GDR's name and even to talk to the other Germany's authorities.

His first meeting with the head of the East German government, Willi Stoph, took place at Erfurt, in the GDR, on 19 March 1970. Erfurt was where the Social Democrats had developed their first Marxist programme in 1891 – a little reminder from the East German government to the Western reformists. Brandt arrived in a special train. The white-haired Stoph, in his austere glasses, was as unwelcoming as expected when he met Brandt at the station. As the two men walked to the hotel where the meeting was to take place, people gathered in the street and chanted: 'Willy! Willy!' Then, because Stoph was also called Willi (though spelled differently), they shouted: 'Willy Brandt! Willy Brandt!' In the square in front of the Erfurter Hof hotel there was a whole crowd shouting: 'Willy Brandt, come to the window!' He was worried that the enthusiastic gathering would provoke the intervention of the security forces: this was a country where any unplanned public expression of opinion was unwelcome. Brandt eventually appeared at the window with a restrained smile. He waved discreetly, less to greet the crowd than to ask them to be quieter. What could he do for them, anyway? He knew he was giving them false hope. 'Tomorrow, I will be in Bonn. Not them,' he thought.[18]

The meeting was unproductive, and the two parties failed to reach agreement on the idea that Germany should never declare war again.[19] The GDR delegates were humiliated by Brandt's audacity in waving to the crowd, and above all by their own inability to prevent the outpouring of enthusiasm, which according to a Stasi report proved that they had underestimated 'the danger of the class enemy'.[20] Brezhnev commented laconically that there was at least one advantage of the Erfurt meeting: 'The world now knows that two German states exist.'[21] In any case, the East Germans had made sure the occasion had the characteristics of an official visit by including a detour to the Buchenwald concentration camp. This had been at the suggestion of Günter Guillaume, one of Brandt's staff at the Chancellery, who was in charge of liaising with the trade unions.[22]

Reassured that it would be possible to make progress towards something resembling a détente, Brandt invited Stoph to Kassel on 21 May 1970. But it was soon clear that the GDR was absolutely not prepared to change its position, and that it was not ready to make any concessions, in substance or in form. The meetings were a complete failure. The two sides decided on a 'pause for reflection', and to restart the conversation at a later date. To make things worse, the talks had been plagued by protesters from the extreme right, shouting insults against the GDR, and cries of 'Down with Brandt!'[23] They were foolish not to see that their protests gave the GDR the perfect opportunity to paint the FRG as a den of Nazis. The East German television channel Schwarzer Kanal had no need to edit or doctor the footage to make it usable in its anti-Western propaganda.

The topic of West Berlin caused yet more tension. The GDR and the Soviets kept trying to undermine the special status it had held since the war by limiting road access to the city. Brandt shared the Western Allies' concern that Moscow was ignoring the responsibilities it held within the quadripartite framework. The East Germans' efforts to disrupt traffic by extending controls at the three road border-crossings into West Berlin was part of the psychological warfare Brandt was so familiar with from his time in Berlin. Many meetings and almost a year of embargo later, the ambassadors of the four powers finally agreed on a more practical way of regulating traffic, while reaffirming the quadripartite system and preserving the Western Allies' legal positions.[24] Brandt was pleased that Washington had been involved in the process, even if the Americans' tenacity was also a sign that they were suspicious of their unruly German protégé: 'I urged Nixon to go along with Brandt's policy and to use our influence to embed it in a wider framework than German nationalism,' Kissinger insisted years later.[25] For the time being, the result suited Brandt. Without the Quadripartite Agreement on Berlin, signed on 3 September 1971, his government would not have been able to ratify the Treaties of Moscow and Warsaw in the Bundestag.

The Ostpolitik marathon was far from over. After a six-month pause for reflection, Brandt asked Bahr to reopen negotiations with East Germany to try and work towards a normalisation agreement. Meanwhile, he was determined to maintain his direct link to Brezhnev. On 17 September 1971, he arrived in Oreanda, in the Crimea, where he stayed with the Soviet leader for three days. The symbolism of the place did not go unnoticed: a few hundred metres away was the Livadia Palace, the tsar's summer residence where the Yalta Agreement had been signed in February 1945. The aim of the meeting was to strengthen their good personal relationship, and to be honest with each other – something that could not always be relied upon when dealing with the Soviets. They had serious discussions about the pursuit of détente and disarmament, and Brandt finally accepted Brezhnev's suggestion of reviving the old idea of a Conference for Security and Cooperation in Europe (CSCE). Brandt was especially in favour of concerted disarmament in Europe, by which he meant not disarmament achieved through force and threat, but, according to an idea that was current at the time, disarmament carried out peacefully and in the mutual interest of all parties. He had wanted to show the world a peaceful Germany when, just one month after his election, he signed the non-proliferation treaty which had caused his predecessor such grief.

Surely nobody could be offended by Brandt's efforts to be a pilgrim of peace? And yet he did manage to irritate people. In Washington, Richard Nixon was more and more annoyed by the liberties this little German Chancellor was taking. In a conversation with Henry Kissinger, he complained, 'Actually Brandt is a little bit dumb.' Kissinger replied: 'Brandt is dumb. And lazy [...] and he drinks.'[26] The Secretary of State's suggestion of setting up a 'back channel' for direct communication between Bonn and the White House was motivated by a desire to keep a close eye on this German Social Democrat, who was becoming more worthy of suspicion as time went on. In June 1971, while preparing for a meeting with Brandt, Nixon suddenly said to Kissinger, 'Good God, if that's Germany's hope, then Germany ain't got much future.'[27]

Georges Pompidou, who had succeeded de Gaulle to the French presidency in 1969, was also displeased that Brandt had simply told him he was going to the Crimea, without asking his opinion. He feared Bonn's contact with the East would lead to a 'German shift'. There was plenty of friction between Brandt and Pompidou, but it would be simplistic to put all the blame for the tension on excessive French suspicion about Ostpolitik. Both men complained about each other's ulterior motives. Brandt was cautious, because he was convinced the French still harboured their age-old ambitions to be the leader of Europe and the West. Moreover, he thought they had been suspicious of him on principle ever since the Germans had started discussions with the Russians. There was some truth in the idea of the 'Rapallo syndrome'[28] – the Western fear of an overly close relationship between Germany and the Soviet Union – but the Germans overestimated its importance and ended up starting a downward spiral of preventive measures.

Pompidou, on the other hand, did not approve of the fact that Brandt was thinking about the German question within the framework of a new security structure in Europe. He had told him as much in January 1970.[29] He found it infuriating that Brandt's Ostpolitik had ambitions to go beyond a simple contribution to détente, and his unilateral initiatives began to get on Pompidou's nerves. It came down to a fundamental difference of opinion. Pompidou totally disagreed with Brandt on the need for concerted disarmament in Europe. Federal Germany had played an active role in Reykjavik in June 1968, when NATO had suggested opening talks on concerted, multilateral force reduction, which would be known as mutual balanced forces reduction (MBFR). France had refused to take part, to avoid French weapons of deterrence being included in the total count of Western forces. On the other hand, France was a strong supporter of the CSCE, while Federal Germany was more reticent. In Bonn the CSCE was seen predominantly as an instrument of the Soviet desire to confirm the status quo, including the division of Germany, and the Germans were not convinced by the idea that the CSCE would make it more difficult for Moscow to use force in its satellite states in Eastern Europe.[30]

The Nobel Prize ... And the Threat of Overthrow

On 20 October 1971, Kai-Uwe von Hassel, the president of the Bundestag, interrupted parliamentary debate: he had just been told that the Nobel Committee had awarded the Nobel Peace Prize to Federal Chancellor Willy Brandt. The MPs of the governing parties, the SPD and FDP, gave him a standing ovation, but very few others joined in. Almost all the CDU/CSU MPs refused to applaud. It was a telling example of the political climate in the early 1970s. Brandt must have been pleased at the thought that the last German to win the Peace Prize had been Carl von Ossietzky in 1936, in much more dramatic circumstances. He gladly received the honour of being placed on an equal footing with the first German Peace Prize holder, Gustav Stresemann, who had won it in 1926 jointly with Aristide Briand.[31] He was pleased by the committee's decision, even though he, like many other politicians, had actually nominated Jean Monnet.

He could not hide a smile of satisfaction at the ceremony in Oslo on 10 December 1971. Oslo! The president of the Nobel Committee announced that he had been awarded the prize because of his commitment to initiatives that supported détente and peace, both as foreign minister and chancellor. In his acceptance speech, Brandt paid tribute to those who had helped him and added how much it meant to him, 'that it is my work "on behalf of the German people" which has been acknowledged; that it was granted me, after the unforgettable horrors of the past, to see the name of my country brought together with the will for peace.' He later remarked that the Protestant Bishop of Berlin had told him that 20 October, the day the prize had been announced, was devoted to a verse from Samuel: 'The Lord had given him rest from all his enemies about him' (2 Samuel 7:1). Some of his listeners understood better than others whom he might have been referring to.

The international response to the prize was celebratory. *Time* magazine had already made him its Man of the Year in January that year, with a front cover showing his face as a bronze statue, with steel bars bolted firmly onto either side of his head, attached to two metal sheets, symbolising the iron curtain, preventing them from sliding too far apart.[32] The Nobel Prize was invaluable for his international image, 'a sort of lifetime canonisation for our secular century'.[33] Within Germany, on the other hand, over 40 per cent of the CDU's supporters thought he did not deserve the prize; there was a rumour that the German secret services had bribed the Nobel Committee, and that anyway the committee was a den of crypto-communists.[34]

The ratification of the Treaties of Moscow and Warsaw triggered a passionate outburst of emotion, fuelled by Axel Springer's extremely hostile response in his various press outlets.[35] Strikingly, even those in similar political spheres had different opinions on the subject. The debate was less about the accuracy of the analysis (let's stop invoking the word 'reunification' as some kind of magic spell, and start actually trying to bring about the conditions for achieving it) than about the idea of surrendering territories that had long been German to the communists. The reproach of treason was not long in resurfacing. It was mainly wielded by Brandt's rivals on the right, but a few Social Democrats and Liberals who did not support his policy also revived it. There were even a few SPD members, from the eastern provinces, who planned to defect. In February 1972 the treaties had their first hearing at the Bundestag. In matters of foreign policy, the Bundestag was only authorised to discuss and ratify.

The head of the opposition's parliamentary group, the Christian Democrat Rainer Barzel, was faced with a dilemma. If the CDU and CSU voted against ratification, it would seem as if they were hostile to the idea of reconciliation with the East, and hostile to the principal victims of Nazism. Moreover, he was personally convinced of the soundness of Brandt's policy regarding the East. How could he show that he agreed with the end, while still disapproving of the means? Barzel, originally from former East Prussia, needed to guide his group towards a coherent position and get them to vote accordingly. There were plenty of opposing voices in the ranks, but also some supporters, among them Richard von Weizsäcker. In his view, ratification of both treaties, especially the Treaty of Warsaw but also the Treaty of Moscow – without which Warsaw would have been impossible – was not merely inevitable, but also the right course of action.[36]

On the morning of 24 April 1972, Marga Sprenger, one of Brandt's two private secretaries, saw him arriving at his office with an unusually expressionless face. Brandt was well liked among his staff because of his courtesy and because he never shouted. His self-control did not extend to hiding his moods, however: he loved telling jokes, but he would also sometimes retreat behind an impassive mask, as was the case on that morning.[37] It was the day after a set of regional elections, which are often held in Germany. The reason for his bad mood was simple: just before the treaties were due to arrive for their second and third hearings, the coalition had been severely weakened. The loss of the election in Baden-Württemberg had cost the government its majority in the Bundesrat, while the defection of two MPs meant the coalition no longer held the majority in the Bundestag. It was the opportunity the CDU/CSU had been dreaming of: a chance to embark on an attempt to overthrow the government, using a mechanism provided in the Constitution. A constructive vote of no confidence meant that, in the absence of a majority, the government could be dissolved without further delay as long as the leader of the opposition immediately formed a replacement team. The idea behind the mechanism, introduced to avoid repeating the problems of the Weimar Republic, was to allow lack of confidence in the government to be expressed, and to lead to political change, but only if the opposition worked to form a majority government that could take over. The plan, therefore, was to oust Brandt and replace him with Rainer Barzel. It was a dangerous plan. What would the CDU do if they succeeded?

Who would they form a coalition with, and what would they do about Ostpolitik?[38] The vote took place on 27 April. The atmosphere in the Bundestag was tense, and Brandt's ministers were already packing their bags. When the result was announced, it was, according to Strauss, nothing less than 'one of the greatest scandals in the history of the FRG':[39] Barzel needed 249 votes to win, and had only received 247. The plan had failed.

The result meant that at least two of the Christian Democrats had voted in favour of Brandt. Outrage. Nobody knew who, or why, until a year later when the CDU MP Julius Steiner confessed in *Die Spiegel* that he had been a double agent, spying on his party for the East and West German secret services. He then accused the general secretary of the SPD, Karl Wienand, of bribing him 50,000 marks to vote for Brandt. It was even possible that he had been bribed twice. Years later, Markus Wolf, the head of the East German Stasi, said that he had given the same amount to Steiner, and his claim was corroborated in the Stasi records. There are some allegations that a second MP was bribed – Leo Wagner, one of Strauss's close supporters at the CSU.[40] The episode ended on 17 May with the definitive vote to ratify the treaties. The CDU/CSU decided the most honourable course of action was to abstain from the vote altogether, and the treaties were ratified. Later, the affair would be remembered as the time the Stasi saved Brandt's government to save Ostpolitik.

The Basic Treaty with the GDR

Brandt was tempted to give up. This new test, together with the obvious fragility of his government and the loss of his majority in parliament almost made him admit defeat. He soon rallied, however: he had a plan. He would deliberately have the Bundestag dissolved and would organise general elections to be held in the autumn, by which time he hoped to be able to win a more comfortable majority. He was one of the few to believe victory was possible, but he was convinced the SPD would be able to profit from Ostpolitik's popularity, as well as the prestige the upcoming Olympic Games, in Munich in September, would give them. Meanwhile, he needed to speed up the negotiations with the GDR, which had been stalling for months. Ulbricht had been replaced on 3 May 1971 by Erich Honecker, who in the position of first secretary of the Central Committee of the SED became the new leader of the GDR. The Soviets had helped him gain power because they thought his unbreakable conviction that West Germany was the class enemy would make him less vulnerable than Ulbricht to contamination by 'social democracy'. Brandt pushed Bahr to hurry things along in his discussions with his East German counterpart, Secretary of State Michael Kohl. Kohl was a very cold man, a typical product of the Communist regime in East Germany. When Bahr returned from their first meeting, he was asked what Kohl was like. 'He makes Gromyko look like a playboy,' he replied.[41] There was amusement at the irony of him sharing a surname with one of the rising stars of the CDU, his polar opposite Helmut Kohl. In German Kohl means 'cabbage' and is a common name. So that they would know which Kohl was being referred to in conversation, in private Brandt's government started calling the Communist Kohl *Rotkohl*, 'red cabbage, which is the name of a popular German side dish.

After a first treaty dealing with matters of transport, the two states finally managed to agree on a text defining the nature of their relationship. It was signed in Bonn and published on 8 November 1972, just in time to allow to the coalition to win the general elections by a large margin. It was a strange treaty because, despite their desire to move beyond their hostile attitudes to each other, the two parties were fundamentally in disagreement. In particular, the FRG did not give in to the East German demand to be fully recognised as a foreign state. Nevertheless, the treaty set down a basic agreement: to develop good neighbourly relations on the basis of the equality of both parties; to refrain from the use of force to settle disputes; to respect each other's borders and territorial integrity; to renounce their claims to speak in each other's names; to develop sectoral cooperation; and to commit to both aspects of détente in Europe – the CSCE and disarmament. There was still one point on which Brandt refused to give way: as the FRG was still unwilling to recognise the GDR in international law, it was out of the question for the two states to exchange ambassadors. The final text refers only to the exchange of 'permanent representatives'; the devil is in the detail. The East Germans, meanwhile, vetoed any mention of German unity within the text, despite the West German delegation's wishes. 'Write us a letter,' Honecker told Bahr, 'and we will take note of your comments.'[42] Bonn immediately added a letter below the signatures, headed 'Letter about German unity', which specified that the treaty did not affect the Federal Republic's primary goal in any way: the re-establishment of the unity of the nation in freedom, as stated in the preamble to the Basic Law. Strikingly, Brandt's team spoke of 'the nation' rather than 'reunification'. As the latter was for the time being impossible, they thought it better not to mislead people about the reality of the division.

Despite these reservations, the Basic Treaty, as this was known, helped the West Germans get under their Eastern neighbours' skin, and to disrupt them in various ways. One example was the accreditation of Western press correspondents in the GDR, which was a step forwards in a country where the authorities had a monopoly on information, and where they regularly harassed those who wanted to know too much. The treaty also enabled the normalisation of relations between the GDR and the Western Allies. In solidarity with West Germany, until then none of the three Western powers had established diplomatic relations with the second Germany. From the GDR's point of view, it was a real triumph to be accepted into the UN in the middle of September 1973, at the same time as the FRG but as a separate member state. East Germany was now able to exchange ambassadors with Washington, London and Paris. Again, however, it was all a question of nuance: the official title of the French ambassador was *Ambassadeur près la RDA*, rather than the more usual *Ambassadeur en RDA*. The apparently small difference was a subtle way of expressing French reservations about the GDR.

Had relations really been normalised? 'Before, we had no relationship with the GDR; now, at least we have a bad one.'[43] Bahr's quip is a good summary of the shift that took place in the early 1970s. After it was officially signed in East Berlin on 21 December, the treaty still could not come into force because of a complaint presented to the Federal Constitutional Court by the government of the Free State of Bavaria. According to the complaint, the treaty was unconstitutional because it violated the principles of the Basic Law, and in particular the items in the preamble: the unity of the nation, the illegitimacy of a second state in Germany, and the injunction to reunification. Brandt had to wait until 31 July 1973 for the Constitutional Court to give its slightly Solomonesque judgement, which did ultimately favour Brandt's government. It was not without satisfaction that he read the document which confirmed his reading of the situation and his caution: the judges felt that, while the Constitution did impose reunification as the objective, the means used to achieve the objective were left to the discretion of politicians.

Anyway, the initiation of relations with another state-like organisation in Germany did not entail the FRG's renunciation of its claim to be the sole successor of the German state as it had been at the end of the nineteenth century, and to be identical to that state within a limited part of its territory. By refusing to recognise the GDR as a foreign country and by exchanging 'permanent representatives' rather than ambassadors, the FRG had 'admitted' but not 'recognised' the division. At any rate, the new measures were intended to facilitate exchanges between the two halves of the one and only German people. Brandt, who had announced in 1969 that he wanted 'to use regulated nearness to work towards true togetherness',[44] reminded people that nothing in the current arrangement precluded future reunification. As the treaty did not rule out the re-establishment of unity in the future, it was constitutional. Strauss could claim a victory in that the judgement had 'got rid of ambiguities',[45] but in the end the judges had authorised the policy of change through rapprochement. Bonn stuck to its guns. Relations with the GDR were 'intra-German' and not 'inter-German', and trade with East Germany would still be categorised as domestic. According to this logic, the GDR would still essentially be a stowaway in the Common Market.

European Revival

Did Brandt's European policy make any sense without Ostpolitik? Under the enormous shadow cast over all other government activity by the success of his diplomatic enterprise in the East, his efforts for European integration seem rather paltry. But we should not hold that against him. There is no suggestion that he desired anything other than to bring about a more-or-less artificial rebalancing of power, while allaying any reservations that the involved parties may have had by reassuring them with phrases like 'Ostpolitik begins in the West'.[46] When Brandt flipped the perspective and wrote to Pompidou that Ostpolitik was 'the eastern component of European politics',[47] he was not just sweet-talking. From the end of the war onwards, he had been pleading the case for European integration, talking about the United States of Europe before Monnet and Schuman had even launched their proposal for the pooling of coal and steel production in 1950. Brandt had been in open opposition to his party during the SPD's period of hostility to the construction of this Europe in the West. It is also unfair to doubt his conviction or to accuse him of having suddenly changed his position. He had proclaimed his belief in the coherence of Eastern policy and the construction of Western Europe in 1946, in his *Criminals and Other Germans*, where he presented European integration as the solution 'to the problem of Germany and the problem of Europe'.[48]

In 1969 his project was still a union of European states. But after the enthusiasms of his youth, he was no longer drawn towards grand, complex structures or the creation of a supranational state; in other words, as he explained to Pompidou: 'neither to institutional perfectionism, nor to integrationist abstracts'.[49] What was needed was pragmatism, and the provision of the necessary tools to make the alliance of European states function. In his view, such an alliance should certainly open its doors to the United Kingdom – no more arguing with the French. In Paris, he thought, they must surely appreciate his honesty; as his involvement in European affairs was directed primarily at gaining Pompidou's agreement for Ostpolitik, he would not also insist on British participation.[50] From the beginning of the 1950s, the SPD had made the case for Great Britain's role in the great European project. Brandt himself, like Schmidt, wanted to include Great Britain because of the long-standing links between Germany and the great power of northern Europe, and also because of Britain's long democratic tradition and the model of its welfare state, which had become part of European identity.

Unlike the French, Brandt did not foresee the difficulties that would follow. In Paris, the general view was that the British would delay political integration and would want to transform the great European project into a simple free trade zone. Eventually, Pompidou yielded to the pressure exerted by other members of the European Economic Community (EEC) and agreed to open negotiations with the United Kingdom and the other candidate nations, Ireland, Denmark and Norway. The French decision to abandon de Gaulle's position was motivated by the new configuration of power relations, particularly in the economic sphere, and especially by the desire to reinforce Western Europe so as to diminish the harmful consequences of opening up to the East. The idea was to make Europe stronger in order to resist the Soviet Union more effectively, and to protect Germany from the dangers of neutralism. When the French President suggested holding a summit of heads of state and government to discuss the triptych of 'completion, deepening and enlargement', Brandt supported him and increased bilateral communication in order to prepare for the summit, which finally took place at The Hague on 1 and 2 December 1969.[51] The leaders managed to arrive at a compromise that satisfied all parties: in exchange for a guarantee of permanent financing for the Common Agricultural Policy that was so important to France, Pompidou agreed to extend the EEC and to open negotiations with the candidate countries.[52] The negotiations took place over the summer of 1971 and resulted in the acceptance of three of the four candidates on 1 January 1963, taking the total number of members to nine. In their referendum in September 1972 the Norwegians voted against joining, disappointing Brandt, who would have loved to see his adopted country in the EEC.

At the start of the 1970s, European integration was progressing on two fronts. The first was in the economic and monetary sphere, where there was nevertheless doctrinal disagreement between the two principal partners, France and Germany. On the French side, the 'monetarist' consensus was that the shared European currency should be introduced as quickly as possible in order to force a convergence of economic practices. German economists, in particular at the independent Bundesbank, held the opposed, 'economist', view that economic differences needed to be reduced before attempting to create an interdependent European entity, of which the shared currency should be the finishing touch. As far as Brandt was concerned it was a chicken or egg question, and he worried that the economists would endlessly be at each others' throats over it.[53] His openness to Jean Monnet's influence led him to favour a pragmatic approach, that a start had to be made somewhere before any progress could be made. In March 1971, the six founding member states of the EEC partially accepted the recommendations of the Werner Plan, presented in October 1970, which suggested gradual progress towards economic and monetary union via several stages. The first stage, which aimed to reduce fluctuation margins between the various European currencies, involved the adoption in the spring of 1972 of a restrictive measure designed to encourage economic coordination: the 'currency snake'. This ran in parallel with developments on the second front of the European project: political integration.[54]

While Pompidou's triptych was taken very seriously in Bonn, in Paris he was opposed by a Gaullist majority, led by Michel Debré, who were strictly '*souverainiste*', wanting to retain national independence rather than being subordinated to a supranational entity. Nevertheless, in October 1970, he managed to establish the European Political Cooperation, which was the mechanism through which foreign ministers could consult each other. The aim was to coordinate foreign policy and approach a political union – at the time thought to be achievable by the end of the 1970s. What form would such a union take? Like Pompidou, Brandt was sure that the first step towards greater coordination should be to organise summits of European leaders, but he wanted to go even further than the creation of a permanent secretariat that would organise intergovernmental meetings. Gradually they came to an agreement and decided in November 1973 to hold regular meetings between the various heads of state and government, in private and without agenda. It was the European Council as Jean Monnet had imagined it, revived by his successors. The French President refused Brandt's other requests, such as more power for the Commission and for parliament in the processes of consultation and decision-making. Brandt also agreed to drop his demand for the European Parliament to be elected by universal suffrage, despite the wishes of the smaller member states and strong public opinion in Germany demanding democratisation in Europe.[55] Overall, Brandt's European track record was a mixed bag. He had failed to persuade Paris to take part in the MBFR disarmament negotiations, which started in Vienna at the beginning of October 1973. In Pompidou's view, the idea of a zone of reduced militarisation in the heart of Europe, comprising the two Germanies, Benelux, Poland and Czechoslovakia, was a hopeless one. It would be like giving Moscow Europe on a plate.

Beyond Europe: The Near East

'Israel welcomes you with the respect due to a man who, during the darkest hours of humanity and the Jewish people in particular, joined those fighting against the Nazis.' Brandt had known Golda Meir, prime minister of Israel, since they had both attended meetings of the Socialist International. 'I am sure we can be honest with each other, as friends.'[56] In Israel, as in Poland, Brandt was one of the rare Germans to be seen positively. It was June 1973, and he was the first German chancellor ever to visit Israel.

Nine months earlier, on 5 September 1972, Germany had been witness to the massacre of Israeli athletes at the Munich Olympic Games. The murders, carried out by the Palestinian Black September Organisation, were also an attack on Germany, Israel's friend, in an attempt to show the Germans' inability to protect Jews in their homeland. It was well known that Palestinian groups like Fatah had given logistical support to the West German terrorist organisation, the Baader-Meinhof gang, who were increasing their attacks on West German institutions. On his 1973 visit, Brandt was representing a Germany that was ashamed, but also sympathetic to and in harmony with Israel. The media focused less on the fact that he narrowly survived a helicopter accident on his arrival in Masada than on his attitude during a visit to Yad Vashem, the memorial to victims of the Holocaust. In a solemn, calm voice, he read a long passage from the Old Testament: 'The

Lord is merciful and gracious, slow to anger and plenteous in mercy.' As he told the Bundestag on his return, it was one of the decisive experiences of his political life.[57] He meant it: his emotions were genuine, and indeed there were plenty of people who were ready to criticise him for being too sensitive.

After the undeniable foreign policy successes of his first years in office, Brandt now faced several difficulties. First of all was his tense relationship with the White House, where Nixon had decreed the 'Year of Europe' on 23 April 1973, at the same time as announcing he wanted the Old World to play a secondary role in world affairs. Washington reacted harshly to what it saw as excessive muscle-flexing on Europe's part. The Europeans were hesitant about the 'Year of Europe' initiative, although they, Brandt among them, officially praised this 'interesting contribution' to the transatlantic conversation. They did not appreciate the way they felt the Americans looked down on them as a regional junior partner, at the same time as demanding that Europe took on a greater share of the Atlantic community's financial responsibilities. Embroiled in the Vietnam War, Nixon threatened to withdraw some of the American troops stationed in West Germany, touching a particularly sensitive nerve in Bonn.[58] The Chancellor continued to support a good transatlantic relationship on principle, but he also hoped the EEC would be able to gain a bit more independence. This balancing act condemned him to work towards making the European construction more thorough at the same time as playing the go-between for France and the United States.

In 1973 the situation deteriorated further with the Yom Kippur War in October. The oil exporters of the Middle East accused the United States and certain other Western industrial nations of being too pro-Israel and announced an embargo. There was a drastic reduction in the available quantities of fuel, and a sharp rise in the price of crude oil. It had serious consequences for budgets, currencies and employment, and it destroyed the macroeconomic equilibrium, convincing everyone that the world was entering a crisis. The fragility of Federal Germany and other developed nations, and their total dependence on foreign imports, became clear. Having largely ceased coal production, they now relied on oil, the fuel of the present, for the majority of their energy needs. The fuel of the future was still undecided: oil or already-controversial nuclear power. In Bonn, it was revealed that the United States Army had secretly used the port facilities in Bremerhaven to ship weapons to Israel, which was under attack. For better or worse, Germany was carried along in America's wake. In Brandt's words, the United States was now treating Germany 'like a colony'.[59] Many Germans only really understood that the FRG was truly suffering from the embargo in December 1973, when they saw pictures of completely empty German motorways. Brandt banned road travel for several Sundays in a row, a predominantly symbolic foray into the world of the car, of material luxury and individual freedom, which acted as a precursor to the crucial 'energy-saving' initiatives to come.

5

'Dare More Democracy' or a Difficult Promise

'In case you, too, take me for an over-sensitive man, I have to tell you that it is a long time since anything hurt me as much (and incidentally caused me as much personal pain) as your nasty phrase "half-chancellor".'[1] Brandt wrote these words to the famous journalist Günter Gaus, editor-in-chief at *Die Spiegel*, who had just published two acerbic columns in the 1 February 1971 edition of his paper, with the title 'Waiting for a Chancellor'. His accusation was simple: Brandt was neglecting domestic politics, especially economic and fiscal policies, and the FRG was in need of a super-minister of economic affairs and finance because the Chancellor preferred focusing on foreign policy 'as if the existence of the government and the well-being of the country depended upon it'. It was a difficult moment for Brandt, who in 1969 had wanted his term in office to be one of reform, and who had dedicated the majority of his inaugural statement to domestic affairs.[2] Had the numerous reforms he had introduced with the slogan 'dare more democracy' not provoked fierce protests from the opposition? Had the CSU, in particular, not furiously accused the socialists of trying to claim that democracy had only begun in 1969, and ignoring everything that had come before? 'All we're missing is a new calendar,' Strauss had quipped.[3]

Nevertheless, Brandt's reaction to Gaus's accusation was all the more bitter for the fact that there was some truth in it, at least where it touched on the economy. Monetary and economic questions were not Brandt's natural preference, and he preferred to delegate these issues to Minister of Economic Affairs Karl Schiller, Minister of Finance Alex Möller or Helmut Schmidt, an economist by training who would later take over both positions. But even if it was undeniable that Ostpolitik had captured much of his attention; even if his own novelist friend Günter Grass had already warned him in March 1970 that he was not making as much impact on domestic politics as he was on foreign policy,[4] Brandt still thought it was unfair to accuse him of failure, or even absence, in half of his job.

What he was ready to admit was that he was not the sole instigator of reform, and that the great project to modernise the country, of which his reforms were a part, was already underway by the time he became chancellor. Alone at the top of the party since the beginning of the 1960s, he had been directing attention to the need for progress in health, town planning, education and civic participation. The grand coalition of which he and the SPD had been a part had already made important advances towards modernising the country. To a certain extent, this made it seem as if his term in office was the simple continuation of a process begun by the coalition of which he had been vice-chancellor. However, his detractors could not deny that since his election in the autumn of 1969 the political culture of the country had undergone a swift and profound transformation. His reforms were pushing Germany rapidly along the same course as other Western nations, which were becoming pluralist societies. This change was taking place amid a sort of reformist euphoria, inspired by Günter Grass's catchy slogan 'dare more democracy'.[5]

For Brandt, impressed by the new forms of mobilisation that modern media made possible, and which had helped him gain power, the change also meant a logical evolution in his relationship to socialism. After having been put off revolutionary socialism during his exile in his youth, and after having helped define 'democratic socialism' during the

1940s and then supported a reformist shift at the Godesberg Congress in 1959, ten years later his goal was now to establish what he called a 'social democracy'. These were weighty words, said the Christian Democrats, and values which they also laid claim to with their model of a social market economy. In Brandt's view, the difference lay in the idea of increased participation, whether it was citizens playing a greater role in community life, employees being given greater say in business decisions or underprivileged classes gaining better access to higher education. It was about humanising social relations, and emphasising the autonomy of an individual freed from authoritarian hierarchies.[6] He was undoubtedly inspired by the Scandinavian model and shared the optimism characteristic of the postwar economic boom, with an unbreakable faith in the possibility of reform and progress.

The grand coalition's major reforms had been in the legal sphere. Marriage and divorce laws had been updated, children born out of wedlock were given more rights, and it was no longer illegal under anti-pimping laws to provide housing to an unmarried couple. Economically and socially, the previous government's track record was not bad either. The techniques of indicative planning and 'concerted action' had strengthened the state's cooperation with more responsible intermediary bodies, reduced conflicts of interest and created a situation in which one group of people worked together towards jointly established goals. This all dovetailed nicely with Brandt's convictions. He considered social progress – for example, statutory sick pay or the extension of social security to all employees – as his personal project.

From 1969 onwards, Brandt and his government continued down the same course, but this time with the FDP liberals as partners. The engine room was undeniably the Chancellery, where a team led by Horst Ehmke carried out Brandt's plans. Brandt was seen as the conductor of the whole reform project, while the individual aspects were actually implemented by his team.[7] The long and varied list of reforms they introduced was a breath of fresh air: lowering the age of majority to 18 gave a greater proportion of the FRG's youthful society the opportunity to participate politically, and the liberal intellectual Ralf Dahrendorf's maxim that the right to education is a fundamental civic right inspired an education policy that gave many more young people access to education, whether academic or professional.[8] The first step was to deal with the traditionally exclusive and academically focused *Gymnasium* schools, which were still only attended by 6 per cent of 13-year-olds in 1960,[9] a number which needed to increase significantly. For the project of 'expanding education', as it was known, to work, Brandt had to get the governments of the *Länder* on board, as they had authority over matters of education. This was easily done. The Chancellor invoked the federation's duty to ensure that all citizens throughout the country were treated equally, and referred to Article 91 of the Basic Law, which defined certain 'joint tasks' that allowed the federation to intervene in the affairs of the *Länder* if it was in the interests of the 'improvement of living conditions'. A joint committee consisting of the federation and the *Länder* was set up in order to implement changes across the federal system and drew up a general plan for education, with the goal of improving the country's scientific and technological level, in part by establishing numerous new educational institutions. The whole reform was carried out in the spirit of the times: there was a general movement towards democratisation by eliminating hierarchies, introducing joint management and encouraging equal opportunities.

Brandt and his life story embodied this new aspiration. His popularity at the beginning of the 1970s was at a record high, and he seemed to be completely in tune with his contemporaries' hopes. It was a skill he had learned in his Berlin years. His style symbolised simplicity at the same time as being full of energy. Opinion polls, and especially reactions to his public appearances, bore witness to the population's genuine enthusiasm for the man they affectionately called 'Willy'. His charisma was praised. He knew what people meant when they called him the 'German Kennedy': he was the face and voice of the population's hopes for progress.

What the opposition saw as an anti-authoritarian shift was, for Brandt, simply the humanisation of authority and the introduction of empathy to government. All his reforms were inspired by the same goal, whether his new penal law which emphasised the rehabilitation of criminals, or his plans for joint management, which aimed to increase employees' power and improve their representation on the governing boards of businesses (although this had to be shelved because of managerial resistance). His reforms were not only aimed at young people. The age of retirement was lowered to 63 in 1973, and there were provisions for improved care for disabled people. However, many promised reforms never materialised – not because they had been promised lightly, but because of the difficulty in getting them past the conservative majority in the Bundesrat, the upper house representing the *Länder* at the federal level. The plan to reform Paragraph 218 of the penal code, concerning abortion, provoked fierce debate. In contrast to most of his party, Brandt was not personally in favour of abortion. Privately, he remembered the circumstances of his own birth, and the choice his mother might have made,[10] although he seemed to have forgotten the fact that abortions were already being carried out in those days, in secret and in horrific conditions.

Changing people's lives, democratising and modernising the country, all required determination and faith in politicians' ability to effect change. Already in 1961, Brandt had bravely declared that the skies above the Ruhr (Germany's biggest industrial region) needed to become blue again, by which he meant taking environmental issues seriously. The environment was gradually becoming part of the modernisation process. Brandt was pleased with the progress of his town planning programmes, aimed at reorganising cities and transport. To an even greater extent than the rest of Europe, Germany was seized by a frenzy of organisation and planning which was in tune with Karl Schiller's rationalisation of economic policy. The adoption of Keynesian doctrine was a logical corollary of the spirit of the times: faith in the future and in the capacity of men to take control of their own condition.[11]

Brandt was no economic expert, and he counted on the nation's finances holding out. But reforms are expensive, especially when several are carried out at the same time. Many of his reforms failed due to lack of finance, and not only because each minister demanded significant investment in his or her own area. Clearly, the weak point of Brandt's policy was that it relied on sustainable growth. The monetary crisis that began in 1971, and the economic crisis that followed the 1973 oil shock, brought dreams of 'more democracy' to an abrupt end. Public discourse was overrun with technical reports and specialist economic vocabulary. Problems now had names like 'inflation', 'unemployment', 'depression'; they brutally circumscribed a horizon that had until recently seemed limitless. Brandt did not enjoy seeing his social modernisation projects fail in this new reality, with its problems caused by events happening elsewhere. The soft currency that flowed into the Bundesbank's coffers in exchange for the marks that were so coveted on the market, along with the high price of unemployment and depression, made the economic policies Schiller had implemented under the grand coalition unworkable. Federal Germany had only three main goals: healthy finance, growth and stability. In the ideal situation, according to macroeconomic theoreticians, these goals should miraculously form a 'magic square' in which moderate growth, price stability, high levels of employment and a healthy external balance of trade are all in harmony. But the internationalisation of the economy revealed the extent to which national governments were at the mercy of global events. The crisis also heightened internal conflicts within the government; the fiscal reform aiming at a more equitable division of labour failed in 1972, and Schiller resigned from his post as 'super-minister' of the economy and finance on 2 July, to be replaced by Helmut Schmidt.[12] Brandt was on his third minister of finance.

He knew that his problems were not totally unrelated to his own character and his management style. Although widely admired abroad, and despite the great moral authority he had in his party and in public opinion, within the SPD Brandt had great difficulty preventing fissures from appearing. He was not an authoritarian leader, which did have certain advantages when it came to encouraging people to speak their minds, making sure everyone was included, and maintaining harmony. He had also managed to bring many intellectuals and artists round to the idea of power.[13] However, his biggest weakness was that he avoided personal confrontation. His plans were undermined by disagreements, particularly within the SPD. Sometimes these were caused by personality clashes or ambition, and sometimes by the increasing ideological differences between the two less and less compatible wings of the party. As well as being chancellor, Brandt was still chairman of the SPD, and it was his responsibility to keep the party together and give it coherence.

The left wing of the party, and especially the young socialists, gave him the most trouble. The opposition were mistaken when they implied that Brandt had opened the doors of power to the 1968 youth movement. There was none of the revolution that was so celebrated by Marxists and Maoists in the model he was defending, which followed the Scandinavian model that had converted him to democratic socialism years ago, and was inspired by the reformist socialism of Eduard Bernstein. He was an advocate of evolution rather than revolution:

> The SPD is still a reformist party. There is not one single course of action, but several different ones, that will improve the rule of law, create the welfare state, and introduce more democracy to the state and to society [...] Democratic socialism is – I repeat – not a dogma.[14]

Despite all his open-spiritedness and his empathy for the younger members, some of the demands made by the left wing of the party, such as giving local authorities the power to allocate private housing, were unacceptable.[15]

Brandt also had to manage the secondary effects of the almost unbelievable growth of his party during the 1970s. The view of the world he put forward, his plans and his promises, all meant that the number of SPD members increased vertiginously, passing 1 million in 1976. In 1969 there had been 90,000 new members, and in 1972 there were 160,000, mostly people under 30. This sudden expansion was also in part due to the transformation of the working population and the strengthening of the middle class. In 1959 almost 55 per cent of the SPD's members had been blue-collar workers, but by 1972 this proportion had dropped to 27.6 per cent, while the bulk of the members were white-collar workers, intellectuals and students. Brandt had to keep this heterogeneous party under control and satisfied, which meant placing greater weight on the more educated social classes, who preferred theoretical debates and passionate radicalism to involvement in the labour movement.[16] Brandt was willing to show some understanding for the party youth, the more radical *Jusos* (Young Socialists) of his sons' generation. But he was ambivalent about the young protesters who wanted to strengthen the Marxist orientation of the party: he wavered between wanting to seem open to new ideas and receptive to criticism, and his instinctive reaction of wanting to stop political debate being eclipsed by verbal or intellectual violence.[17]

He refused to let democracy be undermined by intolerance or extremist dogmatism. His hostility to Marxist–Leninism, and to all extreme left-wing sectarianism, remained unchanged. Moreover, he saw the need to protect himself from the criticism of conservatives who suggested that his Ostpolitik would lead him to collaborate with the communists. He yielded to the pressure and brought in a series of measures designed to keep enemies of democracy out of public life. He would regret his decision soon enough. On 28 January 1972, together with the minister-presidents of the *Länder*, he decided to impose an 'anti-radical decree'. This required government officials and public sector employees to show 'active loyalty to the Constitution', by which was meant adherence to fundamental rights and to the principles of pluralism in a parliamentary democracy. The decree revealed his obsessive fear of a 1930s-style violent overthrow. The Basic Law made provision for the legal prohibition of political parties whose programmes – or the behaviour of whose members – would endanger democratic order.[18] A few activists from the 1968 movement had veered towards terrorism, and the danger of political extremism in Federal Germany was no figment of the imagination. The 'anti-capitalist' Red Army Faction, which formed in 1970 around Andreas Baader, Gudrun Ensslin and Ulrike Meinhof, was not only responsible for bank robberies and several bomb attempts, but also gained the support of many people who were on the lookout for 'fascist' tendencies in the West German political, economic and military 'system'. The authorities saw them as a serious threat to the state, its institutions and the values of West German society.

The 1972 anti-radical decree did not go down well with the general population, and quickly became known as the *Berufsverbot* (professional ban) because, in practice, the decree prevented certain professionals – such as schoolteachers – from carrying out their jobs. Ironic voices began to question how much threat a communist postman could really pose to democratic order. The critics were not only on the extreme left, but also within the SPD, specifically among those who wanted to defend the liberal order. Many Social Democrats, referring to the tradition of criminal law whereby acts rather than intentions are what matters, saw the decree as ideological repression which punished thought crime and disregarded the principle of 'innocent until proven guilty'. They believed simple membership of a group deemed to be radical should not lead automatically to exclusion from the public sector; instead, individuals should be judged according to their behaviour. At the SPD Party Congress in Hanover in 1973, the party distanced itself decisively from its leader and demanded that the exclusion should be lifted wherever it had been applied, unless backed up by proven facts.

The affair dragged on. As the years went by criticism began to come from the international community as well. Unexpectedly, and very unpleasantly for Brandt, who had already reviewed his position, a public attack on Federal Germany and the SPD came from a friendly direction. On 28 May 1976, a 'Committee for the Protection of Fundamental Freedoms in the FRG' was created in France, headed by the first secretary of the French Socialist Party (PS), François Mitterrand, who was in the process of trying to unite the French left. It was supported by the majority of the PS's members. At their party congress in Dijon on 16 May, Mitterrand had declared himself 'the first signatory against the witch hunt in the German public sector'. The SPD steering committee invited a delegation from the PS's executive board to Bonn to discuss the matter, but the damage was done. For Brandt, the attack from the SPD's sister party was treacherous, and he felt Mitterrand had betrayed their friendship. Just at the moment when the German authorities were fighting against extremist left-wing terrorists and being criticised on all sides, just when Brandt and his successor Schmidt were wrestling with the paradox of having to limit some freedoms into order to protect the population as a whole, this French committee set itself up as the defender of freedom in Europe and received demands for help from all over Germany from people who had been excluded from jobs in the public sector. A particularly well-publicised case, in France as well as in Germany, was that of a teacher from Hesse, Silvia Gingold. She was the daughter of a German communist who had been part of the French Resistance, and had lost family members in the Holocaust. The incident was resolved after an exchange of letters between the leaders of the two parties, but Brandt was angry.[19] There was a deep rift between the SPD, who wanted to differentiate themselves from the communists of East Germany, and the PS, who wanted to form an alliance with the communists and disparaged half-hearted 'social democratism'.

The relationship between Brandt and Mitterrand was complex, and the Chancellor's dealings with France ran less smoothly than before. The two men had plenty in common, such as their roles in the modernisation of their respective parties (Brandt at Godesberg, Mitterrand at Épinay), their long-standing occupation of the political centre, their capacity to inspire enthusiasm, and their pragmatic relationship to power. But, despite the secretive aspects of Brandt's character, Mitterrand was infinitely more mysterious and unpredictable, especially in the personal relationship they built up over the years.[20] Mitterrand was happy to admit that his relation to Brandt had 'not always been easy. I confess that I did not put much energy into it.'[21] That was even the case in the early 1970s, when Mitterrand was still a long way from taking power, and Brandt was at the peak of his popularity and efficacy in government. They would meet again soon.

Re-Election

The legislative elections, which the government had arranged by forcing President Heinemann's hand and persuading him to dissolve the Bundestag, took place in November 1972. The governing coalition had deliberately placed themselves in the minority to provoke a new election, in which they hoped to obtain better results. During the six weeks of the election campaign Brandt travelled around the whole country, covering about 25,000 kilometres in a special train: the famous Salonwagen 10205. Originally built for Hermann Göring, it had been salvaged and used by Adenauer for his first trip to the USSR in 1955, since when it had been the official train for all German chancellors.[22] As chancellor campaigning for his own re-election, Brandt gave between five and eight hours' worth of speeches every day, which were only partly pre-written, and which he improvised with the help of a few notes in his characteristically round handwriting, always in green ink. He addressed the crowd, made sure his voice was heard, and savoured his undeniable popularity. His talents as an orator were well known within the party and beyond. He knew how to enthuse an audience by making people feel that he was talking directly to them, with a mixture of empathy and moral demands, encouragements and warnings.[23] From the beginning of the election campaign, where he attracted crowds of supporters, up to the evening when the results were announced, the elections seemed more and more like a plebiscite for 'Willy'. He inspired affection with his simplicity and his big smile, as well as with his darker, more silent side. His ability to get close to people was not an affectation. According to the tabloid press, so fond of articles on his lifestyle, his habit of inviting ordinary citizens to his annual summer party in his family garden was not just for show. His modest, warm smile did away with any ambiguity in the call to national pride adorning the SPD's election posters: 'Germans, we can be proud of our country. Vote for Willy Brandt.' On the evening of 19 November, his party achieved the best result of their history with 45.8 per cent of the votes, from a record turnout of over 90 per cent.[24] Brandt's SPD candidates had clearly profited from the coming-of-age of a new set of first-time voters between aged 18 and 21: 60 per cent of them voted for the SPD, 10 per cent for the FDP and only 30 per cent for the Christian parties. At a time when Ostpolitik seemed to be succeeding, it was a mark of approval for the governing coalition, which now held a comfortable majority of 46 seats in the Bundestag.

Brandt had given so many speeches that he needed an operation on his vocal cords. He was unable to speak, and there was an anxious moment when the operating surgeon discovered a tumour. It turned out to be benign, but Brandt was traumatised by the respiratory complications he experienced while under local anaesthetic. As he was conscious during the surgery, he had felt himself suffocating. He was forced to rest for two weeks just when he was most needed to form the new government, negotiate with the liberals and balance various people's ambitions. It was a strange situation. He was forbidden to talk and could only communicate with the party management in writing, trying not to imagine what deals Wehner and Schmidt would be cooking up while he was on the side-lines.[25] The worst thing, for him, was not being able to drink and, especially, smoke – a veritable torture! His efforts to give up smoking eventually succeeded after a long and arduous two years. As far as alcohol was concerned, he no longer drank whisky or aquavit, and had to content himself with good red wine.[26]

A few weeks later, on 14 December, the Bundestag re-elected him as chancellor. He went on holiday with Walter Scheel to the Canary Islands in January. Photographs show them walking: the elegant Scheel with his trousers rolled up and Brandt at his side, relaxed in a polo shirt. When he returned, his tanned face was once more displayed in the gossip pages. But from 1973 onwards, things started to go downhill.

Sobering Up and Disappointment

The party was a still a constant source of worry, with its internal rifts, the difficult relationship with the *Jusos*, and the growth of the left wing, which was prominent at the party congress in Hanover in the middle of April 1973. Despite this, and in contrast to the rigid stances of men like Schmidt and Leber, Brandt's willingness to debate with the dissenters meant that he retained his popularity. At the Hanover congress, where the sounds of rebellion were unmistakable, he was re-elected as head of the SPD with an impressive 404 votes out of 428.

In the following months, he was criticised by the top echelons of the party, and even some of his friends reproached him for slowing down and delegating power to other people in most areas. He managed to keep up appearances on the international scene, making several trips abroad, and it was then that he seemed happiest; but when the situation in Germany deteriorated towards the end of 1973, he appeared exhausted. Every autumn he suffered from fatigue and despondency, and this year the newspapers reported that he was suffering from flu. There were rumours that he was overworked and going through another phase of depression and sudden melancholy. His body was defending itself against the constant pressure he put on himself. He withdrew from public life completely. Only a few of his closest advisers, like the always loyal Egon Bahr, who helped Rut every time Brandt was ill, and his friend Horst Ehmke were allowed to see him and say: 'Willy, get up. We have a government to run!'[27]

That autumn of 1973 was too much for him. On top of the oil crisis, a growing wave of strikes and public sector unions demanding a 15 per cent pay rise, he had to deal with a nasty blow from Wehner, the head of the SPD's parliamentary wing. A group of German MPs, including Wehner, had visited Moscow between 24 September and 1 October. Wehner had said to the assembled journalists that Brandt was just drifting along: 'The Chancellor likes to take lukewarm baths [...] with plenty of foam.' *Die Spiegel* gave a detailed analysis of the conflict between the two party giants and, quoting Wehner, titled the article, 'What the Government is Missing is a Head'.[28] Brandt had just given an important speech in New York, to mark the entry of his country into the UN, when he heard the news. He was beside himself: 'That's enough; it's him or me.'[29] Two months later, *Die Spiegel* continued the theme by putting a picture of Brandt's head turned to stone on the cover, with the headline, 'The Chancellor in Crisis', and titled its leading article, 'Willy Brandt at 60. The Monument is Crumbling'.[30] In private, Augstein, the editor-in-chief of

Die Spiegel, criticised Brandt's depression, accusing him of being resigned and not putting up any resistance. Brandt was furious that Augstein had played a part in his downfall.[31] But why did he still not split from Wehner after what was clearly a betrayal, if not for the fact that, as always, he wanted to avoid confrontation?[32] Wehner was one of the people encouraging him to run for federal president, a position that would correspond well with his prestige and moral stature. It would also be a good way of resolving his difficulties cleanly while ending on a high note. It was understood that Walter Scheel, who was thinking of running for the presidency, would step aside for Brandt. However – inevitably, given the bitterness in their relationship – the more Wehner advised Brandt to do it, the less attractive it seemed. He refused to countenance the idea of giving up the leadership of the party.

By the Christmas of 1973, though, he did begin to think about resigning. Horst Ehmke, Schmidt's sworn enemy, was no longer in charge at the Chancellery after Schmidt had taken advantage of the formation of the new government in 1972 to replace him with someone more obliging. Brandt now preferred to travel abroad than to stay in Germany, the source of all his troubles, where inflation was climbing, and tempers were frayed because of an ongoing strike of air-traffic controllers that had paralysed the country.

Betrayal and Resignation

It was 24 April 1974; it was Easter and spring was on its way. In a plane returning from Cairo after a five-day official trip to Algeria and Egypt, Brandt and Bahr discussed the possibility of reshuffling the government, and their plans for the coming years. When they arrived at the airport, an unusually large group had gathered to meet them. Brandt saw the minister of the interior, Genscher, approaching. Genscher blurted out, 'They arrested Guillaume this morning. He has already confessed.' It was one more shock to endure. Brandt did not need to hear the word 'spy' to know what had happened.

Although Günter Guillaume was generally the sort of person to blend into the woodwork, his name stood out because of his unusual surname, a legacy of his Huguenot ancestors who had been expelled from France and settled in Prussia more than three centuries previously. Out of necessity, Brandt spent quite a lot of time with him: Guillaume was on his staff and had accompanied him on his election campaign and on several journeys. However, Brandt knew very little about him, other than that he had arrived in Federal Germany as a refugee from the GDR in 1956, along with his wife Christel. His employee dossier noted that he had joined the SPD in Frankfurt am Main, where he had held various positions before following the minister Georg Leber to Bonn in 1969. He had joined the Chancellery, on the recommendation of Horst Ehmke, as deputy chief of service, before finally finding a job as one of the 25 people working in the Chancellor's office. But this rather bland biography of a hard-working Social Democrat did not completely match up to reality.

Guillaume, originally a Berliner, was part of the generation that had been particularly badly affected by Nazism. Born in 1927, he had grown up with the dictatorship and joined the Nazi Party in the last months of the war, when he was sent to fight at the front. His generation of the Hitler Youth saw their world collapse in 1945, and Guillaume suffered particularly, due to his Nazi father's suicide. As an only child whose relationship with his mother was cold, the Communist Party gave him a new ideal and a new opportunity for commitment; it became his world and his substitute family. He became a photographic technician and joined the SED in 1953 by way of pacifism and anti-nuclear activism, which in the GDR was the same thing as anti-Americanism. From 1952 onwards he was an 'unofficial collaborator' of the Stasi – a secret informer – and then got a full-time job at the GDR's foreign intelligence service, the Main Directorate for Reconnaissance (HVA).

Along with his wife, who had joined him in his new activities, he prepared to set out on a mission to the West, where he would live under the code name *Hansen* as a 'resident', to use the Stasi's jargon. He had the ideal profile for a spy. He was married, which lowered the risk that he might stray from his mission because of a love affair with a class enemy. Moreover, he had no family in Federal Germany who could weaken his convictions. As a photographer he had a useful skill, and he was physically nondescript. The Stasi offered him a reconnaissance job, which was a big promotion for someone who had never been to secondary school. The final deciding factor was his mother-in-law, who was useful for two reasons: firstly, she was a confirmed anti-fascist whose Dutch husband had been killed by the Nazis; and secondly, she herself had Dutch nationality, which allowed her to move to West Germany through official refugee channels, and to bring her daughter and son-in-law to join her following the standard procedure for family reunification. This meant Guillaume and his wife could move to West Germany without undergoing thorough questioning.

The three infiltrators arrived in Frankfurt in May 1956, with instructions to spy on the SPD and to encourage opposition on the extreme left in the hope of destabilising the reformist party.[33] In order to evade the notice of the West German intelligence service, Guillaume aligned himself with the right wing of the party. He gained Georg Leber's trust. Leber was elected as an MP in 1965 and was appointed minister in 1966. Guillaume supported him successfully in his legislative election campaign in 1969. Leber asked Guillaume to go with him to the Federal Ministry of Telecommunications as part of his team, but under civil service rules Guillaume's lack of secondary school education disqualified him from the job. When the Chancellery, under Horst Ehmke's leadership, was expanded at the beginning of 1970, he was hired to manage trade union relations. His background was investigated, but nothing was found to suggest he was of any danger.[34] The higher Guillaume rose in the hierarchy, helped by his reassuringly efficient and diligent work ethic, the rarer his messages to East Berlin became, and the more he tried to present a positive image of the SPD and Ostpolitik. It seems that he genuinely grew attached to the Chancellor, to whom he looked up as a father.[35] If he continued to spy, it was perhaps because the Stasi threatened to destroy their agents' lives if they tried to 'hang up'. Guillaume's career continued to improve, and he was promoted ahead of his colleagues. Eventually, at the end of 1972, he entered Brandt's office, the Kanzlerbüro, replacing Reuschenbach, who was leaving to become an MP. His job was to manage relations with the party, which essentially meant organising the Chancellor's meetings and travel arrangements in his capacity as chairman of the SPD.

Brandt had little in common with Günter Guillaume. He found him dull company, uneducated and uncultured. They could spend hours together without talking.[36] Brandt disliked personal clashes, and asked to be rid of the awkward, silent presence in his office. The problem was that, just as Brandt made his request, in the spring of 1973, the authorities had started investigating Guillaume and his wife as potential spies, and they asked the Chancellor not to move Guillaume elsewhere in case it put him on his guard and hindered the investigation. Their suspicions had been raised by chance, while cross-checking Guillaume's details. What happened next is a good illustration of the logic of the Office for the Protection of the Constitution, the FRG's domestic security agency. Their main concern, in the ongoing war between the two intelligence services, was above all not to let the HVA know that their coded messages were being listened to in the West. A report dated 11 May 1973 records the decision to start very discreet surveillance operations on Guillaume's wife. Genscher had been informed of the suspicions, although the head of the security agency, Nollau, had not given him all the details.[37] The Chancellor was also warned that Guillaume would be under surveillance, but that he must at all costs avoid making any changes in the Chancellery, because the secret services wanted to catch the potential spy red-handed. Brandt could almost be described as the bait. The affair caused him considerable annoyance, as he was sure that Guillaume was not a spy, but he followed their instructions nonetheless. He agreed to go ahead with his plan to spend his holidays in Hamar, in Norway, where Guillaume was to accompany him as an aide. During the whole of July 1973, Guillaume and his family would therefore be on holiday with the Brandts. Significantly, it was his job to give Brandt messages that had been deciphered by intelligence agents. He had plenty of time to read and copy tens of messages, of which a dozen were classified in the top two levels of confidentiality. Correspondence between Nixon and Kissinger was among them.

In the following months the two spies were not completely at ease. Christel felt as if she was being watched, and refused to pass on the Norway messages to another agent. In 1974, the couple kept calm, although they knew they were being observed while on a trip to Sainte-Maxime in France: this time, it was the French Directorate of Territorial Surveillance watching them, at the request of the German secret services. When the Germans finally decided to launch 'Operation Tango' and to request a warrant to search Guillaume's home in Bonn, on 24 April 1974, Guillaume, a very probable spy, had been allowed to carry on as normal for ten months. What was worse, he had been working as close as it was possible to get to the Chancellor!

At Bonn airport, Brandt had immediately understood what Genscher meant. The rest of the day, 24 April, was taken up by a crisis meeting; the next day rumours started to circulate; and by the 26th the scandal was on the front pages of all the newspapers. Brandt feared that everything would come out, giving the opposition plenty of ammunition. A spy at the heart of power was a catalyst for suspicions of treason.

The discovery of this spy from the East immediately revived fears of the Communist threat, of the hidden enemy within, and the Social Democrats were yet again accused of being 'people with no Fatherland', as Bismarck had described them in 1878. Brandt carried on as normal, and on 26 April he was in the Bundestag to defend the abortion law, after having spent much of the night preparing his speech. The weekend did not bring him any respite, as he was suffering from toothache and had to have two teeth pulled on the 29th, a Monday. He barely slept. The Guillaume affair was gradually taking up all his time, and there were numerous political files needing his attention. He also needed to discuss a long-awaited ministerial reshuffle with his team. That Monday evening, he called Ehmke in Stuttgart and asked him to drive the 250 kilometres to Bonn so they could talk face to face. They were up until 2 a.m. Brandt told his friend that he was ready to face the political consequences of what had clearly been an unforgivable mistake.[38] He was even more ready when the police started interrogating his bodyguards. They wanted to find out exactly what had been able to filter through to the East, and that meant a close examination of Brandt's private life. The bodyguards described, perhaps exaggerating slightly, the comings and goings of various women in his hotel rooms or his train, on his numerous journeys across Germany; they talked of female journalists, necklaces left behind. There was a suggestion that Guillaume had been 'supplying him with girls'. The police began to fear that Guillaume and the Stasi would start to blackmail Brandt. Wehner was called in to persuade him to resign.[39] Brandt defended himself, but he was shaken by the speed with which the stories were being fabricated, based on a 'Slavic-sounding name' which he had never heard before, or 'a certain Swedish woman' – who turned out to be a journalist who had interviewed him for Scandinavian television during his last election campaign. From his point of view, it seemed to be a well-organised operation run by the police, the secret services and Wehner: a stitch-up. A letter he received from Bauhaus, the head of his bodyguard team, on 10 May, strengthened this suspicion: 'My colleagues and I have the feeling that during our questioning the Office for the

Protection of the Constitution deliberately infringed certain rules, and that we were forced into making statements whose real significance we only understand now. I suspect that these officers were acting under orders.'[40]

During the weekend of 4 and 5 May, the whole SPD leadership met with Brandt at Bad Münstereifel. The meeting had originally been planned to discuss tensions with the trade unions but on the way there, in the car driven by Hans Simon, his chauffeur since 1966, Brandt knew that the main question would be whether he should stay or go. Helmut Schmidt, his logical successor, wanted him to pull himself together and stay, not wanting to take his place just yet.[41] As for Bahr, he thought it would be better to resign as soon as possible, without waiting to be pushed out. The support he might have expected from Wehner never came. For Brandt, there was no doubt: he needed to recuperate, and extricate himself from an unmanageable situation.[42] On the evening of 5 May 1974, Brandt wrote his resignation letter to President Heinemann, dating it 6 May. The news was made public early on the 7th: 'Chancellor Brandt has resigned.'

His decision inspired respect and sympathy rather than the disgrace he feared; 43 per cent of Germans would have preferred him not to resign. Brezhnev was informed at once, and told Bahr that he would never forgive Honecker for having let Guillaume carry on his mission after the Treaty of Moscow and the re-establishment of trust. Much later, in 1985, Honecker told Brandt that he had not been aware of any of it at the time.

Historians can now reconstruct Guillaume's story and his activity thanks to a file of microfilms containing the records of the Stasi's foreign espionage branch. The file was given the pretty code name 'Rosenholz' (Rosewood) when it was returned to Germany, having been saved from destruction by a CIA agent in 1990. It contained information on the identity of spies and could be cross-referenced with the electronic files and documents that East German spies had sent to the Stasi headquarters in East Berlin. The original file, code named 'Sira', had been destroyed when the Communist regime fell, but the Stasi's meticulousness meant that a copy had been made when it was entered into a more efficient filing system during the 1980s.[43] Thanks to these files, we also know about the GDR's intervention in the spring of 1972, when they bribed conservative MPs to stop Brandt being overthrown. They had saved him in 1972, and caused his downfall in 1974. But it was not as simple as that. The Guillaume affair may have been the immediate motive for Brandt's resignation, but for months he had been feeling more and more isolated and under attack, and he already felt he had lost control of economic and financial policy.[44] On 16 May his successor Helmut Schmidt was elected chancellor by the Bundestag, the day after Scheel's election as the new federal president. On 8 May, Brandt had announced on television: 'I will remain as leader of my party, and I will put all my energy into policies that serve the people and serve peace.'[45]

6

After Power

Taking and announcing the decision to resign is one thing, but living through it and facing the consequences are something else altogether. Brandt had to negotiate a range of different reactions, remembering that some of them might be feigned. He managed not to show it, but he was far from convinced when Wehner loudly and awkwardly paid tribute to him in front of the SPD parliamentary wing and clumsily handed him a bouquet of red roses. In Germany it is traditional to dress a bouquet as if it had just been cut, but the roses the slippery Wehner gave Brandt were suffocating in cellophane, like flowers left in a cemetery.[1] When he received a 25-kilo barrel of caviar from Leonid Brezhnev, Brandt could only ponder that gifts reflect the giver and can tell us a lot about relationships. He had happy memories of hours spent talking and drinking quantities of neat spirits with the Kremlin leader. On one occasion Brezhnev had decided to try out a new Mercedes at night, on the steep road that zigzagged down from the Hotel Petersberg near Bonn – it was a miracle it had not ended badly.

In May 1974, the former Chancellor's feelings were mixed, although it was relief that dominated. He now had to come to terms with what had happened, accept defeat and, most difficult of all, admit that he was not completely free of blame in his own downfall. Publicly, he stuck to his habit of hiding anything that really touched him: he put the notes he had taken in the days of that last week, recording his conviction that there had been a conspiracy against him headed by Wehner and Honecker, in a firmly sealed envelope. He spent the summer writing a deliberately toned-down account of the whole affair, which was hastily published with the title *Über den Tag hinaus: ein Zwischenbilanz* (*The Long Term: A Provisional Appraisal*). It was a mistake to try and simplify the matter, however, and soon anyone who knew more details or secrets started publishing their own revelations, which poisoned his first autumn free from political responsibilities. He also needed to reorganise his private life. There were material concerns relating to the family's move out of the Chancellor's residence, but Brandt left these entirely to Rut, who teased him gently: 'he contented himself with carrying his old-fashioned overcoat to the new house.'[2] There were also more intimate matters. He refused to give Rut the explanations she was waiting for. She promised to help and support him through the difficult time he was having, and also, as he did not offer to talk about it, never to question him again about his new attachments. It was 'the beginning of the end', in her eyes.[3]

Suddenly being free from governmental responsibility for the first time in 20 years was a difficult change to get used to, but Brandt's resignation did not mark the end of his career or his political commitments. He had announced that he wanted to dedicate himself to the SPD. He quickly showed that his commitment was serious, but also that he was thinking on an even bigger scale. It was European social democracy that interested him, especially the possibility of applying its values to relationships between rich and poor countries. He was active in this regard at several different levels: he retained his seat in the Bundestag, he was still in the SPD, he joined the Socialist International, he wrote the Brandt Report on the global North–South divide and he was involved with the European Parliament.[4]

A New Equilibrium

Italy aside, the European Community was still very much centred in the north in the mid-1970s. Many of the southern

European countries were still trying to rid themselves of authoritarian regimes, which had long delayed their political and economic development. In April 1974 Marcelo Caetano, the Portuguese prime minister and the dictator António Salazar's successor, was overthrown by the military, which then formed a government together with the socialists and communists. How could the Germans help the Portuguese socialists establish themselves firmly, when the Lusitanian communists were threatening to exclude them? With the financial and logistical support of the SPD, the Portuguese Socialist Party (Partido Socialista) was founded in the middle of April 1973 at Bad Münstereifel. Its leader was Mário Soares, who had been in exile in France until then. Starting in the autumn of 1974, Brandt tried to use his prestige and his contacts to help Soares and to prevent Portugal falling under a new dictatorship, this time an extreme left-wing one. He made a point of attending the first Partido Socialista congress in Lisbon at the end of 1974 and put his lifelong experience of opposition to communism at the service of his socialist friends. He was motivated to help the Portuguese not just out of solidarity between social democrats, but also because of his more general commitment to pluralist democracy. He spoke to Brezhnev about the problem during a visit to Moscow on 3 July 1975 and asked the Soviets to control their subordinates in the Iberian Peninsula.

In Washington, Kissinger thought the whole of southern Europe was on its way to becoming Marxist. For Brandt, it was clear that either an American intervention or the resurgence of the Portuguese right were likely consequences of the extreme left seizing power in Lisbon.[5] At a meeting of socialist heads of government and leaders of social democratic parties in Stockholm, Brandt proposed the creation of the Friendship and Solidarity Committee for Democracy and Socialism in Portugal, and took charge of it in September 1975. It was crucial that it was Europeans who strengthened democracy in Portugal. The strategy paid off at the Portuguese elections in 1976 – thanks to public support, but also to a massive, secret programme to finance the Partido Socialista through the SPD's Friedrich Ebert Foundation. These German funds, paid into bank accounts or given as cash to emissaries visiting the Chancellery discreetly, were shared out between Portugal and Spain.[6]

Spain was in a similar situation to Portugal, and it was a situation which posed a threat to the equilibrium in Europe, demanding the mobilisation of democrats and justifying the dissemination of the Spanish left's demands.[7] When he visited the Partido Socialista congress in Lisbon in the autumn of 1974, Brandt had met Felipe González, the young secretary general of the Spanish Socialist Workers' Party (PSOE), with whom he immediately formed a good relationship. For Brandt, supporting the establishment of the PSOE in the new Spanish political landscape was an important part of his struggle against the trauma caused by Franco's victory at the end of March 1939. He felt he had to help make up for the European democrats' weaknesses against Francoism, but it was also a personal matter for him. 'If one of the duties of a politician is to hide his emotions, you can see that at this precise moment, I am no politician,' he admitted, before continuing his speech, in Spanish, at the first PSOE party congress to take place in Spain, on 5 December 1976.[8] His memories of Barcelona came flooding back – the Hotel Falcon, the disappearance of his friend Mark Rein, his feeling of impotence.

His intuitions about the Communists' methods, formed during his brief time in Spain, had been confirmed by the actions of the later Soviet Bloc. He had needed great perseverance to save Ostpolitik and maintain détente, and then to reach a compromise with Moscow and the Eastern European countries over the course of two years of negotiations, between 1973 and 1975. On 1 August 1975, Brandt was overjoyed to hear that the Helsinki Accords, the first act of the Conference for Security and Cooperation in Europe (CSCE), had been signed. It was the continuation of his Ostpolitik. Both sides were happy. The Eastern Bloc saw their gains in the 'first basket' (inviolability of borders and non-intervention in internal affairs) as a victory and hoped it would stop the West protesting about what went on behind their borders, while the Western European countries were pleased that the 'third basket' imposed respect for human rights and fundamental freedoms on all the signatory states.[9] Dissidents in Poland, the GDR and Czechoslovakia would be able, with the help of the democratic states, to invoke the text to demand more freedom of expression. Charter 77 in Prague, Solidarność in Poland, and GDR dissidents would confirm Brandt's analysis that Helsinki's strategy of 'softening up' the East was the crowning moment of his Ostpolitik. If similar progress could be made on the question of disarmament in the MBFR negotiations in Vienna, there was much cause for hope – except that France was still refusing to participate.

Released from his obligations in the West German leadership, Brandt could now devote himself to his two related passions, the cause of social democracy, and international relations.[10] His only task was a privilege: exercising his influence as an internationally renowned elder statesman. At the end of May 1975, having returned from a trip to South America, where he had met politicians on both ends of the political spectrum, he met up with two of his closest social democrat friends, as he did fairly regularly. Bruno Kreisky, whom he had known since his exile in Sweden, was the Austrian chancellor, and Olof Palme, 14 years younger than him, was prime minister of Sweden. The three men shared more than just the experience of power; they had the same vision of a moderate socialism, were all leaders of their respective parties and – this amused them – had chosen the same names for their children: Kreisky's son was called Peter, like Brandt's eldest, and Palme's second son was called Mattias, like Brandt's youngest. On 24 May 1975 they talked in Kreisky's garden in Vienna. Kreisky was opposite Brandt, while Palme sat on a striped swing seat. Brandt explained his idea of forming an international network 'to improve cooperation between social democrats and others with similar goals all over the world. Our International is not yet quite up to the task.

We would need to find a more flexible way of working together with such groups around the world.'[11] The task was to put an old principle of socialism into practice, namely solidarity with colonised peoples. In any case, it was important to include the Third World in the plans and structures of moderate socialism. Under Brandt's leadership, the socialists would be willing to abandon their demand that their sister parties took America's side in the Cold War. In other words, the European socialists could cooperate with the United States' enemies, as long as they were not actually Moscow's allies.

The forum dreamed up in that Vienna garden met for the first time in Caracas one year later, in May 1976, with delegates from 13 European countries and 15 from Latin America. The topics of discussion were justice, equality and the work to be done in the sphere of education. Brandt emphasised what they had in common: the values of Godesberg, the rejection of right- or left-wing dictatorship, respect for self-determination and the rejection of interventionism, and a shared goal of a better global economic order.[12] Putting all this into practice, which meant supporting struggling socialist movements, such as the opposition to Pinochet in Chile, the Sandinistas in Nicaragua, the National Revolutionary Movement (MNR) in El Salvador and the New Jewel Movement (NJM) in Grenada, would end up causing open conflict between the International and the Reagan administration. Reagan used all possible means, including embargo, to stop the socialists exercising power.[13] In 1976, Kreisky asked Brandt to accept the presidency of the Socialist International, which would thus be given a new lease of life; he was helped by Palme, Soares and Kreisky as vice-presidents. He also had the support of François Mitterrand and Harold Wilson, the prime minister of Great Britain up until April 1976. Brandt gave a new face to the institution, which had been remodelled in 1951 as a successor to the Labour and Socialist International, and which until now had kept a relatively low profile. The new President's priority was to open the Socialist International up to countries which had recently become independent, and to improve North–South relations.[14] He also wanted to use the Socialist International's influence to help establish peace, for example in the Middle East, where he tried to find a balanced position between Israel and Palestine, while maintaining Germany's special sense of responsibility to Israel.[15]

In Europe itself, relationships between the various socialist parties were not always smooth. Brandt tried to calm down the heated relationship between Chancellor Schmidt and the French Parti Socialiste, led by François Mitterrand. Schmidt was annoyed with the French because on 18 January 1976, at a meeting of the Socialist International in Helsingør, in Denmark, Mitterrand had argued strongly in favour of making alliances between socialist and communist parties, in the image of his strategic union of the left in France. Schmidt had protested vehemently, accusing the Frenchman of being naive and not understanding the situation in Germany.[16] Brandt believed it was important to have Mitterrand in the Socialist International. He was less horrified than Schmidt by Mitterrand's suggestion, but nevertheless he stated publicly that such an alliance was out of the question for the SPD, which still needed to differentiate itself from the Eastern Communists.[17] A few weeks later, Mitterrand and Brandt had dinner together, and the French First Secretary explained his strategy for gaining power in France, which had 5 million communist voters.[18] Brandt was persuaded. The two men understood each other well. On several occasions he told Mitterrand, as he did Palme and Kreisky, how much their friendship mattered to him.[19] But it took him 18 months to convince Schmidt to meet with Mitterrand. Many people in the SPD feared that their party's relations with the PS, who were on the verge of gaining power in Germany's most important neighbour, had been incurably soured. Schmidt was biased against the French left, who were strong critics of his methods in the fight against terrorism; he had particularly not appreciated Sartre visiting Andreas Baader in

Stammheim Prison in December 1974, when the philosopher had denounced the 'inhuman conditions' in the prison, while taking everything the most notorious terrorist in Europe said at face value.

The exceptional police powers put in place to fight against the Red Army Faction and its supporters were causing murmurs of discontent even within the SPD. In February 1978, the new anti-terrorism laws were almost voted down in the Bundestag. Brandt had to call his party's parliamentary group to order. As leader of the SPD, he was still responsible for holding together a party which seemed to disagree about everything except the fact that he was its leader. He undoubtedly had a unique moral and political authority, even among the opposition. Although he preferred mediation to exercising this authority, sometimes he was forced to speak bluntly.[20] Differences of opinion within the party were unavoidable. A journalist who interviewed him on 7 April 1976 for the radio station Südwestfunk provoked him, and he replied, 'The SPD is not a Prussian military formation. In a party with more than a million members, there will always be groups of various sorts, and different movements.'[21] He wanted to ensure that the SPD, which still held power as part of the social-liberal coalition under Schmidt, kept its political inventiveness, at the same time as being realistic and responsible. 'Our state, vigilant and ready to fight enemies of democracy, needs authority. The sort of authority that rests on the values and the support of its citizens, which is founded on elections, which is accountable and which is legitimised by moral capacity and intellectual honesty,' he said in 1975 at the celebrations to mark the hundred and fiftieth anniversary of the birth of Ferdinand Lassalle, the SPD's founding father.[22] The question of the state's authority was not the only one troubling the party, with its left-wing electorate. Towards the end of the 1970s, the SPD was confronted with a stream of new demands, especially from the youth.

Youth and age differences were certainly topics of interest and even annoyance to those who saw Brandt appearing more and more often in the company of a young blonde woman, 33 years his junior, who had recently joined the SPD's press office. Brigitte Seebacher had studied history and German literature, and was interested in the history of the labour movement. She was preparing a doctoral thesis on Erich Ollenhauer, supervised by Ernst Nolte. She certainly shook things up in Brandt's life. Many of his friends reproached him for preferring a woman they thought of as a cold, social-climbing intellectual to the faithful and patient Rut, who was still well liked in political circles. Moreover, it seemed as if this new companion wanted to cut him off from his social life and his friends. On the other hand, some people saw her as a form of rejuvenation therapy for a mid-life crisis. She was certainly a challenging debate partner and a link to the youth he was trying to understand and manage at the SPD. At her side, Brandt started visiting younger Social Democrats in their thirties, such as Oskar Lafontaine and his wife,[23] and Scharping, Engholm and Schröder. People described them as Brandt's 'grandchildren'. He and Brigitte travelled a lot to France, 'through the Auvergne and Brittany, Burgundy and Savoie, Provence and the Côte d'Azur,' and Mitterrand introduced them to Gascony and the Atlantic coast.[24] This new connection to the landscape, to nature and to the French people calmed him down. It was refreshing not to be recognised in the street all the time. He seemed visibly younger, and Brigitte was convinced that the diet she had put him on was doing him good. When he was in Bonn and working in his office at the Bundestag or the party headquarters, he often smoked a small cigarette and drank a glass of wine. His colleagues would watch, amused, as he then tried to hide the smell on his breath so his new companion would not notice.[25]

One good reason to stick to his new healthy lifestyle was an episode hinting that his heart and arteries were not well. He had been in New York at the end of October 1978, and despite feeling ill had continued his journey to Vancouver.

It was not until his return to Bonn that he was diagnosed with an infarction. After a spell in hospital in Germany, an acquaintance at the Ministry of Health recommended that he went to France to rest, and with Simone Veil's help he found a cardiologist in Hyères. He was warmly welcomed by the gentle late December sun of the Côte d'Azur, but he soon learned that it was actually a matter of two infarctions. He stayed there to convalesce for six weeks, all the while waited on hand and foot by the French.[26] Abroad, in peace and quiet, he was able to put things in perspective.

There was still no question of him stepping down as leader of the SPD, which, along with Europe, was still his true passion. More and more, he found himself sympathising with the non-aligned countries who wanted to establish a new, fairer economic and commercial order.[27] In 1977 he had accepted an invitation from the president of the World Bank, Robert McNamara, to take charge of the Independent Commission for International Development Issues. Known as the North–South Commission, it was set up to try and break the deadlock between the rich and poor nations in the discussion about development. Brandt had personally picked the members of this new forum, most of whom were from developing countries. Representatives from the developed world included conservatives like former British prime minister Edward Heath and democrats like Olof Palme, as well as others with a variety of different backgrounds, horizons and sensibilities. As soon as the forum was launched in December 1977, it became obvious that a change of approach and discourse was necessary. Instead of talking about development 'aid', both sides needed to recognise that development in the South was in their mutual interest. At a series of conferences, Brandt emphasised the principles that would form the backbone of their future approach: development and the problem of poor countries' access to markets should be treated as questions of global equilibrium, rather than social justice; and development policies should be seen as both the condition for and guarantee of world peace.

It was this aspect of interdependence and global security that gave the 'Brandt Report', published in 1980, its undeniable status as a trailblazer.[28] The key idea was to balance the creation and distribution of wealth, while protecting the environment, in order to combat over-population, famine, migration caused by hunger and war, and the ecological catastrophes that were predicted for the future. Among the suggestions were the abolition of customs barriers for products imported into industrialised nations from the Third World ('or should I say from Two-Thirds of the World?'[29]); the creation of a price-stabilisation fund that would protect raw-material revenues from fluctuation; an increase of 1 per cent in development aid; support for an increase in food production; the imposition of an international tax; and an increase in the amount of credit made available by the World Bank for investment in the Third World. These initiatives, which asked a great deal of the North, were accompanied by the requirement for the southern nations to put the social justice they demanded for themselves on the world stage into practice within their own borders.

The report received a mixed welcome. It was not until two decades later that Brandt's analysis and recommendations started to be recognised as just. The heightening of East–West tension during the 1980s distracted attention from the problem. Brandt developed his idea of a North–South conflict that would be *the* new social question par excellence in a book published in 1985 with the title *Organised Madness: Arms and Hunger*.[30] On 1 March 1989, in a letter he wrote together with Shridath Ramphal, he asked President Bush to organise a global summit, including the Soviet Union, on the model of the Cancun Conference of 1981.[31] Bush ignored the request. It was clear that, coupled with his engagement in Latin America and the Caribbean, Brandt's position on the North–South relationship had done serious damage to his friendship with the United States. In the preface to his report, he had written that the most powerful country in the world should not sit on the side-lines while the rest of the world came together to try and improve everybody's future. He no longer felt that there was anybody in London or Washington who would listen to him. He was completely at odds with Reagan's and Thatcher's new economic and business orientation. He failed to persuade Reagan to go back on his decision to reduce the United States' financial contribution to the International Development Association (IDA), which granted low-rate credit to developing countries.[32] It seemed as if the trust between the former Chancellor and the White House had been destroyed. Reagan was exasperated when Brandt accused him of being unpredictable and that his security and defence policies actually increased global insecurity. To get his own back on Brandt, whom he saw as an unbearable do-gooder, Reagan refused to meet him when he made an official visit to Federal Germany in 1985.

The Trials of Youth

In the early 1980s, Brandt was also dealing with major concerns about his party. The Brandt–Schmidt–Wehner troika was still in place at the SPD, but disagreements were cropping up more and more often as the ecological and pacifist movements gained ground. He spent hours in his office discussing the problem with his closest friends: Schmidt, the SPD vice-chairmen Hans Koschnick and Johannes Rau, and Egon Bahr, who had succeeded Hans-Jürgen Wischnewski and Holger Börner to the position of secretary general, which he would shortly lose to Peter Glotz in 1981. The Soviet invasion of Afghanistan in December 1979 made it impossible to deny that tension in the East–West relationship was increasing and seemed to prove the pessimists right. Schmidt had already sounded the alarm in a celebrated speech in London in October 1977. He had denounced the increasing lack of military equilibrium in Europe, and his words accelerated NATO's realisation of the severity of the situation, leading to their 'Double-Track' decision on 12 December 1979: the West invited the Soviets to negotiations and demanded that they withdraw their new SS-20 nuclear missiles, which had disturbed the balance of power. If the Soviets had not withdrawn them by 1983, equivalent American missiles, the Pershing II, would be deployed in Western Europe. The West German pacifists, among whom were a significant number of people close to the SPD, believed this carried a large risk of Europeans being dragged into a conflict that might break out elsewhere but that would be militarily controlled in Europe. People started saying the threat had changed sides: America, the traditional protector, was now seen as a dangerous power potentially responsible for transforming Germany into a nuclear battlefield. In contrast to Schmidt, who showed little understanding of his party's doubts, and who remained in favour of rebalancing and rearmament, Brandt continued to promote détente. He rallied Wehner and Bahr to his cause, and they confronted the Chancellor and the minister for defence, Hans Apel. But Schmidt was convinced that Brandt was in fact in favour of the double-track decision, and that he had simply changed his tune for the sake of keeping the youth on his side.[33]

For Brandt, the decisive factor was the new political configuration demanding his attention: the explosion of the Greens onto the West German political landscape, with the creation in January 1980 of a new party that combined the forces of the 'new social movements', as they were known: the anti-nuclear movement, the ecological movement, the feminists and the new left. This new entity's main supporters came from the youth, whom Brandt – remembering his traumatic experience under the Weimar Republic – feared the SPD would lose altogether. To avoid this, he wanted to open social democracy up and to take heed of the desire for a 'first-person politics'.[34] He was growing more and more defiant towards Washington, first towards Jimmy Carter and then even more so after the election of the 'hawkish' Ronald Reagan at the end of 1980. He still tried to plead the case for détente and, evoking de Gaulle, for Europeans to put their faith in the ongoing efforts to work towards peace.[35] He decided to open up a sort of parallel diplomacy, and went to meet Brezhnev in July 1981. He also thought he would be able to count on his friend François Mitterrand, who had been elected French president on 10 May 1981, to share his viewpoint. Two months earlier, the two men had shared a symbolic, moving journey across the GDR, driving along the route Mitterrand had taken when he had escaped from a German prisoner-of-war camp in 1941.[36]

Brandt was right behind Mitterrand on 21 May, when the new President walked up Rue Soufflot in Paris, carrying a rose. With Pierre Bérégovoy and André Rousselet on either side of him, arms linked in his, Brandt was all smiles. Was it because he was counting on an alliance with Paris against the American plan for rearmament? After all, the PS had already expressed an anti-missile commitment.[37] However, once he was elected, Mitterrand changed his stance on the balance of power in Europe and adopted his predecessor's position.[38] Citing France's special position within NATO, he refused to let France's strike force be counted. Paris's reasoning was simple: their nuclear missiles were an important deterrent in case France was ever under threat. It was a way of preserving France's special status, following the same course as de Gaulle had when he pulled out of plans for military integration with NATO in 1966, but without adding to the Western Bloc's overall count of weapons. But Brandt was convinced it was crucial to see things from Moscow's point of view, and count the French weapons. Over the following months, Brandt and Mitterrand fell out badly. The French were worried about the German pacifist movement, which was seen in Paris as the malaise of a tortured nation, the expression of an outdated romanticism, or evidence of their strange relationship to nature. The French government advisers supported Schmidt, and explicitly accused Brandt of playing a dangerous game that might lead to neutralism and turn the SPD into Moscow's helper. If the SPD leaders were letting themselves be manipulated like this by the Kremlin, it must be a sign of Germany's extreme fragility, and so a grave threat for the security of Western Europe.[39]

On 10 October 1981, the television cameras of Europe were all trained on the hundreds of thousands of people attending an enormous demonstration in Bonn against the stationing of the Pershing missiles in the FRG. From the SPD's point of view, these were the supporters they were at risk of losing to the ecological and pacifist movements; Brandt tried to establish the party's official position with the phrase: 'Rearmament is not the way to security.'[40] However, his friend Richard Löwenthal started circulating a petition at the same time, asserting that the ecological and pacifist movements were marginal, and calling for a focus on the SPD's traditions. It had many signatures, especially from trade unionists.[41]

Brandt's relationship with Mitterrand's PS deteriorated after Poland declared a state of martial law on 13 December 1981. For Brandt, Jaruzelski's coup was a lesser evil compared to an armed intervention from Moscow, and he was happy to have avoided a repeat of what had happened in Berlin in 1953, Budapest in 1956 and Prague in 1968. Mitterrand seemed to share this opinion, but Lionel Jospin, the first secretary of the PS, publicly criticised Brandt's muted reaction to the crisis.[42] Once more, the relationship between the two parties had become electric. As for the two governments, it was clear that belonging to the same political family was no guarantee of harmony or real cooperation. The Social Democrat Chancellor Schmidt and the Socialist President Mitterrand took great care to avoid the subject of the economy, so wide was the rift between, on the one side, the left-leaning Mitterrand's nationalisations and his policy of public spending, and on the other, the centrist Chancellor's convictions: he declared that 'today's profits are tomorrow's investments and the jobs of the day after tomorrow.'[43] Brandt could have mediated between the two leaders if he had not been so distrusted in Paris because of his attitude towards the East–West question.

The year 1982 started badly. The domestic situation in Germany was deteriorating, and the SPD–FDP coalition was crumbling. Although the coalition had worked well when renewed in 1976 and 1980, the liberals had been gradually withdrawing from it, and distancing themselves from Schmidt, who was too Keynesian for their liking. The liberal minister of economic affairs, Count Lambsdorff, was explicit in his criticism. Eventually the tension broke, and there was a constructive vote of no confidence in the Bundestag on 1 October 1982. The procedure that had failed to oust Brandt in 1972 succeeded this time against Schmidt: without a majority in the Bundestag, he had to step down and let the leader of the CDU, Helmut Kohl, take his place as chancellor. Because Brandt was a former chancellor and the leader of the SPD, and also because he believed fair play was an important pillar of parliamentary democracy, he was one of the first to congratulate Kohl, but his face was impassive.[44]

He was pleased to discover that the new centre-right coalition would continue with the Ostpolitik they had once fought against, justifying Brandt and Schmidt's strategy. However, the SPD now found itself in opposition, after 13 years of power. The mood was sombre. It was up to Brandt to boost the crowd's morale at the SPD party conference at Kiel in November, after the Greens achieved their first electoral success in Hesse.[45] The day the votes were counted, he published the first volume of his memoirs, titled *Links und Frei* (*Left and Free*), which covered his life up until 1950. His youth was seen through the filter of his later years, when he had learned to soften the contours of his journey: he decided to abandon his first, more controversial idea for the title: *Red or Brown*.[46]

It was icy on 20 January 1983. Brandt would rather have been walking in the French countryside than in Bonn. All the MPs were gathered in the Bundestag to hear Mitterrand make a solemn speech to mark the twentieth anniversary of the signing of the Élysée Treaty. His account of Franco-German history was vivid and well told, but then he moved on to the absolute necessity of re-establishing a balance of military power in Europe. Without mincing his words, Mitterrand called on the German MPs to speak out in favour of the deployment of Pershing missiles in Germany at the parliamentary vote that would be held that autumn. Kohl, the new chancellor, was pleased. Schmidt, now a mere MP, felt himself vindicated. Brandt's face, on the other hand, was like stone. He was appalled that his French friend was trying to interfere in German domestic policy, and that he was taking the exact opposite stance to the SPD. What use would it do to tell the press that 'nobody can make our decision for us'? Mitterrand's speech had an enormous impact.[47] As the end of 1983 approached, and with it the deadline for the Soviets to withdraw their missiles, the bad feeling between Brandt and Mitterrand grew ever more obvious. Brandt continued to say, 'we need to transform the East–West confrontation into a peaceful order in Europe,' but the French President hit the nail on the head with his sly observation, 'I am against the Euromissiles. But I see two simple facts: pacifism is in the West, and the missiles are in the East. That seems like an unequal relationship.'[48] In October 1983, there were more large demonstrations in the major cities of Germany; a federation of groups under the umbrella of the peace movement managed to form a human chain 108 kilometres long protesting against the missiles. But when Brandt nervously approached them to offer them the SPD's support, he had to endure the insults of one of the leaders, Petra Kelly, who accused him publicly of not being deeply enough involved in the cause. It seemed as if his efforts had gone unnoticed.[49]

On 22 November, the new Christian-liberal majority in the Bundestag, which had been voted in at the early elections held in the spring of 1983, approved the stationing of Euromissiles in Germany. It came as no surprise. Brandt's only consolation was that his party had remained loyal to him. An internal vote at the SPD party congress in Cologne in November was a landslide victory for Brandt: out of the 400 delegates, only 13 had supported Schmidt and voted in favour of the Pershing missiles; all the rest had voted with Brandt against their deployment.[50] After completing his term as an MP, Schmidt would withdraw from political life in 1987. Wehner had retired. Brandt was the only one of the troika who seemed to be unsinkable. However, he too started to think about passing the baton. He was more and more reliant on the group of men in their forties, who were known as his heirs – those dynamic 'grandchildren' who were either already leaders of the *Länder* or were vying with each other for power. They included Oskar Lafontaine in Saarland, Björn Engholm in Schleswig-Holstein, Rudolf Scharping in Rhineland-Palatinate and Gerhard Schröder, who was elected as minister-president of Lower Saxony in 1990.[51] Brandt put his favourite, Lafontaine, forward as a potential chancellor candidate for the 1987 elections, but Lafontaine declined. For the moment, the party preferred Johannes Rau and Hans-Jochen Vogel, who were slightly older. Rau was the obvious choice, having just achieved an impressive electoral victory in the enormous *Land* of North Rhine-Westphalia, with 52 per cent of the votes. He was no match for Helmut Kohl, however, and finished his career as president of the Federal Republic.

In his private life, Brandt's divorce from Rut had been confirmed shortly before Christmas in 1980, and he built himself a hideaway in France. In 1983 he bought an old house in the Cévennes, on the triple border of Lozère, Gard and Ardèche. The little house near Gagnières, called Le Mézy, was built of dry stone and had a flat, tiled roof that he and Brigitte renovated. He loved the wild scenery and his good-natured neighbours, whom he would join for a pastis, talking French in his gravelly Nordic accent. He pottered about in the garden and chopped wood, and his grandchildren came to stay. On 9 December 1983, he married Brigitte in Unkel, near Bonn. It was his third wedding. Ten days later, he celebrated his seventieth birthday.

He was still involved in politics in various ways: at the SPD, the Socialist International, the North–South Commission or the European Parliament. He used his position in these institutions to develop his ideas about his favourite subjects: socialism, freedom, German history, the true nature of Nazism, the mistakes of the Weimar Republic and resistance to Hitler from across the political spectrum.[52] Since 1955 he had spoken of the failed 20 July 1944 plotters as his 'dead friends', and 30 years later he called Julius Leber 'the man who saved the nation's honour'.[53] In 1986, under his leadership, the SPD started to reform their party programme, prioritising employment, gender equality, European integration, the environment and, as always, more democracy.[54] On the international stage, Brandt honed his rhetoric. 'Socialism without human rights is like Christianity without Jesus,'[55] he declared at the Socialist International congress in Lima in 1986. In Germany, he caused a stir by calling reunification 'the great sham of the 1950s',[56] now that meetings between the SPD leadership and the East German SED were becoming more and more frequent. It seemed as if he thought that the effort to reunite the German nation had been confined to the dungeons of history or been postponed indefinitely.

Nevertheless, change was happening – without anybody being able to say exactly what effect it would have. Brandt approved of Mikhail Gorbachev's appointment as the new secretary general of the Central Committee of the Communist Party of the Soviet Union (CPSU), after Chernenko's death on 10 March 1985. Thanks to Bahr's connections in Moscow, Brandt was soon able to establish a relationship with Gorbachev and made an official visit to meet him in May.[57] He found Gorbachev's ideas of 'common security' and the 'common European home' reassuring. He went on a tour round most of the European capitals, but waited until September 1985 to accept an invitation that Honecker had sent him two years previously. Nothing had changed in East Germany, where, to avoid another enthusiastic welcome of the sort Brandt had received at Erfurt 15 years previously, on his first visit to the GDR, the Stasi gathered together hundreds of their collaborators to pretend to be ordinary people in the streets.[58] During their meeting, Brandt and Honecker discussed the humanitarian problems of a state where hundreds of citizens were in prison because they had tried to leave their country, and where only retired people were allowed to travel to the West. Honecker also swore that he had known absolutely nothing about the spy in the Chancellery; governments are interested in information, but not the people who obtain it.[59]

The elections in January 1987 did not bring the hoped-for success. The SPD only received 37 per cent of the vote, behind the coalition of Kohl's CDU and the liberals, with 45 per cent and 9 per cent respectively. Brandt felt he had been proved right: Rau had not been the right man for the job, and it was now time to appoint Lafontaine as the party's future candidate, and Vogel as the party leader.[60] It was certainly time for Brandt to pass the baton, after 23 years at the head of the SPD. He knew he should leave before he was pushed out. He was well aware that the party was struggling with a deep internal rift. In the spring of 1987, there was uproar: Brandt tried to appoint a young woman in her thirties, a complete unknown, as party spokeswoman. Margarita Mathiopoulos was the daughter of Greek intellectuals who had sought asylum in Germany, victims of the Greek military junta. She held a PhD in history and political science and was a talented journalist. She was also a dark-haired beauty. What she was not, however, was a member of the SPD, or a German national. In private, Brandt's friends – Bahr, Ehmke, Verheugen and most of the rest of the party office – tried to dissuade him, but to no avail. He thought the party should open itself up to young democrats and to intellectual women, and try and attract those who were being tempted away by the liberals or the Greens. The SPD needed to adapt to the media age and rejuvenate social democracy's slightly musty image. But when it was discovered that Mathiopoulos's studies had been financed by the FDP's foundation, and that moreover she was engaged to a CDU activist who worked with Weizsäcker, there was such outrage that she withdrew her candidacy. Brandt received letters full of xenophobic hate, which profoundly disturbed the internationalist in him.

He had had enough. He announced at the political bureau on 23 March 1987:

> When a prop that has remained in place for a long time will no longer hold, when a personal issue becomes a major matter of state, and I see an influential minority of elected representatives falling out of line, then I think, at my age, that it is time to turn the page.

Combative as ever, he added, 'Let there be no misunderstanding: I am leaving the deck, but not the ship. I will continue to put my long experience, and the freedom of speech I exercise, at the service of German and European social democracy.'[61] Even Chancellor Kohl was shocked by the way the SPD had pushed their historic leader out, the man who had been chancellor as well as party chairman.[62] It only remained to orchestrate a graceful exit at a special congress. On 14 June 1987, Brandt was elected 'honorary chairman for life', and Hans-Jochen Vogel became the new SPD chairman. In the Beethovenhalle in Bonn, Brandt gave his farewell speech, somewhere between a reckoning and a will:

> If I had to choose one thing which, alongside peace, is the most important thing in the world, I would not hesitate for a moment: it is freedom. Freedom for all, and not just for the few. Freedom of conscience and of thought. But also freedom in the sense of being free from fear or poverty.[63]

His relationship with Helmut Schmidt had never recovered from the Euromissiles debate. In his resignation speech,

Brandt publicly criticised his former friend, who had tried to push him out. Schmidt thought Brandt had been leader of the party for too long.[64] Things got even worse when two separate ceremonies were organised at the start of 1989, one to celebrate Brandt's seventy-fifth birthday, the other for Schmidt's seventieth. Neither man was invited to the other's party.

Brandt was delighted with the welcome he received from President Weizsäcker at the beginning of January 1989, and was especially pleased with the photograph taken of the party standing on the steps of the presidential palace in Bonn, the beautiful white Villa Hammerschmidt. Brandt is standing in the middle of the front row, waving, flanked by his wife Brigitte and by Weizsäcker who, despite political differences (he was a CDU politician), had always been supportive of Brandt. On the same step there are the three socialists François Mitterrand, Mário Soares and Shimon Peres. Behind them are Helmut Kohl and Jacques Delors, Gro Harlem Brundtland and Hans-Jochen Vogel, Rainer Barzel and Hans-Dietrich Genscher. Bruno Kreisky, Walter Scheel, Oskar Lafontaine, Egon Bahr and many others among Brandt's friends, were also there. Everyone was smiling and clapping, and the crowd of photographers sang, 'Happy Birthday, dear Willy!' Weizsäcker paid tribute to 'one of the world's leading figures since World War II; a headstrong and thoughtful maverick who never liked playing the hero. He was often attacked cruelly, and he did not have a tough skin. He was a powerful man, but he never abused his power.'[65]

7

The End of the Story?

The joy and surprise of the years 1989 and 1990 masked an insistent question: had the SPD abandoned their goal of joining the two halves of Germany into a single state? Had Ostpolitik failed? Brandt, for one, refused to countenance reunification if it involved establishing Germany as it had been prior to and during the Reich; it would be anachronistic and foolish to think it was possible to go back to 'Bismarck's nation-state'.[1] It was as impossible as it was reprehensible – and so reunification was a 'sham'.

Over the course of the 1980s, the conversation between the SPD and the communist SED had become institutionalised, and it seemed as if the division was now a permanent and acknowledged one; that the East German party was a legitimate partner; and that the two systems were of equal status. They had published a joint paper in 1987.[2] On the right, the Social Democrats were accused of digging reunited Germany's grave. Traitors once more? This time, however, Brandt was absolved by Kohl, who believed that, although he had accepted the necessity of talking to the SED because he had lost hope, deep down the former Chancellor was still attached to the idea of German unity.[3] Anyway, there was hardly anyone left who believed in the possibility of reunification at the end of the 1980s. A poll in 1987 showed that only 3 per cent of West German citizens still thought it might happen.[4]

And yet, was the logic of 'change through rapprochement' not proved right by the fact that the East German regime could not prevent the West exerting an irresistible attraction over the population of the GDR? In May 1989, public protests took place in many of the GDR's cities in reaction to rigged municipal elections. Small groups started daring to demand free elections and respect for the Helsinki principles. Alongside this clandestine movement, hundreds of GDR citizens made the most of the summer months to escape to the socialist states which had managed to rebel against Moscow. On 10 August, the border between Hungary and Austria was opened, and a veritable exodus to the West began. 'I feel as if an era is ending,' Brandt said to the Bundestag on 1 September, on the fiftieth anniversary of the beginning of World War II. He was no visionary; he was referring to the end of the 'politics of small steps', and he still did not suspect that the Soviet Union might release the jewel in its crown, the GDR.[5]

However, the pace of events accelerated after the fortieth anniversary of the foundation of the GDR, on 7 October. Brandt began to sense that the East German regime was getting weaker. Amazingly, he still distrusted the alternative political groups which had been officially established, one after the other, to rebel against the status quo. When he visited the GDR in 1985 he had not followed his eldest son Peter's advice to meet with these opposition groups.[6] He respected their courage, certainly, but he did not understand these intellectuals, whose meetings were held in Protestant places of worship. Besides, they wanted to reform the GDR, which meant preserving it as a separate state. They dreamed of a 'third way'. What a ridiculous idea, he thought, to try and create a new social democratic party in the GDR, the SDP, instead of once more taking up the torch of the SPD, which had been so cruelly snuffed out in 1946! What Brandt did not understand was that he was the absolute reference point for these socialists in the East.[7] He was far more moved by the masses of ordinary people taking to the streets in peaceful protest. On 16 October, he received an honorary doctorate from the Lomonosov Moscow State University, and in his acceptance speech he called for a new form of cooperation between East and West. The following day, he and Bahr, with

Gerhard Schröder, the former leader of the young socialists and now leader of the opposition in Lower Saxony, and Hans Koschnick, president of the Bundestag's Committee on Foreign Affairs, all visited Gorbachev. Brandt spoke cautiously of 'a certain common ground where the two German states could cooperate'. Astonishingly, Gorbachev was just as explicit about 'serious changes' that were starting to take place in the GDR. He mentioned the meeting of the SED's political bureau and central committee that was due to take place the next day, where Honecker would be forced to resign,[8] to be replaced by Egon Krenz, another dyed-in-the-wool communist.

In Bonn, 9 November 1989 was an ordinary day. Brandt spent the morning in his office at the Bundestag, as he did every other working day. During the evening sitting, while the MPs were in the chamber to attend a vote, incredible news was heard: the SED's political bureau had just announced that a law had been passed, with immediate force, giving East German citizens freedom of movement! It would allow them to leave their country and cross the border, freely. The MPs stood up and sang the German national anthem, the third verse of the 'Deutschlandlied', whose words are unity, justice and freedom. The chairman of the SPD, Vogel, announced on the microphone: 'This decision means that after 28 years, the wall has lost its meaning; you will understand if at this moment, I look to Willy Brandt.'[9] It was not until a few hours later, however, that Brandt and many others truly understood that the Berlin Wall would literally open up before the flood of East Germans wanting to make sure the news was true. The first crossings took place as night fell, but the Brandts were unaware of what was happening, as their television had not been connected yet. They had just moved to a new house in Unkel, on the banks of the Rhine, south of Bonn. In the early hours of the morning, at about 5 o'clock, the former Chancellor was woken by a phone call from a journalist who told him that the wall was open; Brandt gave her an interview and finished the conversation with the words: *Das ist es* (So, that's it).[10]

The End of the Berlin Wall

The fall of the wall brought a tumult of emotions and images, as if it was now possible to rewrite the whole strange history. A British military plane carried Brandt to Berlin on the morning of 10 November, and he was immediately driven to the Brandenburg Gate. He remembered standing there on 13 August 1961, looking at the first barbed wire, and then again with Kennedy in 1963. He repeated the same words over and over for the journalists: 'Now what belongs together will grow together.' In 'his' city hall in Schöneberg, where he met the Mayor Walter Momper, Chancellor Kohl and Minister Genscher, Brandt spoke of 'bringing Germans back together'. It was the phrase 'what belongs together' which caught on, however, to the extent that he added it retrospectively to his speech at the city hall when it came to be published.[11]

That evening, he and Kohl both received the same message from Gorbachev, asking them to intervene to 'try and prevent any potentially undesirable or dramatic further developments'.[12] Brandt may well have shared Gorbachev's desire to avoid a violent reaction from the East German police, but privately he remarked, amused, 'They have opened the wall, but they know not what they do.' In the GDR, the opening of the wall was seen as liberation, and as a recovery of the socialism that had been warped by communism. Brandt was not surprised that the slogans changed every time there was a new demonstration, when hundreds of thousands of people would descend on the streets of the GDR: after 'We are the people!', which dismissed the SED's claim to speak in the people's name, came 'We are one people!' and then, by the middle of November, 'Germany, a united nation!' The message was loud and clear: the people wanted unity. Unlike many other Social Democrats, Brandt approved Kohl's ten-point plan, presented to the Bundestag on 29 November, which sketched out the possible phases of cooperation leading to the ultimate, still-distant goal of reunification. Kohl was sure his reaction had been the appropriate one; he said as much to the press in response to Lafontaine's reproach that he had not consulted the Allies first.[13] Either way, Brandt struggled to understand their European neighbours' nervous reactions. Margaret Thatcher raised fears about renascent German imperialism, and Giulio Andreotti, prime minister of Italy, had harsh words for the overly impatient Germans, while François Mitterrand showed no enthusiasm for any swift change in Germany's situation. While on an official visit to the GDR, Mitterrand seemed to want the division between the two states to be made permanent. Brandt publicly criticised 'the heads of state who seem unable to fulfil the commitments laid down on paper by their predecessors'.[14] The last few years had seen several disagreements between Brandt and Mitterrand, especially when it came to the question of nuclear defence.[15] This time, Brandt reproached the British and French for being stuck in the past; in an article in *Die Zeit* he reminded Mitterrand that the Germans had a right to self-determination too.[16] If the people wanted unity, they should have it. Brandt still refrained from talking about reunification, however. Throughout Ostpolitik he had always tried to emphasise that the Basic Law and its preamble mentioned unity, but not reunification.[17] Mitterrand was aware of this detail and, according to his adviser Attali, would have been pleased to note Brandt's insistence on the necessity of creating 'something new' by 'new-unification' rather than reunification.[18]

Like Kohl, who was welcomed as a saviour in the GDR, Brandt was met by crowds wherever he went in East Germany. On 6 December 1989, St Mary's Church in Rostock, on the shore of the Baltic Sea, was full to bursting. Brandt had been invited there by the pastor, Joachim Gauck, who had opened his parish up to protesters months before and had become a figurehead in the 'citizens' movement'. There were almost 40,000 people gathered around the church, eager to see Willy Brandt: he was a veritable legend, and not only because his family came from the same area. In his speech, he called on the crowd to support social democracy and explained why the 'third way' would never work.[19] It was a strange situation: he was pleading social democracy's cause, but his relationship with the SPD was deteriorating.

The SPD party congress in Berlin on 18 December was an opportunity for him to have a dig at the Kohl administration for their vagueness about the legitimacy of the Oder–Neisse line, but he did not spare the SPD either, and spoke as freely as he had done when he had resigned as chairman. He warned his colleagues about their negative attitude, and told them that it was not a question of *if* there should be unity, but *when*.[20] Even his relationship with his 'heir', Oskar Lafontaine, deteriorated when Lafontaine said it would better to focus on improving social justice in the GDR and the FRG rather than working towards reunification. Günter Grass did not fare much better. Brandt's long-standing friend told the congress that the division was the price Germany had to pay for Auschwitz, and that to reunite Germany would be to repeat the accumulation of power that had led to the worst massacre in history. Their old friendship was shattered.[21]

In the first months of 1990, Brandt had a hard time understanding what Gorbachev was trying to achieve; he seemed to be constantly blowing hot and cold. At the beginning of February, Brandt received a five-page letter in which the Russian leader explained that he was indeed willing to leave the division of Germany in the past, but that in return he demanded neutrality from reunited Germany.[22] Brandt, like the federal government, was resolutely against the idea of military neutrality. He was shocked to hear his party discussing the possibility of a reunified Germany leaving NATO. He shared Genscher's vision of Germany remaining in the Atlantic alliance, but with the territories of the GDR excluded from its integrated structures.[23] Mitterrand expressed his agreement when the two men met in Paris on 8 March. The question of whether unified Germany should belong to a military bloc was still undecided throughout the first half of the year, while the external aspects of reunification – namely the end of Germany's postwar special status – were dealt with in the 'Two plus Four Treaty', which united the two Germanys and the four Allies. Brandt was involved in the negotiations. He thought it was important to make sure the Polish were satisfied, and to reassure all of Germany's various neighbours, and he tried to organise a 'Two plus Nine' conference. He was ignored. He went on a grand tour of the GDR in the run-up to the elections on 18 March, the first free elections held in the territory since 1932. Wherever he spoke, he was greeted by huge crowds. The results of the vote were clearly in favour of reunification, but disastrous for the SPD, who only received 21.9 per cent of the votes. Brandt was sure it was because the people had rejected Lafontaine's stance against rapid economic and monetary union of the GDR and FRG. The East German population were moving in large numbers to the West, and there was a saying at the time that, 'If the Deutschmark will not come to us, we will go to the Deutschmark.'

Summer brought some relief – Gorbachev finally yielded and approved the future Germany's membership of NATO – and also much emotion. On 22 June, Brandt and Genscher were invited by the ministers of foreign affairs of the four Allies to watch Checkpoint Charlie being dismantled. For Brandt, Berlin was the obvious choice to be the German capital once more. Within the SPD, people were critical of the forced march to unity. But on 23 August, the freely elected East German MPs voted to join the Federal Republic according to Article 23 of the Basic Law, and the West German MPs validated the treaty of union in the Bundestag on 22 September. Even if, at first, Brandt had stressed the importance of Article 146, which required a new constitution to be drawn up for the reunited nation, now he publicly expressed his support for Kohl's choice of a quick solution, as well as his disagreement with Lafontaine's continuing criticism of the government. On 3 October, the day of reunification, Brandt's former 'heir' noted bitterly that

Brandt ostentatiously refused to shake his hand. The two men never spoke again.[24]

That evening was one of the most moving occasions of Brandt's life. He shared his emotion with the important figures gathered around him before the Reichstag in Berlin: President Weizsäcker, Chancellor Kohl, Minister of Foreign Affairs Genscher, and thousands of others. Shortly before midnight, 14 young people carried a huge red, black and gold flag down the Reichstag steps, while in the distance the 'liberty bell' at Schöneberg city hall, a recent gift from the Americans as a sign of solidarity, could be heard ringing out. The flag of democratic Germany was raised into the night, while Weizsäcker pronounced the words of the preamble to the constitution:

> Conscious of their responsibility before God and men, animated by the resolve to serve world peace as an equal partner in a united Europe, the German people have adopted, by virtue of their constituent power, this Basic Law. The Germans [...] have achieved the unity and freedom of Germany in self-determination.

As the national anthem played and fireworks in Germany's colours went off, Brandt visibly struggled to keep his emotions under control.[25]

After the general elections on 2 December, when the SPD only received 33.5 per cent of the vote compared to the CDU/CSU's almost 44 per cent, Brandt encouraged his party to be its own worst critic. He had been re-elected as an MP, and it was up to him, as the elder statesman, to open the first Bundestag at which MPs from West and East were present: 'We must now work towards Germany's complete internal unity, as well as the unification of Europe, and we must show ourselves worthy of our increased global responsibility.' Unifying Germany internally meant facing the challenge of how to integrate the communists. Brandt remembered how he had admired

Mitterrand for seeing that bringing the French communists on side, and including them in his government in 1981, would take some of the sting out of their campaign.[26] Brandt did not suggest going quite that far, but he took pains to emphasise the difference between communism and true socialism, between communist socialism and democratic socialism.[27] Going back to his postwar reflections on how to deal with Nazism, when he had differentiated between being a criminal and being obedient, he argued for reconciliation. He was inspired by the energy of Eastern Europeans like Václav Havel, the renowned dissident author, who invited him to Prague. In Brandt's view, Havel was an exceptional figure in the campaign for peace, alongside Nelson Mandela, who had recently been freed after 27 years in prison, and whom Brandt met in June 1990.[28]

Illness and the Hour of Reckoning

During his summer holiday in France in 1991, Brandt was troubled by an insistent pain in his legs that made him unable to walk. He had an operation in Germany at the beginning of October, after it was discovered that he had intestinal cancer. His wife was the only other person who knew that the tumour was malignant, and that it was terminal.[29] To try and preserve his health, he resigned as president of the Socialist International, which under his leadership had been more important than it had ever been before, or would be again. It took several months to find a suitable successor. Pierre Mauroy, who had recently resigned as first secretary of the French PS, was chosen in September 1992. 'One does not replace Willy Brandt,' he said respectfully, 'one comes after him.'[30]

There was still the problem of Europe. Germany's reunification had put the complicated question of nationhood back on the agenda, especially the question of how to combine it with the European project. In the 1970s, Brandt had already explained that 'to build Europe means preserving the values of national identity, and laying the structure of a European government over them.'[31] The return of the nationalist element in a democracy which had been established according to post-national values made it more important than ever for Brandt, the European patriot, to reiterate his vision of Europe. His commitment was extremely long-standing: in Oslo in 1939, before a crowd of emigrants, he had made a speech about a possible economic and political reorganisation of the European continent.[32] In his Norwegian publications he had deliberately used the term 'United States of Europe', while still preferring a pragmatic approach towards achieving the unity he considered as 'necessary in itself'.[33] Later, he had insisted on the importance of 'Europeanising Europe' and keeping greater distance from the United States of America, an opinion he had repeated during the Euromissiles crisis.[34] He called for strengthened military cooperation between the autonomous European states, which were capable of uniting in diversity to rise to the challenge posed by the new global situation.[35] The foreign affairs section he helped write for Kiesinger's keynote policy speech in 1966 had been subtly inflected with this attitude, when he spoke of nationhood, Europe and peace as interwoven strands of the same thread.[36] What should progress towards European unity look like, once the Maastricht Treaty had been signed in February 1992? Brandt thought it needed gradual steps, following Monnet's advice that 'the accomplishment of meaningful progress is more important than the pursuit of perfectionist goals.'[37] Anyway, Brandt usually preferred to talk in terms of intensifying progress, rather than using grand terms like integration.[38] He saw the need for patience, as he had done when supporting Britain's membership of the European Community against French opposition. On 4 May 1992, he gave his final speech in Luxembourg, restating his guiding principles once more: the necessity of Europe after the catastrophe of Nazism, the Franco-German relationship as its central axis, and always, always, the search for a 'new architecture for Europe'. He ended with these words, looking towards the future: 'Openness, understanding and willingness to help will be repaid one day, but looking at the world with a closed spirit will come back to haunt us. I believe it is important that we do not leave this idea of a shared European direction by the wayside.'[39]

His health was getting worse. On 27 August, Helmut Kohl visited him at home in Unkel. 'Why are you out of bed and dressed, when you're in so much pain?' Kohl asked, astonished. 'When my Chancellor pays me a visit,' Brandt replied, his gaze unwavering, 'I will not stay in bed.'[40] They talked for a long time. Brandt spoke of his coming death and described what he wanted for his funeral. He asked Felipe González, the Spanish prime minister, to give the eulogy. Later, it was said that he drank his last glass of red wine with his Spanish 'adopted son'.[41]

Willy Brandt died at home, in the afternoon, on 8 October 1992. His wife told Helmut Kohl, in accordance with Willy's wishes, that the Chancellor should announce his death. An official ceremony was held a few days later at the Reichstag, attended by all the great and good of the country, and Felipe González finished his speech with the words '*Adios, amigo Willy.*' Willy's former wife, Rut, the mother of his three sons, received no invitation to the national funeral.

Herbert Frahm is dead. But Brandt's name is carried by his three sons: the historian Peter Brandt, the author and screenwriter Lars Brandt, and the actor Matthias Brandt. As for Willy, the man and his values live on in his political legacy. He is buried in plot F24 in the Waldfriedhof, a cemetery in the Berlin-Zehlendorf forest. His grave is marked only by a rough stone slab, with his name engraved in big capital letters, the name he gave himself and which accompanied him throughout his life:

WILLY BRANDT

Notes

Preface

1 Egon BAHR, *'Das musst Du erzählen'. Erinnerungen an Willy Brandt*, Berlin, 2013, p. 36.

Prologue

1 According to his words in 1960, Willy BRANDT, *Links und frei. Mein Weg 1930–1950*, Hamburg, 1982, pp. 175–8 and *Mein Weg nach Berlin*, with L. LANIA, Munich, 1960, pp. 84–93; Willy BRANDT, *My Life in Politics* (trans. Anthea Bell), London, 1992, pp. 95–6; Brigitte SEEBACHER, *Willy Brandt*, Munich, 2004, p. 115.

2 Letter from Brandt to Ording, adviser at the Norwegian Ministry of Foreign Affairs, 27.12.1941, Willy BRANDT, *Berliner Ausgabe, Band. 2: Zwei Vaterländer. Deutsch-Norweger im schwedischen Exil – Rückkehr nach Deutschland 1940–1947*, ed. Einhart LORENZ, Bonn, 2000 (hereafter *BA 2*), pp. 65–72, p. 68.

3 BRANDT, *My Life in Politics, op. cit.*, p. 98.

4 Article in the *Lübecker Volksbote*, 11.3.1930, Willy BRANDT, *Berliner Ausgabe, Band 1: Hitler ist nicht Deutschland. Jugend in Lübeck – Exil in Norwegen 1928–1940*, ed. Einhart LORENZ, Bonn, 2002 (hereafter *BA 1*), pp. 83–4.

I Between Attachment and Emigration

1 BRANDT, *Links, op. cit.*, p. 22, Gregor SCHÖLLGEN, *Willy Brandt. Die Biographie*, Berlin, 2001, p. 16. Peter MERSEBURGER, *Willy Brandt 1913–1992. Visionär und Realist*, Munich, 2002, p. 18.

2 BRANDT, *My Life in Politics, op. cit.*, pp. 73–4.

3 BRANDT, *Mein Weg nach Berlin, op. cit.*, p. 33.

4 This view is expressed by SEEBACHER, *op. cit.*, p. 90, and SCHÖLLGEN, *op. cit.*, p. 10.

5 Wismar is in northern Germany, on the Baltic coast, slightly to the east of Lübeck in the direction of Rostock.

6 Brandt, *Links*, *op. cit.*, pp. 21–2, cited by Merseburger, *Brandt*, *op. cit.*, p. 18 and Schöllgen, *op. cit.*, p. 18.

7 The Spartacist uprising in Berlin, in the first week of January 1919, was the culmination of the '1918–19 German revolution'. A general strike and armed battles in the streets were supressed by the Freikorps, a counter-revolutionary paramilitary group, at the orders of the head of the Social Democratic government, Friedrich Ebert. Karl Liebknecht and Rosa Luxemburg, the leaders of the Spartacist League, an extreme left Marxist revolutionary group, were captured by the Freikorps and murdered on 15 January.

8 The Freikorps (free corps) were extreme-right paramilitary organisations raised after World War I to fight against the newly formed Weimar Republic. They were supported by many German veterans who felt disconnected from civilian life. Although officially disbanded in 1920, many Freikorps attempted, unsuccessfully, to overthrow the government in the Kapp Putsch of March 1920.

9 Letter from Heinz Neumann, a former classmate, to Brandt, 1.5.1970, Willy Brandt Archive, in the Archive of Social Democracy in the Friedrich Ebert Foundation in Bonn (hereafter WBA), BK, 15. In May 1930 Frahm published an article discussing the importance of family and social background, article in *Lübecker Voksbote,* 6.5.1930, *BA 1, op. cit.*, pp. 85–8.

10 'Republik, das ist nicht viel, Sozialismus ist das Ziel', Frahm in an article in *Lübecker Voksbote*, 24.9.1930, *BA 1, op. cit.*, pp. 88–91.

11 Schöllgen, *op. cit.*, p. 21.

12 Article in *Lübecker Volksbote*, 12.12.1928, *BA 1, op. cit.*, p. 80.

13 Article 'Sie schänden den Namen des Proletariats!', *Lübecker Volksbote*, 28.4.1931, *Ibid.*, pp. 92–4. He did not see any difference between the KPD's methods and those of the Nazis.

14 According to Brandt, who was made an honorary citizen of Lübeck on 29.2.1972. A copy of his school report of 26.2.1932 is on display at the Forum Willy Brandt Berlin, run by the Federal Chancellor Willy Brandt Foundation.

15 Brandt paid tribute to him by dedicating a chapter of his memoirs to 'The emperor of the little people', Brandt, *Links*, *op. cit.*, p. 12.

16 Brandt, *My Life in Politics*, *op. cit.*, p. 74.

17 Letter from Martha Kuhlmann (Frahm), 7.2.1947, WBA, B 25, 213. Facsimile in Seebacher, *op. cit.*, p. 90.

18 Brandt, *My Life in Politics*, *op. cit.*, p. 74; Einhart Lorenz, *Willy Brandt. Deutscher, Europäer, Weltbürger*, Stuttgart, 2012, p. 11.

19 Merseburger, *Brandt*, *op. cit.*, p. 39.

20 'Die Todesursachen des deutschen Sozialdemokratie', in Dorothea Beck/Wilfried F. Schoeller (eds), *Julius Leber, Schriften, Reden, Briefe*, Munich, 1976.

21 Brandt, *Links, op. cit.*, p. 60. His distancing from the SPD is clear in his writings of 1932, *BA 1, op. cit.*, pp. 110–12.
22 Lorenz, *Brandt. Deutscher, Europäer, op. cit.*, p. 21.
23 Seebacher, *op. cit.*, pp. 112–13.
24 According to Heinrich Bruhn, a comrade of Brandt's from the time, writing in *Stern*, 13.12.1973. Pamphlets in the Willy Brandt Archive, cited in Merseburger, *Brandt, op. cit.*, p. 52.
25 Seebacher, *op. cit.*, p. 107.
26 Brandt, *Links, op. cit.*, p. 72.
27 Brandt, *My Life in Politics, op. cit.*, pp. 83–4.
28 Brandt's presentation at the SAP conference in Dresden, *BA 1, op. cit.*, pp. 114–15. Mentioned in *Links, op. cit.*, pp. 64–5.
29 Lorenz, *Brandt. Deutscher, Europäer, op. cit.*, p. 18.
30 Hans Georg Lehmann, *In Acht und Bann. Politische Emigration, NS-Ausbürgerung und Wiedergutmachung am Beispiel Willy Brandts*, Munich, 1976, pp. 97–9.
31 He was commissioned to write about this trip in the *Volksbote*, 29.7.1931, *BA 1, op. cit.*, pp. 95–100.
32 Willy Brandt, *Draußen, Schriften während der Emigration*, ed. G. Struve, Munich, 1966, p. 63.
33 *Frankfurter Allgemeine Zeitung* (hereafter *FAZ*), 16.2.1961.
34 Brandt, *Links, op. cit.*, p. 74; Brandt, *My Life in Politics, op. cit.*, p. 85.
35 In 1960, Brandt, *Mein Weg nach Berlin, op. cit.*, p. 72, in 1982, Brandt, *Links, op. cit.*, p. 83.
36 *Ibid.*, p. 70.
37 *BA 1, op. cit.*, pp. 115–20.
38 Brandt, *Links, op. cit.*, p. 77.
39 Peter Koch, *Willy Brandt. Eine politische Biographie*, Berlin, 1988, p. 82.
40 Brandt, *Links, op. cit.*, p. 88.
41 Details about Brandt's exile can be found in Einhart Lorenz, *Willy Brandt in Norwegen. Die Jahre des Exils 1933 bis 1940*, Kiel, 1989.
42 Lehmann, *op. cit.*, p. 128; Merseburger, *Brandt, op. cit.*, pp. 66–7.
43 Details in Brandt, *Links, op. cit.*, pp. 117–23.
44 E. Lorenz in Horst Möller/Maurice Vaïsse (eds), *Willy Brandt und Frankreich*, Munich, 2005, pp. 29–34.
45 In his published articles and his letters to the SAP leadership between October 1936 and Feburary 1937, *BA 1, op. cit.*, docs 36 to 40.
46 Hilde Walter, 'Aus der Chronik des Nobelpreises für Carl von Ossietzky', *Aus Politik und Zeitgeschichte*, 4.10.1969.
47 Letter from Brandt to Walcher, 21.1.1937, *BA 1, op. cit.*, pp. 265–6.

48 Brandt, *Links, op. cit.*, p. 216.
49 Letter from Brandt to the SAP leadership, 31.3.1937, *BA 1, op. cit.*, pp. 294–7.
50 Brandt talked about Marc Rein for the rest of his life, Seebacher, *op. cit.*, pp. 129–30.
51 Report by Brandt for the SAP leadership, 5.7.1937, *BA 1, op. cit.*, pp. 306–42, p. 342.
52 Lorenz, *Brandt. Deutscher, Europäer, op. cit.*, p. 40.
53 Brandt, *My Life in Politics, op. cit.*, p. 73. Details about his loss of nationality can be found in Brandt, *Links, op. cit.*, pp. 261–5.
54 Rut Brandt, *Freundesland. Erinnerungen*, Hamburg, 1992, p. 61.
55 Article written Christmas 1937, *Arbeider-Ungdommen, BA 1, op. cit.*, pp. 352–5. Article written January 1939, *Telegraf og Telefon, Ibid.*, pp. 392–7.
56 Brandt, pamphlet on the foreign policy of the Soviet Union, 1917–39, written October 1939, extracts in *ibid.*, pp. 429–33. See also his article of February 1940, *ibid.*, pp. 459–67.
57 Brandt, *Mein Weg, op. cit.*, p. 134; Brandt, *Draußen, op. cit.*, p. 123, p. 375.
58 Letters from Gertrud Gaasland to W. Brandt and I. Enderle in October 1940 and January 1941, Archive of Social Democracy, Friedrich Ebert Foundation, Bonn (hereafter AdsD), NL Lang, 19.
59 Lorenz, *Willy Brandt. Deutscher, Europäer, op. cit.*, p. 59.
60 Report of Brandt's interrogation, Swedish Security Service archives, used by E. Lorenz, see *BA 2, op. cit.*, p. 337, note 32.
61 Lorenz in Möller/Vaïsse, *op. cit.*, p. 35.
62 WBA, A 5, Allg. Korrespondenz 1942, 1943, 1944, 27, 29.
63 He had used the phrase before, on 28.12.1939, in an article for the *Bergens Arbeiderblad*, in German in *BA 1, op. cit.*, pp. 453–5. For the development of his concept of European unity see E. Lorenz in Andreas Wilkens (ed.), *Willy Brandt et l'unité de l'Europe. De l'objectif de la paix aux solidarités nécessaires*, Brussels, 2011, pp. 45–60.
64 Letter to J. Walcher, 30.6.1942, WBA, A 5, 11.
65 Cited in Merseburger, *Brandt, op. cit.*, pp. 42–3.
66 Brandt, *Links, op. cit.*, pp. 364–75. On his contacts with the resistance within Germany, WBA, B 25, 163.
67 Klaus Schönhoven, *Freiheit durch demokratischen Sozialismus. Willy Brandts Überlegungen zum programmatischen Selbstverständnis der SPD, Gesprächskreis Geschichte 98*, Bonn, 2013, pp. 15–16. For the history of social democratic thought, see Helga Grebing in Horst Heimann (ed.), *Sozialdemokratische Traditionen und Demokratischer Sozialismus*, Cologne, 1993, or Bernd Faulenbach, *Geschichte der SPD: Von den Anfängen bis zur Gegenwart*, Munich, 2012. See also texts written by Brandt

between 1947 and 1972 in Willy Brandt, *Berliner Ausgabe, Band 4: Auf dem Weg nach vorn: Willy Brandt und die SPD 1947–1972*, ed. Daniela Münkel, Berlin, 2000 (hereafter *BA 4*).

68 Rut Brandt, *op. cit.*, p. 61.

69 Karl Jaspers, *The Question of German Guilt*, trans. E. B. Ashton, New York, 1947.

70 Speech on 9.2.1945 to the SPD bureau in Stockholm, *BA 2*, *op. cit.*, pp. 231–9. See also his booklet *The Postwar Policy of the German Socialists*, July 1944, *BA 2*, *op. cit.*, p. 154–205. Lorenz, *Brandt in Norwegen*, p. 30.

71 Cited by Michel in Bernd Rother (ed.), *Willy Brandts Außenpolitik*, Wiesbaden, 2014, p. 101.

72 WBA, Allg. Korrespondenz 1945–1946.

73 Lorenz, *Willy Brandt. Deutscher, Europäer*, *op. cit.*, p. 82.

74 Letter to Szende, 8.10.1946, in *BA 2*, *op. cit.*, pp. 316–18. On his distant relationship to France see Lorenz in Möller/Vaïsse, *op. cit.*, pp. 39–40.

2 In Berlin, at the Heart of the Cold War

1 Brandt, *Links*, *op. cit.*, p. 402.

2 *Ibid.*, p. 450.

3 Letter from Brandt to Walcher, 30.4.1946, *BA 2*, *op. cit.*, pp. 300–4, p. 301.

4 Merseburger, *Brandt*, *op. cit.*, p. 246.

5 Speech given by Schumacher, 27.8.1945, in Willi Albrecht (ed.), *Kurt Schumacher: Reden – Schriften – Korrespondenzen 1945–1952*, Berlin, 1985, pp. 256–86, p. 279.

6 Letter from Brandt to Schumacher, 23.12.1947, *BA 4*, *op. cit.*, p. 86. Lorenz, *Willy Brandt. Deutscher, Europäer*, *op. cit.*, p. 96.

7 Rut Brandt, *op. cit.*, p. 79.

8 *Ibid.*

9 Cited in Merseburger, *Brandt*, *op. cit.*, p. 307.

10 Lorenz, *Willy Brandt. Deutscher, Europäer*, *op. cit.*, p. 93.

11 Schöllgen, *op. cit.*, p. 81.

12 Rut Brandt, *op. cit.*, p. 99.

13 Lorenz, *Willy Brandt. Deutscher, Europäer*, *op. cit.*, p. 98.

14 In February 1949, cited in Helga Grebing, *Willy Brandt: Der andere Deutsche*, Munich, 2008, p. 126.

15 Bonn had been chosen as the provisional capital city partly because of the FRG's new Western centre of gravity, and partly because of Adenauer's links to the region (he was originally from nearby Cologne).

16 Rut Brandt, *op. cit.*, p. 110.

17 Willy BRANDT, *Berliner Ausgabe, Band 3: Berlin bleibt frei. Politik in und für Berlin 1947–1966*, ed. Siegfried HEIMANN, Berlin, 2004 (hereafter *BA 3*), p. 151.
18 Rut BRANDT, *op. cit.*, p. 111.
19 *Ibid.*, p. 80. On Brandt and Western integration during the 1950s, see Wolfgang SCHMIDT in WILKENS, *Unité de l'Europe*, *op. cit.*, pp. 61–81.
20 Adenauer's keynote speech, 20.9.1949, in Klaus STÜWE (ed.), *Die großen Regierungserklärungen der deutschen Bundeskanzler von Adenauer bis Schröder*, Opladen, 2002, pp. 35–47, p. 46.
21 Wilhelm Pieck, a German communist who had lived in exile since 1933, first in France and later in Moscow, became the first president of the GDR in 1949 until his death in 1960. Otto Grotewohl, a former social democrat, together with Pieck formed the new Socialist Unity Party in East Germany in April 1946. He was the first prime minister of the GDR from 1949 until his death in 1964. Ernst REUTER, *Reden, Artikel, Briefe 1949 bis 1953*, Berlin, 1975, pp. 130–45, p. 143.
22 Speech at the Bundestag, second Bundestag session, 146th sitting, 30.5.1956.
23 Report by Wehner on the twentieth CPSU Congress, 1.6.1956, AdsD, Papiers Menzel R 30. August H. LEUGERS-SCHERZBERG, *Die Wandlungen des Herbert Wehner: Von der Volksfront zur Großen Koalition*, Berlin, 2002.
24 Wolfgang SCHMIDT, 'Die Wurzeln der Entspannung: Der konzeptionelle Ursprung der Ost- und Deutschlandpolitik Willy Brandts in den fünfziger Jahren', *Vierteljahrshefte für Zeitgeschichte,* 51 (2003), pp. 521–63, p. 557.
25 Speech at the SPD Congress in Berlin, 8.5.1949, *BA 4*, *op. cit.*, pp. 99–130, p. 101.
26 SCHMIDT in WILKENS, *Unité de l'Europe*, *op. cit.*, pp. 61–81.
27 Rut BRANDT, *op. cit.*, pp. 115–16.
28 In his memoirs, Franz Josef Strauss remembers 'agreeable evenings passed in Willy Brandt's company, up until 1953', *Die Erinnerungen*, Berlin, 1989, p. 401.
29 Details in MERSEBURGER, *Brandt*, *op. cit.*, pp. 334–7.
30 *Ibid.*, p. 338; Rut BRANDT, *op. cit.*, p. 118; SCHÖLLGEN, *op. cit.*, p. 99.
31 Brandt's first mayoral declaration to Berlin's Abgeordnetenhaus (House of Representatives), from *Berliner Stimme*, 19.10.1957, cited in LORENZ, *Willy Brandt. Deutscher, Europäer*, *op. cit.*, pp. 106–7.
32 Rut BRANDT, *op. cit.*, p. 123.
33 Charles DE GAULLE, *Memoirs of Hope* (trans. Terence KILMARTIN), London, 1971, p. 174.

34 *Le Monde*, 17.12.1958; *France Soir*, 16.12.1958; *Le Canard Enchaîné*, 25.3.1959; BUFFET in MÖLLER/VAÏSSE, *op. cit.*, p. 49; Daniela MÜNKEL, *Bemerkungen zu Willy Brandt*, Berlin, 2005, p. 145.
35 Günter HOFMANN, *Willy Brandt und Helmut Schmidt: Geschichte einer schwierigen Freundschaft*, Munich, 2012, p. 77.
36 Hans-Peter SCHWARZ, *Axel Springer: Die Biografie*, Berlin, 2008, p. 298.
37 Every individual was allowed to change 60 Reichsmarks for 60 Deutschmarks, but the value of any Reichsmarks over and above that was divided by ten.
38 Willy BRANDT, *Begegnungen und Einsichten: Die Jahre 1960–1975*, Munich, 1978, p. 9; Rut BRANDT, *op. cit.*, p. 130.
39 Statistics in Damian VAN MELIS/Henrik BISPINCK (eds.), *'Republikflucht': Flucht und Abwanderung aus der SBZ/DDR 1945 bis 1961*, Munich, 2006, pp. 225–59; Hannes ADOMEIT, *Die Sowjetmacht in internationalen Krisen und Konflikten: Verhaltensmuster, Handlungsprinzipien, Bestimmungsfaktoren*, Baden Baden, 1983, pp. 274–7; Joachim SCHOLTYSECK, *Die Außenpolitik der DDR*, Munich, 2003, p. 20.
40 Cited in Hervé ALPHAND, *L'étonnement d'être, Journal 1939–1973*, Paris, 1977, p. 361.
41 According to his adviser Klaus Schütz, in interview with AstFilm productions, Bundeszentrale für politische Bildung; BRANDT, *Begegnungen, op. cit.*, pp. 12–13.
42 On the limits of the agreement between Brandt and Kennedy, see Judith MICHEL in ROTHER, *Außenpolitik, op. cit.*, pp. 113–18.
43 *Ibid.*, p. 19.
44 The Vopos were members of the GDR's national police force, the Volkspolizei (People's Police).
45 BRANDT, *Begegnungen, op. cit.*, p. 24.
46 Letter from Brandt to Kennedy and speech at the Schöneberg city hall, 16.8.1961.
47 BRANDT, *My Life in Politics, op. cit.*, p. 11.
48 Rut BRANDT, *op. cit.*, p. 134; BRANDT, *Begegnungen, op. cit.*, pp. 32–3.
49 Edgar WOLFRUM, *Die Mauer: Geschichte einer Teilung*, Munich, 2009, p. 19. Figures in Bernd EISENFELD/Roger ENGELMANN, *13.8.1961: Mauerbau: Fluchtbewegung und Machtsicherung*, Berlin, 2001, p. 37; Edgar WOLFRUM, 'Die Mauer', in E. FRANÇOIS/H. SCHULZE (eds), *Deutsche Erinnerungsorte, Band 1*, Munich, 2001, pp. 552–68, p. 552.
50 BRANDT, *Begegnungen, op. cit.*, p. 9.
51 Ulbricht on 12.8.1961, cited in *FAZ*, 13.8.2007. Matthias UHL/Armin WAGNER (eds), *Ulbricht, Chruschtschow und die Mauer, eine Dokumentation*, Munich, 2003, p. 50.

52 Ulbricht, radio address on 15.6.1961.
53 Erich Honecker, *From My Life* (tr. Aus meinem Leben), Oxford, 1981.
54 Film cited in Wolfrum, Mauer, *op. cit.*, p. 55.
55 Uhl/Wagner, *op. cit.*, docs 34–42.
56 Reiner Marcowitz, *Option für Paris? Unionsparteien, SPD und Charles de Gaulle 1958 bis 1969*, Munich, 1996, p. 230; Andreas Wilkens, *Der unstete Nachbar: Frankreich und die deutsche Ostpolitik 1969–1974*, Munich, 1990, pp. 123–76.
57 Letter from Toulouse to Margerie, 24.9.1963, *Documents diplomatiques français 1963, Tome II (1er juillet–31 décembre)*, Bern, 2003 (hereafter *DDF 1963*), p. 330.
58 Rut Brandt, *op. cit.*, p. 142.
59 Brandt's notes on this meeting, *BA 3*, *op. cit.*, pp. 417–19.
60 Brandt, *My Life in Politics*, *op. cit.*, p. 60.
61 Buffet in Möller/Vaïsse, *op. cit.*, p. 59.
62 He said this openly to Brandt in 1965, although in 1963 he had claimed that the government of the FRG had not invited him to go to Berlin. Apart from members of the government, Brandt was the German politician who met de Gaulle most frequently, Marcowitz, *op. cit.*, p. 104.
63 Brandt's notes on this meeting, 24.4.1963, WBA, Reg. Bürgermeister, 74, also in *BA 3*, *op. cit.*, pp. 412–17, p. 415. Also in Brandt, *Begegnungen*, *op. cit.*, p. 136.
64 Note from Bahr to Brandt, 11.2.1963, AdsD, Fonds Bahr a, 173, also cited in Egon Bahr, *Zu meiner Zeit*, Munich, 1996, p. 172.

3 From Party Chairman to Foreign Minister

1 Thomas Mergel, *Propaganda nach Hitler. Eine Kulturgeschichte des Wahlkampfs in der Bundesrepublik 1949–1990*, Göttingen, 2010; Daniela Münkel, *Willy Brandt und die 'vierte Gewalt'. Politik und Massenmedien in den 50er bis 70er Jahren*, Frankfurt am Main, 2005; Anja Kruke, *Demoskopie in der Bundesrepublik Deutschland. Meinungsforschung, Parteien und Medien, 1949–1990*, Düsseldorf, 1997; Münkel, *Bemerkungen*, *op. cit.*, pp. 113–33, 161–85; Wienand Gellner, *Ideenagenturen für Politik und Öffentlichkeit. Think Tanks in den USA und in Deutschland*, Opladen, 1995.
2 Details in Lorenz, *Willy Brandt. Deutscher, Europäer*, *op. cit.*, pp. 118–21; Brandt, *Begegnungen*, *op. cit.*, p. 48; Mergel, *op. cit.*, pp. 289–96. Münkel, *Bemerkungen*, *op. cit.*, pp. 211–35.
3 One of the CDU's 1961 election posters showed a picture of Adenauer pointing his finger, with this phrase: 'Everything that has happened in Berlin since 13 August is the result of Khrushchev

deliberately helping the SPD and their candidate Willy Brandt, alias Frahm,' see SEEBACHER, *op. cit.*, p. 195.

4 STRAUSS, *op. cit.*, p. 397. The Stasi had given the CDU/CSU much 'useful material' on Brandt's past, Markus WOLF, *Spionagechef im geheimen Krieg, Erinnerungen*, Munich, 1997, p. 272; Hubertus KNABE, *Die unterwanderte Republik. Stasi im Westen*, Berlin, 2001.

5 Peter MERSEBURGER, *Rudolf Augstein. Biographie*, Munich, 2007, p. 209.

6 Cited in Egon BAHR, *Willy Brandt und die Nation*, Schriftenreihe der BWBS, 16, Berlin, 2008, p. 17.

7 Reproduced in LORENZ, *Willy Brandt. Deutscher, Europäer*, *op. cit.*, p. 120.

8 MERSEBURGER, *Augstein*, *op. cit.*, p. 208.

9 *BA 3*, *op. cit.*, p. 71.

10 BRANDT, *Koexistenz – Zwang zum Wagnis*, Stuttgart, 1963.

11 Brandt's speech at the Tutzing Evangelical Academy, 15.7.1963, *BA 3*, *op. cit.*, pp. 419–49, p. 435.

12 BRANDT, *My Life in Politics*, *op. cit.*, p. 63.

13 As told in BAHR, *Zu meiner Zeit*, *op. cit.*, pp. 155–7.

14 *Ibid.*, p. 162.

15 Interview for *Panorama* on the ARD channel, 30.12.1963.

16 SCHWARZ, *Springer*, *op. cit.*, p. 379.

17 *BA 3*, *op. cit.*, p. 72. In 1964, 89 per cent of West Berliners declared themselves satisfied with Brandt's politics and personality, *ibid.*, p. 70.

18 Jean Monnet Foundation, Brandt's interview with Hanns J. Küsters, 20.6.1983.

19 Gérard BOSSUAT in WILKENS, *Unité de l'Europe*, *op. cit.*, pp. 85–121; Eric ROUSSEL, *Jean Monnet*, Paris, 1996, p. 824.

20 Georges Pompidou, 8.5.1964, *Documents diplomatiques Français 1964, Tome I (1er janvier–30 juin)*, Bern, 2002, p. 488.

21 Press conference at the Élysée, 25.3.1959, *Documents diplomatiques Français 1959, Tome I (1er janvier–30 juin)*, Paris, 1994, docs 211 and 213.

22 HEIMANN in MÖLLER/VAÏSSE, *op. cit.*, p. 80

23 *BA 3*, *op. cit.*, pp. 459–69, p. 462.

24 Brandt, speech given at the Evangelische Akademie in Tutzing, 15.7.1963, *ibid.*, p. 421. On the evolution of the SPD see Beatrix BOUVIER, *Zwischen Godesberg und Großer Koalition. Der Weg der SPD in die Regierungsverantwortung. Außen-, sicherheits- und deutschlandpolitische Umorientierung und gesellschaftliche Öffnung der SPD 1960–1966*, Bonn, 1990.

25 Cited in BAHR, *Brandt und die Nation*, *op. cit.*, p. 32.

26 There is no family connection between Gerhard Schröder (1910–89), Christian Democrat, and Gerhard Schröder (1944–),

SPD, chancellor between 1998 and 2005. The elder Schröder was minister of the interior, of foreign affairs and then of defence between 1950 and 1960.

27 Klaus Schönhoven, *Wendejahre. Die Sozialdemokratie in der Zeit der Großen Koalition, 1966–1969*, Bonn, 2004, p. 41.

28 Interview with the British journalist Prittie, 21.8.1972, in *BA 4, op. cit.*, pp. 360–2.

29 He was succeeded as mayor of Berlin in October 1967 by his friend Heinrich Albertz, who until then was senator (i.e. minister of a city-state) of the interior, and then by Klaus Schütz.

30 Letter from Brandt to the party members in *Vorwärts*, 7.12.1966, reproduced in *BA 4, op. cit.*, pp. 392–95, p. 394.

31 On 7 November 1968, during the CDU congress in Berlin, the young woman slapped the Chancellor 'in the name of the 50 million people who died in the war', as a public denunciation of his Nazi past.

32 Eugen Kogon, 'Das Recht auf den politischen Irrtum', *Frankfurter Hefte* 2 (1947), pp. 641–55, p. 655.

33 For details on the Brandt's worries about Peter, see Rut Brandt, *op. cit.*, pp. 181–204. On the subject of generational conflict in the labour movement see Klaus Schönhoven/Bernd Braun (eds), *Generationen in der Arbeiterbewegung*, Munich, 2005.

34 Brandt's notes from their meeting on 2.6.1965, *BA 3, op. cit.*, pp. 480–6, p. 483.

35 Maurice Vaïsse in Möller/Vaïsse, *op. cit.*, p. 112.

36 François Seydoux, *Dans l'intimité franco-allemande. Une mission diplomatique*, Paris, 1977, pp. 91–2.

37 Klaus Hildebrandt in Möller/Vaïsse, *op. cit.*, p. 120. See also Henning Türk, *Europapolitik der Großen Koalition 1966–1969*, Munich, 2006. For a more positive analysis, see Claudia Hiepel in Wilkens, *Unité de l'Europe, op. cit.*, pp. 213–29.

38 Michel in Rother, *Außenpolitik, op. cit.*, p. 124. In his notes after a meeting with Nixon in 1971, in which they had discussed Vietnam, Brandt wrote: 'Other people's advice, annoyingly, was not welcome', Brandt, *Erinnerungen, op. cit.*, p. 399.

39 Lorenz, *Willy Brandt. Deutscher, Europäer, op. cit.*, p. 147; Brandt, *Begegnungen, op. cit.*, pp. 183–4.

40 Peter Bender, *Die 'Neue Ostpolitik' und ihre Folgen vom Mauerbau bis zur Vereinigung*, Munich, 1996, pp. 138–47.

41 Schönhoven, *Wendejahre, op. cit.*, p. 668.

42 *Ibid.*, p. 486.

43 Mergel, *op. cit.*, pp. 162–70; *BA 4, op. cit.*, p. 56.

44 Kurt Sontheimer, *So war Deutschland nie: Anmerkungen zur politischen Kultur der Bundesrepublik*, Munich, 1999, pp. 134–5; Münkel, *Bemerkungen, op. cit.*, pp. 187–209.

45 Arnulf BARING, *Machtwechsel. Die Ära Brandt-Scheel*, Stuttgart, 1982, p. 194.
46 *Ibid.*, p. 175. See an interview Brandt gave on live television, 28.9.1969, in Willy BRANDT, *Berliner Ausgabe, Band 7: Mehr Demokratie wagen. Innen- und Gesellschaftspolitik 1966–1974*, ed. Wolther von KIESERITZKY, Bonn, 2001 (hereafter *BA 7*), pp. 197–200.
47 BAHR, *Zu meiner Zeit*, *op. cit.*, p. 270; BAHR, *'Das musst Du erzählen'*, *op. cit.*, p. 73.
48 MERSEBURGER, *Brandt*, *op. cit.*, p. 581
49 Cited in *Der Spiegel*, 27.10.1969. Also in BRANDT, *My Life in Politics*, *op. cit.*, p. 250, and BRANDT, *Begegnungen*, *op. cit.*, p. 296.
50 *L'Express*, 27.10.1969. On the evolution of Brandt's image in French public opinion, see Rachèle RAUS in WILKENS, *Unité de l'Europe*, *op. cit.*, pp. 187–210.
51 Cited in HUSSON in MÖLLER/VAÏSSE, *op. cit.*, p. 216.

4 The Chancellor of Ostpolitik

1 BAHR, *Zu meiner Zeit*, *op. cit.*, p. 275.
2 Ernst Friedländer had been president of the European Movement and of the German section of the Union of European Federalists (UEF) during the 1950s. See Katharina FOCKE, 'Erinnerungen an Jean Monnet', in Andreas WILKENS (ed.), *Interessen verbinden. Jean Monnet und die europäische Integration der Bundesrepublik Deutschland*, Bonn, 1999, pp. 23–30.
3 As told in BAHR, *Brandt und die Nation*, *op. cit.*, p. 20.
4 Pierre DE VILLEMAREST, *Polyarnik. Histoire d'un chef d'État, espion épisodique de Moscou*, Paris, 1999.
5 BAHR, *'Das musst Du erzählen'*, *op. cit.*, p. 33.
6 *BA 2*, *op. cit.*, p. 238; STÜWE, *op. cit.*, pp. 163–80. For the reaction of the French ambassador in Bonn: François Seydoux de Clausonne to Maurice Schumann, 29.10.1969, *Documents diplomatiques français 1969, Tome II (1er juillet–31 décembre)*, Bern, 2013, pp. 682–6.
7 Statement on 28.10.1969, in STÜWE, *op. cit.*, pp. 163–80.
8 Cited in BAHR, *Zu meiner Zeit*, *op. cit.*, p. 289.
9 BAHR, *'Das musst Du erzählen'*, *op. cit.*, p. 97.
10 Letter from Dönhoff to Brandt, 1.12.1970, WBA, 4; Marion Gräfin DÖNHOFF, *Weit ist der Weg nach Osten. Berichte und Betrachtungen aus fünf Jahrzehnten*, Munich, 1988, p. 207, p. 213.
11 Gérard SAINT-PAUL, *L'agenouillement au ghetto*, Paris, 2012, pp. 9–12.
12 Cited in Richard VON WEIZSÄCKER, *Vier Zeiten*, Berlin, 2002, p. 212, who agrees with the analysis. Similarly phrased in *Der Spiegel*, 14.12.1970.

13 Rut BRANDT, *op. cit.*, p. 244; BAHR, *Zu meiner Zeit, op. cit.*, p. 341; BAHR, *'Das musst Du erzählen', op. cit.*, p. 105.
14 Martin KÖLBEL (ed.), *Willy Brandt und Günter Grass. Der Briefwechsel*, Göttingen, 2013.
15 BRANDT, *My Life in Politics, op. cit.*, p. 200. He had already explained to the Herzl Institute in New York in 1961 that no reparation would be ever be able to atone for the abominable crimes committed in the German people's name, in Willy BRANDT, *Im Zweifel für die Freiheit. Reden zur demokratischen und deutschen Geschichte*, ed. Klaus SCHÖNHOVEN, Bonn, 2012, pp. 704–16.
16 *Der Spiegel*, 14.12.1970. For other reactions see Alexander BEHRENS (ed.), *'Durfte Brandt knien?' Der Kniefall in Warschau und der deutsche-polnische Vertrag. Eine Dokumentation der Meinungen*, Bonn, 2010, pp. 108–10.
17 WILKENS, *Der unstete Nachbar, op. cit.*, pp. 70–8.
18 BRANDT, *My Life in Politics, op. cit.*, p. 211; BRANDT, *Begegnungen, op. cit.*, pp. 490–3; Rut BRANDT, *op. cit.*, p. 244.
19 Brandt's report on the meeting, 19.3.1970, in Willy BRANDT, *Berliner Ausgabe, Band 6: Ein Volk der guten Nachbarn. Außen- und Deutschlandpolitik 1966–1974*, ed. Frank FISCHER, Bonn, 2005 (hereafter *BA 6*), pp. 281–8.
20 Archive of the State Security Services of the GDR – Bundesbeauftragten für die Stasi-Unterlagen, Berlin, www.bstu.bund.de (hereafter BStU), Z 1832, MfS, Sekr. d. Min., cited in SEEBACHER, *op. cit.*, p. 220.
21 Cited in Ulrich VÖLKLEIN, *Honecker. Eine Biographie*, Berlin, 2003, p. 291.
22 Eckard MICHELS, *Guillaume, der Spion. Eine deutsch-deutsche Karriere*, Berlin, 2013, p. 114.
23 MERSEBURGER, *Brandt, op. cit.*, p. 606. For Brandt's image in the GDR, see Christoph KLESSMANN in Bernd ROTHER (ed.), *Willy Brandt. Neue Fragen, neue Erkenntnisse*, Bonn, 2011, pp. 34–5. Brandt's report on the meeting, 21.5.1970, *BA 6, op. cit.*, pp. 309–15.
24 Georges-Henri SOUTOU in MÖLLER/VAÏSSE, *op. cit.*, p. 136; WILKENS, *Der unstete Nachbar, op. cit.*
25 Henry KISSINGER, *White House Years*, New York, 1979, p. 530.
26 *FAZ*, 25.1.2000, cited in MERSEBURGER, *Brandt, op. cit.*, p. 625. According to P. Winand, Kissinger gave the great power countries like France favourable treatment in comparison to 'little' Germany, in WILKENS, *Unité de l'Europe, op. cit.*, pp. 385–6.
27 15.6.1971, in *Foreign Relations of the United States, 1969–1976, Vol. 40*, ed. D.C. GEYER, Washington, 2008 (hereafter *FRUS*), p. 741.
28 BRANDT, *My Life in Politics, op. cit.*, p. 177.
29 SOUTOU in MÖLLER/VAÏSSE, *op. cit.*, p. 128.

30 Du Reau in Wilkens, *Unité de l'Europe, op. cit.*, pp. 391–400.
31 Brandt had paid tribute to Stresemann and Rathenau as inspirational role models for foreign affairs, in 1967 and 1968, speech in Brandt, *Im Zweifel, op. cit.*, pp. 594–613 and pp. 614–30.
32 *Time* magazine, 4.1.1971.
33 Hans-Peter Schwarz, in Möller/Vaïsse, *op. cit.*, p. 160.
34 Lorenz, *Willy Brandt. Deutscher, Europäer, op. cit.*, p. 167; Merseburger, *Brandt, op. cit.*, pp. 640–1.
35 Schwarz, *Springer, op. cit.*, p. 488 and pp. 508–33.
36 Weizsäcker, *op. cit.*, pp. 215–17.
37 On his secretarial office, see Merseburger, *Brandt, op. cit.*, pp. 595–6.
38 These were Barzel's words to Schmidt, Helmut Schmidt, *Weggefährten. Erinnerungen und Reflexionen*, Berlin, 1996, p. 512.
39 Strauss, *op. cit.*, p. 444.
40 Merseburger, *Brandt, op. cit.*, pp. 689–90; Wolf, *op. cit.*, p. 261; *Die Spiegel*, 27.11.2000; *Bild Zeitung* published the 'Rosenstock dossier', which implicated Wagner, on 2.8.2000; Andreas Grau, 'Auf der Suche nach den fehlenden Stimmen 1972', *Historich-Politische Mitteilungen*, 16 (2009); Baring, *op. cit.*, pp. 580–9.
41 Bahr, *Zu meiner Zeit, op. cit.*, p. 358.
42 *Ibid.*, p. 406.
43 *Ibid.*, p. 424.
44 The German phrase is more striking: 'über ein geregeltes Nebeneinander zu einem Miteinander zu kommen', 28.10.1969, in Stüwe, *op. cit.*, p. 164.
45 Strauss, *op. cit.*, pp. 449–55.
46 Claudia Hiepel, *Willy Brandt und Georges Pompidou, Deutsch-französische Europapolitik zwischen Aufbruch und Krise*, Munich, 2012; Loth in Rother, *Neue Fragen, op. cit.*, pp. 114–34; Wilkens in Möller/Vaïsse, *op. cit.*, p. 199: meeting between Brandt and Pompidou, 30.1.1970, AN, 5 AG 2, 104.
47 Letter from Brandt to Pompidou, 27.11.1969, in F. Eibl and H. Zummerman (eds), *Akten zur Auswärtigen Politik der Bundesrepublik Deutschland, 1969, Band 2*, Munich, 2000 (hereafter *AAPD* 1969, II), doc. 380.
48 Willy Brandt, *Verbrecher und andere Deutsche. Ein Bericht aus Deutschland 1946*, Bonn, 2007, p. 347.
49 Brandt, *Begegnungen, op. cit.*, p. 345; Meeting with Pompidou 25.1.1971, Archives nationales, Paris (hereafter AN), 5 AG 2, 105.
50 Wilkens in Möller/Vaïsse, *op. cit.*, p. 203. Brandt saw Great Britain as 'an element of democratic stability in our Europe', notes for a speech he gave on 28.6.1965, cited by Hiepel in Wilkens, *Unité de l'Europe, op. cit.*, p. 216. It was also important to keep the anglophile countries of the EEC happy, p. 223.

51 BOSSUAT in *ibid.*, pp. 85–121; WILKENS in *ibid.*, pp. 247–82; Jean MONNET, *Mémoires*, Paris, 1976, p. 582; *DDF* 1969, II; *AAPD* 1969, II.
52 RÜCKER in MÖLLER/VAÏSSE, *op. cit.*, p. 182; BRANDT, *Begegnungen*, *op. cit.*, p. 321; Guido THIEMEYER in WILKENS, *Unité de l'Europe*, *op. cit.*, pp. 231–45.
53 WILKENS in MÖLLER/VAÏSSE, *op. cit.*, p. 209.
54 Brandt rekindled the discussion about the monetary question with Pompidou. His role is now well known, BOSSUAT in WILKENS, *Unité de l'Europe*, *op. cit.*, p. 95. On his role in the political aspects of the European project see *ibid.*, pp. 101–9. On his suggestions regarding social policy see Sylvain SCHIRMANN in *ibid.*, pp. 311–23.
55 LOTH in ROTHER, *Neue Fragen*, *op. cit.*, p. 132.
56 'Mrs. Meir Greets Brandt as a Fighter against Nazism', Jewish Telegraphic Agency, 8 June 1973, available at www.jta.org/1973/06/08/archive/mrs-meir-greets-brandt-as-a-fighter-against-nazism (accessed 11 August 2016).
57 Excerpts from his speech at the Bundestag on his return from Israel, 18.6.1973, in *BA 6*, *op. cit.*, pp. 484–5.
58 On his foreign policy difficulties, see SOUTOU in MÖLLER/VAÏSSE, *op. cit.*, p. 149. On the Year of Europe, see Pascaline WINAND in WILKENS, *Unité de l'Europe*, *op. cit.*, pp. 367–90.
59 Cited by Klaus HARPPRECHT, *Im Kanzleramt. Tagebuch der Jahre mit Willy Brandt*, Hamburg, 2000, p. 375.

5 'Dare More Democracy' or a Difficult Promise

1 Letter from Brandt to Günter Gaus, 15.2.1971, WBA A 8/6.
2 Statement partially reproduced in *BA 7*, *op. cit.*, pp. 218–24.
3 STRAUSS, *op. cit.*, p. 538.
4 He admitted this during an interview with the radio station Südwestfunk, 30.12.1969, WBA, A 3, 330. On Grass, see *BA 7*, *op. cit.*, p. 46.
5 Peter BRANDT in Horst EHMKE, *Reformpolitik und 'Zivilgesellschaft'*, Schriftenreihe der BWBS 9, Berlin, 2001, p. 14. Grass wrote about his relationship with the Chancellor in his novel *From the Diary of a Snail*. On modernisation see Axel SCHILDT/Detlef SIEGFRIED/Karl-Christian LAMMERS (eds), *Dynamische Zeiten. Die 60er Jahre in den beiden deutschen Gesellschaften*, Hamburg, 2000.
6 Speech to the Tutzing Evangelical Academy, 13.7.1971, *BA 7*, *op. cit.*, pp. 272–82.
7 *BA 7*, *op. cit.*, p. 48. For a full list of the reforms announced see MERSEBURGER, *Brandt*, *op. cit.*, p. 580.

8 Ralf Dahrendorf, *Bildung ist Bürgerrecht. Plädoyer für eine alternative Bildungspolitik*, Hamburg, 1965.

9 And 3–4 per cent in 1950, Axel Schildt, *Moderne Zeiten. Freizeit, Massenmedien und Zeitgeist in der Bundesrepublik der 50er Jahre*, Hamburg, 1995, p. 60.

10 He spoke privately on the subject to Helmut Kohl, for example: Helmut Kohl, *Erinnerungen 1990–1994*, Munich, 2007, p. 485.

11 Gabriele Metzler, *Konzeptionen politischen Handelns von Adenauer bis Brandt. Politische Planung in der pluralistischen Gesellschaft*, Paderborn, 2005.

12 Brandt mentioned the difficulty he was having controlling internal conflict in a note on 3.3.1972, *BA 7*, *op. cit.*, pp. 299–301.

13 *Ibid.*, p. 40.

14 Willy Brandt, *Über den Tag hinaus. Eine Zwischenbilanz*, Hamburg, 1974, p. 110. He had already said something similar in his speech to the SPD regional congress in 1954, *BA 4*, *op. cit.*, pp. 150–76. On Bernstein, see Thomas Meyer, *Bernsteins konstruktiver Sozialismus. Eduard Bernsteins Beitrag zur Theorie des Sozialismus*, Bad Godesberg, 1977; Klaus Schönhoven, Introduction to Brandt, *Im Zweifel*, *op. cit.*, pp. 7–62.

15 Hofmann, *op. cit.*, p. 139.

16 Schönhoven, Introduction to Brandt, *Im Zweifel*, *op. cit.*, p. 33; Rudolph in Willy Brandt, *Berliner Ausgabe, Band 5: Die Partei der Freiheit. Willy Brandt und die SPD 1972–1992*, ed. Karsten Rudolph, Bonn, 2002 (hereafter *BA 5*), pp. 17–20. Source *Jahrbuch der SPD, vol. 1958–1959*, p. 267; *vol. 1968–1969*, p. 258; *vol. 1973–1975*, p. 269.

17 *BA 4*, *op. cit.*, p. 60.

18 The Federal Constitutional Court confirmed the constitutionality of the decree on 22.5.1975, evoking the particular importance of loyalty for people working in the public sector.

19 Hélène Miard-Delacroix in Möller/Vaïsse, *op. cit.*, pp. 231–45.

20 Brandt's last wife, Brigitte Seebacher, paints a bitter picture of Mitterrand in her memoirs, Seebacher, *op. cit.*, pp. 27–40.

21 Hubert Vedrine, *Les Mondes de François Mitterrand*, Paris, 1996, p. 126.

22 Alfred Gottwaldt, *Salonwagen 10205. Von der Schiene ins Museum*, Bonn, 1997.

23 *BA 5*, *op. cit.*, p. 20.

24 The exact figure is 91.1 per cent. For details of the results and congratulations, see Brandt, *Begegnungen*, *op. cit.*, p. 577.

25 He gave instructions via notes addressed to Wehner and Schmidt, reproduced in *BA 7*, *op. cit.*, pp. 384–404; Baring, *op. cit.*, pp. 509–12. On these arrangements, see Merseburger, *Brandt*, *op.*

cit., p. 659; Harmut SOELL, *Helmut Schmidt, Vol. 2: Macht und Verantwortung*, Munich, 2008, p. 197.

26 MERSEBURGER, *Brandt*, *op. cit.*, p. 659.

27 BAHR, *Zu meiner Zeit*, *op. cit.*, p. 218; Rut BRANDT, *op. cit.*, p. 192; BAHR, *'Das musst Du erzählen'*, *op. cit.*, p. 131. According to Schmidt, we can only understand Brandt if we recognise the importance of this aspect of him, HOFMANN, *op. cit.*, p. 12.

28 *Der Spiegel*, 8.10.1973.

29 Cited in BAHR, *'Das musst Du erzählen'*, *op. cit.*, p. 151.

30 *Der Spiegel*, 10.12.1973.

31 MERSEBURGER, *Augstein*, *op. cit.*, p. 449.

32 MERSEBURGER, *Brandt*, *op. cit.*, p. 658.

33 MICHELS, *op. cit.*, pp. 12–60; Günter GUILLAUME, *Die Aussage. Wie es wirklich war*, Munich, 1990, p. 74.

34 MICHELS, *op. cit.*, pp. 99–100; Horst EHMKE, *Mittendrin. Von der Großen Koalition zur Deutschen Einheit*, Berlin, 1994, p. 232.

35 Ingrid KERZ-RÜHLING/Thomas PLÄNKERS, *Verräter oder Verführte. Eine psychoanalytische Untersuchung Inoffizieller Mitarbeiter der Stasi*, Berlin, 2004.

36 Details in MICHELS, *op. cit.*, pp. 140–220.

37 Hans-Dietrich GENSCHER, *Erinnerungen*, Berlin, 1995, p. 197.

38 Brandt's memos from 24 April to 6 May, in *BA 7*, *op. cit.*, pp. 508–37, p. 512.

39 *Ibid.*, pp. 520–1. Brandt suspected that Wehner and Honecker had formed an alliance to try and oust him. On the week leading up to his resignation, see SEEBACHER, *op. cit.*, pp. 270–82, and on their suspicions of collusion between Wehner and Honecker, pp. 237–82.

40 Letter from Bauhaus to Brandt, 10.5.1974, WBA, B25, 172, reproduced in SEEBACHER, *op. cit.*, p. 278.

41 Schmidt has often confirmed this. HOFMANN, *op. cit.*, p. 11; BARING, *op. cit.*, pp. 748–55.

42 SEEBACHER, *op. cit.*, p. 280.

43 BStU website; Helmut MÜLLER-ENSBERG, *'Rosenholz'. Eine Quellenkritik*, Berlin, 2007.

44 Hermann SCHREIBER, *Kanzlersturz. Warum Willy Brandt zurücktrat*, Munich, 2003.

45 Televised statement, 8.5.1974, *BA 7*, *op. cit.*, pp. 538–40.

6 After Power

1 MERSEBURGER, *Brandt*, *op. cit.*, p. 740; BAHR, *'Das musst Du erzählen'*, *op. cit.*, p. 161.

2 Rut BRANDT, *op. cit.*, p. 272.

3 *Ibid.*, p. 271.

4 He was elected president of the Socialist International in 1976, president of the North–South Commission in 1977 and member of the European Parliament in the first direct elections in 1979.
5 Meeting with Brezhnev, Willy BRANDT, *Berliner Ausgabe, Band 8: Über Europa hinaus. Dritte Welt und Sozialistische Internationale*, ed. Bernd ROTHER and Wolfgang SCHMIDT, Bonn, 2006 (hereafter *BA 8*), pp. 131–3. Analysis in BRANDT, *Begegnungen, op. cit.*, pp. 630–3.
6 On this financial support, see *ibid.*, pp. 629–35; Bernd ROTHER in WILKENS, *Unité de l'Europe, op. cit.*, pp. 403–14; also in ROTHER, *Außenpolitik, op. cit.*, p. 279; MERSBURGER, *Brandt, op. cit.*, pp. 748–51.
7 These were: liberation of political prisoners, freedom of press and freedom of assembly, abolition of 'anti-terrorist' laws, and freedom to establish unions and political parties, BRANDT, *Begegnungen, op. cit.*, p. 631 and p. 634.
8 On Brandt and González, see ROTHER in WILKENS, *Unité de l'Europe, op. cit.*, p. 409.
9 The different topics were organised into three groups called 'baskets'. The second basket, not mentioned here, dealt with European cooperation between the two blocs. The conference was attended by 35 states, including the United States, Canada, the USSR, and all the European states except Albania and Andorra. On Brandt and the CSCE, see DU REAU in WILKENS, *Unité de l'Europe, op. cit.*, pp. 391–400.
10 *BA 8, op. cit.*, p. 98.
11 Discussion in Vienna, 24.5.1975, Willy BRANDT/Bruno KREISKY/Olof PALME, *Briefe und Gespräche 1972 bis 1975*, Frankfurt am Main, 1975, pp. 131–3. See also *BA 8, op. cit.*, p. 28.
12 Brandt's speech at the Caracas conference, 23.5.1976, *BA 8, op. cit.*, pp. 141–9.
13 Details in ROTHER in ROTHER, *Außenpolitik, op. cit.*, pp. 310–20.
14 Speech in Geneva, 26.11.1976, *BA 8, op. cit.*, pp. 161–77.
15 ROTHER in ROTHER, *Außenpolitik, op. cit.*, p. 323.
16 Helmut SCHMIDT, *Die Deutschen und ihre Nachbarn*, Berlin, 1990, pp. 242–52; BRANDT, *My Life in Politics, op. cit.*, p. 491; also see *Le Monde, Le Figaro, France Soir, Le Quotidien, Aurore*, 20.1.1976.
17 Interview with Brandt for ARD, Tagesschau, 18.1.1976, and Deutschlandfunk, 19.1.1976. Interview with Schmidt for Deutsches Fernsehen, Tagesschau, 19.1.1976. Press conference at Helsingør, 19.1.1976 and SPD press and communications bulletin, 20.1.1976.
18 Working dinner for Brandt and Mitterrand, 26.3.1976, WBA, F, 17.
19 Letter from Brandt to Mitterrand, 13.11.1978, WBA, F, 17; details in MIARD-DELACROIX in MÖLLER/VAÏSSE, *op. cit.*, pp. 231–45.

20 *BA 5*, *op. cit.*, pp. 21–2. He had always struggled with opposition, Schönhoven, Introduction to Brandt, *Im Zweifel*, *op. cit.*, p. 38.
21 SPD press and communications bulletin, 7.4.1976.
22 Speech on 11.4.1975, in Brandt, *Im Zweifel*, *op. cit.*, pp. 140–6.
23 His meetings with Lafontaine are quoted in Merseburger, *Brandt*, *op. cit.*, p. 774.
24 Seebacher, *op. cit.*, p. 11.
25 Interview in Merseburger, *Brandt*, *op. cit.*, p. 776.
26 *BA 8*, *op. cit.*, p. 35; Seebacher, *op. cit.*, p. 13.
27 Details in *BA 8*, *op. cit.*, pp. 18–20. The documents in this volume reflect Brandt's intense international activity after 1974.
28 The 'Brandt Report', or Independent Commission on International Development, *North–South: A Programme for Survival. The Report of the Independent Commission on International Development Issues under the Chairmanship of Willy Brandt*, London, 1980, was translated into 21 languages.
29 Brandt's opening speech at the Commission's first meeting in Bonn, 9.12.1977, *BA 8*, *op. cit.*, pp. 209–13, here p. 212.
30 Willy Brandt, *Der organisierte Wahnsinn. Wettrüsten und Welthunger*, Cologne, 1985.
31 Letter reproduced in *BA 8*, *op. cit.*, pp. 465–8.
32 Correspondence between Brandt and Reagan, cited by Michel in Rother, *Außenpolitik*, *op. cit.*, p. 148.
33 Hofmann, *op. cit.*, p. 13.
34 Speech in Berlin, 4.4.1981, *BA 5*, *op. cit.*, pp. 336–48, p. 343. On the effects of the Euromissiles crisis on the SPD, see Bernd Faulenbach, *Das sozialdemokratische Jahrzehnt. Von der Reformeuphorie zur neuen Unübersichtlichkeit. Die SPD 1969–1982*, Bonn, 2011, pp. 709–23.
35 Interview in *Der Spiegel*, 14.1.1980.
36 Ulrich Lappenküper, *Mitterrand und Deutschland. Die enträtselte Sphinx*, Munich, 2011, pp. 141–4.
37 PS manifesto, 24.1.1981, and 110 proposals for France in François Mitterrand, *Politique II*, Paris, 1981, pp. 305–13, pp. 313–24.
38 Pierre Melandri in Serge Berstein/Pierre Milza/Jean-Louis Bianco, *François Mitterrand. Les années du changement 1981–1984*, Paris, pp. 220–52.
39 Hélène Miard-Delacroix in *ibid.*, pp. 295–311.
40 W. Biermann's note, 6.12.1982, WBA, SPD-Parteivorsitz, 109.
41 *BA 5*, *op. cit.*, p. 51.
42 Lappenküper in Möller/Vaïsse, *op. cit.*, pp. 267–8. This positive attitude towards Jaruzelski and the refusal to meet Lech Walesa, who would receive the Nobel Peace Prize in 1983, are among the SPD leadership's mistakes and failures. Summary and footnotes in Willy Brandt, *Berliner Ausgabe, Band 10: Gemeinsame Sicherheit.*

Internationale Beziehungen und deutsche Frage 1982–1992, ed. Uwe Mai/Bernd Rother/Wolfgang Schmidt, Bonn, 2009 (hereafter *BA 10*), pp. 44–53; *BA 8*, *op. cit.*, p. 40.
43 Hélène Miard-Delacroix, *Partenaires de choix. Le chancelier Schmidt et la France, 1974–1982*, Bern, 1993; Matthias Waechter, *Helmut Schmidt und Valéry Giscard d'Estaing. Auf der Suche nach Stabilität in der Krise der 70er Jahre*, Bremen, 2011.
44 Helmut Kohl, *Erinnerungen 1982–1990*, Munich, 2005, pp. 21–2.
45 18.11.1982, WBA, A3, 895; *BA 5*, *op. cit.*, pp. 393–405.
46 Hofmann, *op. cit.*, p. 20.
47 Miard-Delacroix in Andreas Schulz (ed.), *Parlamentarische Kulturen in Europa – das Parlament als Kommunikationsraum*, Berlin, 2012, pp. 177–93; Miard-Delacroix in Antoine Mares and Marie-Pierre Rey (eds), *Mémoires et émotions. Au cœur de l'histoire des relations internationales*, Paris, 2014, pp. 55–64.
48 Brandt on 5.5.1983, *BA 10*, *op. cit.*, pp. 130–6, Mitterrand in Brussels, 13.10.1983, 'Le pacifism est à l'ouest et les euromissiles sont à l'est', available at www.ina.fr/video/I09082528 (accessed 25.5.2016).
49 Hofmann, *op. cit.*, p. 223.
50 *Ibid.*, p. 9.
51 Matthias Micus, *Die 'Enkel' Willy Brandts. Aufstieg und Politikstil einer SPD-Generation*, Frankfurt am Main, 2005.
52 Speeches in Brandt, *Im Zweifel*, *op. cit*: 15.6.1979 in Munich, pp. 300–16; 9.9.1982 in Bonn, pp. 317–36; 30.1.1983 in Berlin, pp. 242–51; 19.3.1983 in Berlin, pp. 252–64.
53 At the Berlin-Plötzensee memorial, 19.7.1955, in *ibid.*, pp. 337–44; at Ahrensburg, 16.1.1985, pp. 363–74.
54 Statement, 30.6.1986, *BA 5*, *op. cit.*, pp. 423–7.
55 SPD Press Office, Funk, TV 340/86, 20.6.1986.
56 Speech at the Munich Kammerspiele, 18.11.1984, *BA 10*, *op. cit.*, p. 195.
57 Wilfried Loth in Wilkens, *Unité de l'Europe*, *op. cit.*, p. 419. Report of their meeting on 27.5.1985 in *BA 10*, *op. cit.*, pp. 219–30. The two men became friendly and wrote to one another regularly, WBA, A9, 10, e.g. 26.8.1985 and 20.1.1986. Mikhail Gorbachev, *Memoirs*, trans. Georges Peronansky and Tatjana Varsavsky, London, 1997, p. 551.
58 Siegfried Suckut, 'Willy Brandt in der DDR', *Jahrbuch für historische Kommunismusforschung*, 16 (2008), pp. 170–82.
59 Michels, *op. cit.*, p. 185. Note on his meeting with Honecker, 19.9.1985, *BA 10*, *op. cit.*, pp. 256–8; Wolfgang Krieger and Jürgen Weber (eds), *Spionage für den Frieden? Nachrichtendienste in Deutschland während des Kalten Krieges*, Munich, 1997.
60 Münkel, *Bemerkungen*, *op. cit.*, p. 239.

61 Statement on 23.3.1987, *BA 5, op. cit.*, pp. 446–51; BRANDT, *My Life in Politics, op. cit.*, p. 338; MERSEBURGER, *Brandt, op. cit.*, pp. 799–802.
62 KOHL, *1982–1990, op. cit.*, pp. 537–8.
63 Speech published in Willy BRANDT, *Die Abschiedsrede*, Berlin, 1987, here p. 13.
64 HOFMANN, *op. cit.*, p. 195 and p. 221; *BA 5, op. cit.*, p. 448.
65 WEIZSÄCKER, *op. cit.*, p. 450.

7 The End of the Story?

1 Brandt at a hearing for Members of the US Congress in Washington, 29.9.1983, *BA 10, op. cit.*, pp. 157–71, p. 170. He imagined a possible rapprochement between the two Germanys in the future, but 'would leave it to the next generation'.
2 Brandt agreed to the exchange of experts in March 1983. The SPD was represented by the Friedrich Ebert Foundation. Letter from Brandt to Honecker, 9.3.1983, *BA 10, op. cit.*, p. 129. See also the summary in *ibid.*, pp. 34–5. The opposition noted 130 such meetings between 1982 and 1988, KOHL, *1982–1990, op. cit.*, p. 539.
3 *Ibid.*, p. 973; and KOHL, *1990–1994, op. cit.*, p. 78 and p. 111.
4 Silke JANSEN, 'Zwei deutsche Staaten – zwei deutsche Nationen? Meinungsbilder zur deutschen Frage im Zeitablauf', *Deutschland Archiv*, 22/x (1989), pp. 1132–43.
5 Speech to the Bundestag, 1.9.1989, in Willy BRANDT, *'... was zusammengehört'. Reden zu Deutschland*, Bonn, 1990, pp. 15–21; SEEBACHER, *op. cit.*, p. 289.
6 *BA 10, op. cit.*, p. 41.
7 This became clear at their congress on 24.2.1990, where the SDP renamed itself as the SPD.
8 Meeting with Gorbachev, 17.10.1989, *BA 10, op. cit.*, pp. 369–79, p. 377.
9 Deutscher Bundestag, 174th sitting, 9.11.1989, p. 13221.
10 SEEBACHER, *op. cit.*, p. 296. Brandt told the story in a speech on 1.2.1992, in *'... was zusammengehört', op. cit.*, pp. 147–8.
11 *Ibid.*
12 Message from Gorbachev to Brandt, 10.11.1989, *BA 10, op. cit.*, pp. 391–2.
13 Interview in *Stern*, 7.12.1989; SEEBACHER, *op. cit.*, p. 304.
14 Speech to the Berlin congress, 18.12.1989, *BA 10, op. cit.*, p. 419.
15 LAPPENKÜPER in MÖLLER/VAÏSSE, *op. cit.*, p. 274.
16 *Die Zeit*, 17.11.1989. On Mitterrand and reunification, see two opposing views in Frédéric Bozo, *Mitterrand, la fin d la guerre*

froide et l'unification allemande: De Yalta à Maastricht, Paris, 2005, and LAPPENKÜPER, *op. cit.*, pp. 259–302.

17 He said this in an interview with Deutschlandfunk, 20.5.1985, *BA 10, op. cit.*, pp. 215–18.

18 Jacques ATTALI, *Verbatim III, 1988–1991,* Paris, 1995, pp. 368–70 and p. 377. In German the word is *Neuvereinigung,* a term Brandt used after unification, SCHÖNHOVEN, Introduction to BRANDT, *Im Zweifel, op. cit.*, p. 50.

19 Speech in Rostock, 6.12.1989, WBA, A3, 1064.

20 Speech to the Berlin congress, 18.12.1989, *BA 10, op. cit.*, pp. 417–24; SEEBACHER, *op. cit.*, pp. 308–14.

21 Letter from Brandt to Grass, 24.8.1990, *BA 10, op. cit.*, p. 456.

22 Cited in SEEBACHER, *op. cit.*, pp. 317–19, note 64.

23 *BA 10, op. cit.*, pp. 87–91.

24 Oskar LAFONTAINE, *Das Herz schlägt links,* Berlin, 1999, p. 32.

25 KOHL, *1990–1994, op. cit.*, pp. 241–2.

26 Egon BAHR in WILKENS, *Unité de l'Europe, op. cit.*, p. 25.

27 SCHÖNHOVEN, Introduction to BRANDT, *Im Zweifel, op. cit.*, p. 37.

28 SEEBACHER, *op. cit.*, p. 329.

29 *Ibid.*, pp. 348–76.

30 *Le Monde,* 17.3.1992.

31 Interview in Oriana FALLACI, *Intervista con la Storia,* Milan, 1985, p. 353; Andreas WILKENS in WILKENS, *Unité de l'Europe, op. cit.*, pp. 11–17, p. 15.

32 *BA 1, op. cit.*, p. 428.

33 Draft speech, 17.11.1966, WBA, publizistische Äußerungen, 243.

34 Article in the *New York Times,* 29.4.1973; SPD press release, 29.3.1984, *BA 10, op. cit.*, pp. 175–7.

35 Speech in Beijing, 30.5.1984, *BA 10, op. cit.*, pp. 178–86.

36 'Préserver les droits de notre people, construire l'Europe, garantir la paix par une détente sans illusions', cited in BAHR in WILKENS, *Unité de l'Europe, op. cit.*, pp. 19–34, p. 25; STÜWE, *op. cit.*, pp. 148–60.

37 WILKENS in WILKENS, *Unité de l'Europe, op. cit.,*, pp. 247–82, p. 248.

38 HIEPEL in WILKENS. *Unité de l'Europe, op. cit.,* pp. 215–16.

39 Speech in *BA 10, op. cit.*, pp. 533–47. For commentary see WILKENS in WILKENS, *Unité de l'Europe, op. cit.*, pp. 11–17, p. 12.

40 KOHL, *1990–1994, op. cit.*, pp. 486–7.

41 SAINT-PAUL, *op. cit.*, pp. 109–10.

Bibliography

Archives

Archive of Social Democracy – Archiv der sozialen Demokratie, Friedrich Ebert Foundation, Bonn (AdsD).

Archive of the State Security Services of the GDR –Bundesbeauftragten für die Stasi-Unterlagen des Staatssicherheitsdienstes der ehemaligen DDR), Berlin (BStU).

Archives Nationales, Pierrefit (AN).

Forum Willy Brandt, Berlin, run by the Federal Chancellor Willy Brandt Foundation (BWBS).

Jean Monnet Foundation.

Willy Brandt Archive, in the Archive of Social Democracy in the Friedrich Ebert Foundation, Bonn (WBA).

Published Collections of Documents

Brandt, W., *Berliner Ausgabe, Band 1: Hitler ist nicht Deutschland. Jugend in Lübeck – Exil in Norwegen 1928–1940*, ed. E. Lorenz, Bonn, 2002 (*BA 1*).

—— *Berliner Ausgabe, Band 2: Zwei Vaterländer. Deutsch-Norweger im schwedischen Exil – Rückkehr nach Deutschland 1940–1947*, ed. E. Lorenz, Bonn, 2000 (*BA 2*).

—— *Berliner Ausgabe, Band 3: Berlin bleibt frei. Politik in und für Berlin 1947–1966*, ed. S. Heimann, Berlin, 2004 (*BA 3*).

—— *Berliner Ausgabe, Band 4: Auf dem Weg nach vorn: Willy Brandt und die SPD 1947–1972*, ed. D. Münkel, Berlin, 2000 (*BA 4*).

—— *Berliner Ausgabe, Band 5: Die Partei der Freiheit. Willy Brandt und die SPD 1972–1992*, ed. K. Rudolph, Bonn, 2002 (*BA 5*).

—— *Berliner Ausgabe, Band 6: Ein Volk der guten Nachbarn. Außen- und Deutschlandpolitik 1966–1974*, ed. F. Fischer, Bonn, 2005 (*BA 6*).

—— *Berliner Ausgabe, Band 7: Mehr Demokratie wagen. Innen- und Gesellschaftspolitik 1966–1974*, ed. W. von Kieseritzky, Bonn, 2001 (*BA 7*).

—— *Berliner Ausgabe, Band 8: Über Europa hinaus. Dritte Welt und Sozialistische Internationale*, ed. B. Rother and W. Schmidt, Bonn, 2006 (*BA 8*).

—— *Berliner Ausgabe, Band 10: Gemeinsame Sicherheit. Internationale Beziehungen und deutsche Frage 1982–1992*, ed. U. Mai, B. Rother and W. Schmidt, Bonn, 2009 (*BA 10*).

Eibl, F. and H. Zummermann (eds), *Akten zur Auswärtigen Politik der Bundesrepublik Deutschland, 1969, Band 2*, Munich, 2000 (*AAPD*).

Documents diplomatiques Français 1959, Tome I (1er janvier–30 juin), Paris, 1994 (*DDF 1959*).

Documents diplomatiques Français 1963, Tome II (1er juillet–31 décembre), Bern, 2003 (*DDF 1963*).

Documents diplomatiques Français 1964, Tome I (1er janvier–30 juin), Bern, 2002 (*DDF 1964*).

Documents diplomatiques Français 1969, Tome II (1er juillet–31 décembre), Bern, 2013 (*DDF 1969*).

Foreign Relations of the United States, 1969–1976, Vol. 40, ed. D.C. Geyer, Washington, 2008 (*FRUS*).

Newspapers and Magazines

Aurore
Aus Politik und Zeitgeschichte
Bild Zeitung
Le Canard Enchaîné
L'Express
Le Figaro
France Soir
Frankfurter Allgemeine Zeitung
Le Monde
New York Times
Le Quotidien
Der Spiegel
Stern
Time
Die Zeit

Published books and Articles

Adomeit, H., *Die Sowjetmacht in internationalen Krisen und Konflikten: Verhaltensmuster, Handlungsprinzipien, Bestimmungsfaktoren*, Baden Baden, 1983.

Albrecht, W. (ed.), *Kurt Schumacher: Reden – Schriften – Korrespondenzen 1945–1952*, Berlin, 1985.
Alphand, H., *L'étonnement d'être, Journal 1939–1973*, Paris, 1977.
Attali, J., *Verbatim III, 1988–1991*, Paris, 1995.
Bahr, E., *Zu meiner Zeit*, Munich, 1996.
—— *Willy Brandt und die Nation*, Schriftenreihe der BWBS 16, Berlin, 2008.
—— *'Das musst Du erzählen'. Erinnerungen an Willy Brandt*, Berlin, 2013.
Baring, A., *Machtwechsel. Die Ära Brandt-Scheel*, Stuttgart, 1982.
Beck, D. and W.F. Schoeller (eds), *Julius Leber, Schriften, Reden, Briefe*, Munich, 1976.
Behrens, A. (ed.), *'Durfte Brandt knien?' Der Kniefall in Warschau und der deutsche-polnische Vertrag. Eine Dokumentation der Meinungen*, Bonn, 2010.
Bender, P., *Die 'Neue Ostpolitik' und ihre Folgen vom Mauerbau bis zur Vereinigung*, Munich, 1996.
Berstein, S., P. Milza and J.-L. Bianco, *François Mitterrand. Les années du changement 1981–1984*, Paris, 2001.
Bitsch, M-T., *Histoire de la construction européenne de 1945 à nos jours*, Brussels, 2008.
Boll, F. and K. Ruchniewicz (eds), *Nie mehr eine Politik über Polen hinweg. Willy Brandt und Polen*, Bonn, 2010.
Bouvier, B., *Zwischen Godesberg und Großer Koalition. Der Weg der SPD in die Regierungsverantwortung. Außen-, sicherheits- und deutschlandpolitische Umorientierung und gesellschaftliche Öffnung der SPD 1960–1966*, Bonn, 1990.
Bozo, F., *Mitterrand, la fin de la guerre froide et l'unification allemande: De Yalta à Maastricht*, Paris, 2005.
Bracher, K.-D., W. Jäger and W. Link, *Republik im Wandel 1969–1974. Die Ära Brandt*, Stuttgart, 1976.
Brandt, P. and D. Lehnert, *Mehr Demokratie wagen. Geschichte der Sozialdemokratie 1830–2010*, Berlin, 2012.
Brandt, R., *Freundesland. Erinnerungen*, Hamburg, 1992.
Brandt, W., *Mein Weg nach Berlin*, with L. Lania, Munich, 1960.
—— *Koexistenz – Zwang zum Wagnis*, Stuttgart, 1963.
—— *Draußen, Schriften während der Emigration*, ed. G. Struve, Munich, 1966.
—— *Friedenspolitik in Europa*, Frankfurt am Main, 1968.
—— *Reden und Interviews 1969–1971*, Hamburg, 1971.
—— *Reden und Interviews 1971–1973*, Hamburg, 1973.
—— *Über den Tag hinaus. Eine Zwischenbilanz*, Hamburg, 1974.
—— *Begegnungen und Einsichten: Die Jahre 1960–1975*, Munich, 1978.
—— *Links und frei. Mein Weg 1930–1950*, Hamburg, 1982.

—— *Der organisierte Wahnsinn. Wettrüsten und Welthunger*, Cologne, 1985.

—— *Die Abschiedsrede*, Berlin, 1987.

—— '*... was zusammengehört'. Reden zu Deutschland*, Bonn, 1990.

—— *My Life in Politics*, trans. Anthea Bell, London, 1992 (published in German as *Erinnerungen*, Frankfurt am Main, 1989).

—— *Verbrecher und andere Deutsche. Ein Bericht aus Deutschland 1946*, Bonn, 2007.

—— *Im Zweifel für die Freiheit. Reden zur demokratischen und deutschen Geschichte*, ed. K. Schönhoven, Bonn, 2012.

——, B. Kreisky and O. Palme, *Briefe und Gespräche 1972 bis 1975*, Frankfurt am Main, 1975.

Conze, E., *Die Suche nach Sicherheit. Eine Geschichte der Bundesrepublik Deutschland von 1949 bis zur Gegenwart*, Munich, 2009.

Dahrendorf, R., *Bildung ist Bürgerrecht. Plädoyer für eine alternative Bildungspolitik*, Hamburg, 1965.

De Gaulle, C., *Memoirs of Hope*, trans. Terence Kilmartin, London, 1971 (published in French as *Mémoires d'espoir*).

De Villemarest, P., *Polyarnik. Histoire d'un chef d'État, espion épisodique de Moscou*, Paris, 1999.

Doering-Manteuffel, A. and R. Lutz, *Nach dem Boom. Perspektiven auf die Zeitgeschichte seit 1970*, Göttingen, 2008.

Dönhoff, M. Gräfin, *Weit ist der Weg nach Osten. Berichte und Betrachtungen aus fünf Jahrzehnten*, Munich, 1988.

Ehmke, H., *Mittendrin. Von der Großen Koalition zur Deutschen Einheit*, Berlin, 1994.

—— *Reformpolitik und 'Zivilgesellschaft'*, Schriftenreihe der BWBS 9, Berlin, 2001.

Eisenfeld, B. and R. Engelmann, *13.8.1961: Mauerbau: Fluchtbewegung und Machtsicherung*, Berlin, 2001.

Fallaci, O., *Intervista con la Storia*, Milan, 1985.

Faulenbach, B., *Das sozialdemokratische Jahrzehnt. Von der Reformeuphorie zur neuen Unübersichtlichkeit. Die SPD 1969–1982*, Bonn, 2011.

—— *Geschichte der SPD: Von den Anfängen bis zur Gegenwart*, Munich, 2012.

Focke, K., 'Erinnerungen an Jean Monnet', in A. Wilkens (ed.), *Interessen verbinden. Jean Monnet und die europäische Integration der Bundesrepublik Deutschland*, Bonn, 1999, pp. 23–30.

Gellner, W., *Ideenagenturen für Politik und Öffentlichkeit. Think Tanks in den USA und in Deutschland*, Opladen, 1995.

Genscher, H.D., *Erinnerungen*, Berlin, 1995.

Gorbachev, M., *Memoirs*, trans. G. Peronansky and T. Varsavsky, London, 1997 (published in Russian as *Zhizhn' i reformy*).

—— *Wie es war. Die deutsche Wiedervereinigung*, Berlin, 1999.

Gottwaldt, A., *Salonwagen 10205. Von der Schiene ins Museum*, Bonn, 1997.

Grau, A., 'Auf der Suche nach den fehlenden Stimmen 1972', *Historisch-Politische Mitteilungen*, 16 (2009), pp. 1–18.

Grebing, H., *Willy Brandt: Der andere Deutsche*, Munich, 2008.

Groh, D. and P. Brandt, *'Vaterlandslose Gesellen'. Sozialdemokratie und Nation 1860–1990*, Munich, 1992.

Guillaume, G., *Die Aussage. Wie es wirklich war*, Munich, 1990.

Haftendorn, H., *Deutsche Außenpolitik zwischen Selbstbeschränkung und Selbstbehauptung*, Stuttgart, 2001.

Harpprecht, K., *Im Kanzleramt. Tagebuch der Jahre mit Willy Brandt*, Hamburg, 2000.

—— *Willy Brandt oder der Mut zum Glück*, Reinbek, 2003.

Heimann, H. (ed.), *Sozialdemokratische Traditionen und Demokratischer Sozialismus*, Cologne, 1993.

Hiepel, C., *Willy Brandt und Georges Pompidou, Deutsch-französische Europapolitik zwischen Aufbruch und Krise*, Munich, 2012.

Hofmann, G., *Willy Brandt und Helmut Schmidt: Geschichte einer schwierigen Freundschaft*, Munich, 2012.

Honecker, E., *From My Life*, Oxford, 1981 (published in German as *Aus meinem Leben*).

Independent Commission on International Development, *North–South: A Programme for Survival. The Report of the Independent Commission on International Development Issues under the Chairmanship of Willy Brandt*, London, 1980 ('Brandt Report').

Jahrbuch der SPD (various years)

Jansen, S., 'Zwei deutsche Staaten – zwei deutsche Nationen? Meinungsbilder zur deutschen Frage im Zeitablauf', *Deutschland Archiv* 22/x (1989), pp. 1132–43.

Jarausch, K.H. (ed.), *Das Ende der Zuversicht? Die siebziger Jahre als Geschichte*, Göttingen, 2008.

Jaspers, K., *The Question of German Guilt*, trans. E.B. Ashton, New York, 1947.

Jewish Telegraphic Agency, 'Mrs. Meir Greets Brandt as a Fighter against Nazism', 8 June 1973, available at www.jta.org/1973/06/08/archive/mrs-meir-greets-brandt-as-a-fighter-against-nazism (accessed 11 August 2016)

Kerz-Rühling, I. and T. Plänkers, *Verräter oder Verführte. Eine psychoanalytische Untersuchung Inoffizieller Mitarbeiter der Stasi*, Berlin, 2004.

Kielmansegg, P. Graf, *Nach der Katastrophe. Eine Geschichte des geteilten Deutschland*, Berlin, 2000.

Kissinger, H., *White House Years*, New York, 1979.

Knabe, H., *Die unterwanderte Republik. Stasi im Westen*, Berlin, 2001.

Koch, P., *Willy Brandt. Eine politische Biographie*, Berlin, 1988.

Kogon, E., 'Das Recht auf den politischen Irrtum', *Frankfurter Hefte* 2 (1947), pp. 641–55.

Kohl, H., *Erinnerungen 1982–1990*, Munich, 2005.

—— *Erinnerungen 1990–1994*, Munich, 2007.

Kölbel, M. (ed.), *Willy Brandt und Günter Grass. Der Briefwechsel*, Göttingen, 2013.

Krieger, W. and J. Weber (eds), *Spionage für den Frieden? Nachrichtendienste in Deutschland während des Kalten Krieges*, Munich, 1997.

Kruke, A., *Demoskopie in der Bundesrepublik Deutschland. Meinungsforschung, Parteien und Medien, 1949–1990*, Düsseldorf, 1997.

Lafontaine, O., *Das Herz schlägt links*, Berlin, 1999.

Lappenküper, U., *Mitterrand und Deutschland. Die enträtselte Sphinx*, Munich, 2011.

Lehmann, H.G., *In Acht und Bann. Politische Emigration, NS-Ausbürgerung und Wiedergutmachung am Beispiel Willy Brandts*, Munich, 1976.

Leugers-Scherzberg, A.H., *Die Wandlungen des Herbert Wehner: Von der Volksfront zur Großen Koalition*, Berlin, 2002.

Lorenz, E., *Willy Brandt in Norwegen. Die Jahre des Exils 1933 bis 1940*, Kiel, 1989.

—— *Willy Brandt. Deutscher, Europäer, Weltbürger*, Stuttgart, 2012.

Marcowitz, R., *Option für Paris? Unionsparteien, SPD und Charles de Gaulle 1958 bis 1969*, Munich, 1996.

Mares, A. and M.-P. Rey (eds), *Mémoires et émotions. Au cœur de l'histoire des relations internationales*, Paris, 2014.

Mergel, T., *Propaganda nach Hitler. Eine Kulturgeschichte des Wahlkampfs in der Bundesrepublik 1949–1990*, Göttingen, 2010.

Merseburger, P., *Willy Brandt 1913–1992. Visionär und Realist*, Munich, 2002.

—— *Rudolf Augstein. Biographie*, Munich, 2007.

Metzler, G., *Konzeptionen politischen Handelns von Adenauer bis Brandt. Politische Planung in der pluralistischen Gesellschaft*, Paderborn, 2005.

Meyer, T., *Bernsteins konstruktiver Sozialismus. Eduard Bernsteins Beitrag zur Theorie des Sozialismus*, Bad Godesberg, 1977.

Miard-Delacroix, H., *Partenaires de choix. Le chancelier Schmidt et la France, 1974–1982*, Bern, 1993.

—— *Le défi européen de 1963 à nos jours*, Histoire franco-allemande séries, Villeneuve d'Ascq, 2011.

Michels, E., *Guillaume, der Spion. Eine deutsch-deutsche Karriere*, Berlin, 2013.

Micus, M., *Die 'Enkel' Willy Brandts. Aufstieg und Politikstil einer SPD-Generation*, Frankfurt am Main, 2005.

Mitterrand, F., *Politique II*, Paris, 1981.

Möller, H. and M. Vaïsse (eds), *Willy Brandt und Frankreich*, Munich, 2005.
Monnet, J., *Mémoires*, Paris, 1976.
Müller-Ensberg, H., *'Rosenholz'. Eine Quellenkritik*, Berlin, 2007.
Münkel, D., *Bemerkungen zu Willy Brandt*, Berlin, 2005.
—— *Willy Brandt und die 'vierte Gewalt'. Politik und Massenmedien in den 50er bis 70er Jahren*, Frankfurt am Main, 2005.
Potthoff, H., *Im Schatten der Mauer. Deutschlandpolitik 1961 bis 1990*, Berlin, 1999.
Reuter, E., *Reden, Artikel, Briefe 1949 bis 1953*, Berlin, 1975.
Rother, B. (ed.), *Willy Brandt. Neue Fragen, neue Erkenntnisse*, Bonn, 2011.
—— (ed.), *Willy Brandts Außenpolitik*, Wiesbaden, 2014.
Roussel, E., *Jean Monnet*, Paris, 1996.
Saint-Paul, G., *L'agenouillement au ghetto*, Paris, 2012.
Schildt, A., *Moderne Zeiten. Freizeit, Massenmedien und Zeitgeist in der Bundesrepublik der 50er Jahre*, Hamburg, 1995.
——, D. Siegfried and K.C. Lammers (eds), *Dynamische Zeiten. Die 60er Jahre in den beiden deutschen Gesellschaften*, Hamburg, 2000.
Schmidt, H., *Die Deutschen und ihre Nachbarn*, Berlin, 1990.
—— *Weggefährten. Erinnerungen und Reflexionen*, Berlin, 1996.
Schmidt, W., *Kalter Krieg, Koexistenz und kleine Schritte. Willy Brandt und die Deutschlandpolitik 1948–1963*, Opladen, 2001.
—— 'Die Wurzeln der Entspannung: Der konzeptionelle Ursprung der Ost- und Deutschlandpolitik Willy Brandts in den fünfziger Jahren', *Vierteljahrshefte für Zeitgeschichte*, 51 (2003), pp. 521–63.
Schöllgen, G., *Willy Brandt. Die Biographie*, Berlin, 2001.
Scholtyseck, J., *Die Außenpolitik der DDR*, Munich, 2003.
Schönhoven, K., *Wendejahre. Die Sozialdemokratie in der Zeit der Großen Koalition, 1966–1969*, Bonn, 2004.
—— *Freiheit durch demokratischen Sozialismus. Willy Brandts Überlegungen zum programmatischen Selbstverständnis der SPD*, Gesprächskreis Geschichte 98, Bonn, 2013.
—— and B. Braun (eds), *Generationen in der Arbeiterbewegung*, Munich, 2005.
Schreiber, H., *Kanzlersturz. Warum Willy Brandt zurücktrat*, Munich, 2003.
Schulz, A. (ed.), *Parlamentarische Kulturen in Europa – das Parlament als Kommunikationsraum*, Berlin, 2012.
Schwarz, H.P., *Axel Springer: Die Biografie*, Berlin, 2008.
Seebacher, B., *Willy Brandt*, Munich, 2004.
Seydoux, F., *Dans l'intimité franco-allemande. Une mission diplomatique*, Paris, 1977.
Soell, H., *Helmut Schmidt, Vol. 1: Vernunft und Leidenschaft*, Munich, 2003.

—— *Helmut Schmidt, Vol. 2: Macht und Verantwortung*, Munich, 2008.

Sontheimer, K., *So war Deutschland nie: Anmerkungen zur politischen Kultur der Bundesrepublik*, Munich, 1999.

Sternburg, W. von (ed.), *Die deutschen Kanzler von Bismarck bis Schmidt*, Königstein, 1985.

Strauss, F.J., *Die Erinnerungen*, Berlin, 1989.

Stüwe, K. (ed.), *Die großen Regierungserklärungen der deutschen Bundeskanzler von Adenauer bis Schröder*, Opladen, 2002.

Suckut, S., 'Willy Brandt in der DDR', *Jahrbuch für historische Kommunismusforschung* 16 (2008), pp. 170–82.

Türk, H., *Europapolitik der Großen Koalition 1966–1969*, Munich, 2006.

Uhl, M. and A. Wagner (eds), *Ulbricht, Chruschtschow und die Mauer: Eine Dokumentation*, Munich, 2003.

Van Melis, D. and H. Bispinck (eds), *'Republikflucht': Flucht und Abwanderung aus der SBZ/DDR 1945 bis 1961*, Munich, 2006.

Vedrine, H., *Les Mondes de François Mitterrand*, Paris, 1996.

Völklein, U., *Honecker. Eine Biographie*, Berlin, 2003.

Waechter, M., *Helmut Schmidt und Valéry Giscard d'Estaing. Auf der Suche nach Stabilität in der Krise der 70er Jahre*, Bremen, 2011.

Walter, F., *Die SPD. Vom Proletariat zur Neuen Mitte. Biographie einer Partei*, Berlin, 2009.

Weizsäcker, R. von, *Vier Zeiten*, Berlin, 2002.

Wilkens, A., *Der unstete Nachbar: Frankreich und die deutsche Ostpolitik 1969–1974*, Munich, 1990.

—— *Interessen verbinden. Jean Monnet und die europäische Integration der Bundesrepublik Deutschland*, Bonn, 1999.

—— (ed.), *Willy Brandt et l'unité de l'Europe. De l'objectif de la paix aux solidarités nécessaires*, Brussels, 2011.

Winkler, H.A., *Der lange Weg nach Westen*, 2 vols, Munich, 2000.

Wirsching, A., *Abschied vom Provisorium. Geschichte der Bundesrepublik Deutschland 1982–1990*, Stuttgart, 2008.

Wolf, M., *Spionagechef im geheimen Krieg, Erinnerungen*, Munich, 1997.

Wolfrum, E., 'Die Mauer', in E. François and H. Schulze (eds), *Deutsche Erinnerungsorte, Band 1*, Munich, 2001, pp. 552–68.

—— *Die geglückte Demokratie. Geschichte der Bundesrepublik Deutschland von ihren Anfängen bis zur Gegenwart*, Stuttgart, 2006.

—— *Die Mauer: Geschichte einer Teilung*, Munich, 2009.

Index